DATA SECURITY *in the* AGE OF AI

A Guide to Protecting Data and Reducing Risk in an AI-Driven World

ANAND SINGH, PhD

ISBN: 978-1-968433-01-7
Imprint: Responsible AI Institute Press
Editor: Renée Lautermilch
Cover Design: Mubeen Ahmed
Formatting and Layout: Saqib Arshad

DEDICATION

To my mother, Dr. Tara Devi Singh, whose love of teaching sparked my passion for learning and sharing, and to my father, Dr. Ashok Kumar Singh, whose quiet strength and tireless work ethic shaped the course of my life.

ACKNOWLEDGEMENTS

As I reach the end of this journey, I am filled with gratitude for many individuals whose guidance, encouragement, and support made this book possible. I am deeply thankful to everyone who helped me along the way.

I am especially grateful to my wife, Soma, and my children, Arushi and Arnav. Thank you for your love, your unwavering support, and for being the heartbeat of my life. I am also grateful to Zuko, my partner in crime, who loyally kept me company and ensured I didn't turn entirely into a hermit, mainly by staring into my soul until I took him for a walk.

I am also grateful to my colleagues across the years whose insights and collaboration have shaped my thinking on data security and AI. My experiences at UnitedHealth Group, Target Corporation, Alkami Technology, and Symmetry Systems have all contributed to the perspectives shared in this book.

Special thanks to Dr. Mohit Tiwari, one of the industry's foremost experts on data security, whose ideas and insights profoundly influenced the direction of this book. I'm also grateful to Jay Modh whose instincts around storytelling and messaging played a pivotal role in shaping how this book came to life.

To my cybersecurity community cheerleaders—Cecil Pineda, Jaimin Shah, and Randy Moss—thank you for your thoughtful advice, invaluable feedback, and consistent encouragement, especially during the more arduous phases of the writing process. I'm also thankful to Shashi Mysore, whose encouragement was a steady source of motivation throughout; to Claude Mandy, whose gift for structuring and communicating complex ideas helped me tremendously, and to Lars Delin, whose support and presentation work helped plant the seeds for how to present complicated concepts.

Many others have left a lasting imprint on my professional and intellectual journey. I am especially thankful to:

- Doug Linebarger, my mentor and supervisor since 2018, whose guidance has profoundly shaped my growth and success.
- Dr. David Lilja, my thesis advisor at the University of Minnesota, for laying the foundation of my academic training.
- Dr. Eugene Spafford, who instilled in me a love for cybersecurity during my days at Purdue University.
- George Finney, author and Zero Trust thought leader, for his insightful perspectives and encouragement.
- Yash Sabharwal, for constantly reminding me of the importance of this book and motivating me every step of the way.
- Matt Wilson, whose work in enterprise AI at Alkami helped shape my thinking around governance and adoption.
- Clinton Waner and Justin Hadley, whose spirited conversations on AI and data security illuminated many of the challenges this book seeks to address.
- Dennis Irwin, who helped sharpen my perspective on navigating compliance, governance, and regulatory challenges in AI rollout.
- To all my friends and extended family - too many to name in this limited space - thank you for being the laughter, the lifeline, and the pressure relief valve I didn't know I needed.

TABLE OF CONTENTS

LIST OF ABBREVIATIONS

> *"What do cybersecurity professionals do with all the time they save by using acronyms?"*
>
> —JUNIOR-BEAR-6955 (REDDITOR)

ABBREVIATION	FULL TERM
ABAC	Attribute-Based Access Control
ACL	Access Control List
AI	Artificial Intelligence
AI-PIA	AI Privacy Impact Assessment
ANPD	Autoridade Nacional de Proteção de Dados (Brazil)
APT	Advanced Persistent Threat
API	Application Programming Interface
APAC	Asia-Pacific
APPI	Act on the Protection of Personal Information (Japan)
AWS	Amazon Web Services
AUP	Acceptable Use Policy
BabyAGI	Baby Artificial General Intelligence
BCP	Business Continuity Planning
BPO	Business Process Outsourcing
CAD	Computer-Aided Design
CAPTCHA	Completely Automated Public Turing test to tell Computers and Humans Apart
CASB	Cloud Access Security Broker
CD	Continuous Delivery
CDO	Chief Data Officer
CDSO	Chief Data Security Officer

ABBREVIATION	FULL TERM
CEO	Chief Executive Officer
CFO	Chief Financial Officer
CHD	Cardholder Data
CI	Continuous Integration
CIEM	Cloud Infrastructure Entitlement Management
CII	Critical Information Infrastructure
CIO	Chief Information Officer
CIS	Center for Internet Security
CISO	Chief Information Security Officer
CMP	Consent Management Platform
CNN	Convolutional Neural Network
COO	Chief Operating Officer
COPPA	Children's Online Privacy Protection Act
CPA	Colorado Privacy Act
CCPA	California Consumer Privacy Act
CPPA	California Privacy Protection Agency
CPRA	California Privacy Rights Act
CSL	Cybersecurity Law (China)
CTDPA	Connecticut Data Privacy Act
CTO	Chief Technology Officer
CVE	Common Vulnerabilities and Exposures
CVV	Card Verification Value
DAM	Database Activity Monitoring
DB	Database
DBA	Database Administrator
DBIR	Data Breach Investigations Report (from Verizon)
DHCP	Dynamic Host Configuration Protocol
DID	Decentralized Identity
DKIM	DomainKeys Identified Mail
DLL	Dynamic Link Library
DMARC	Domain-based Message Authentication, Reporting & Conformance
DNA	Deoxyribonucleic Acid

ABBREVIATION	FULL TERM
DOJ	Department of Justice
DPIA	Data Protection Impact Assessment
DPDP	Digital Personal Data Protection (India's privacy law)
DP-FTRL	Differentially Privacy Follow The Regularized Leader
DPO	Data Protection Officer
DPR	Data Protection Regulation
DR	Disaster Recovery
DSL	Data Security Law (China)
DLP	Data Loss Prevention
DSP	Data Security Platform
DSPM	Data Security Posture Management
DSAR	Data Subject Access Request
EEA	European Economic Area
EC2	Elastic Compute Cloud (AWS)
EKS	Elastic Kubernetes Service (AWS)
ETL	Extract, Transform, Load
FERPA	Family Educational Rights and Privacy Act
FTP	File Transfer Protocol
GAN	Generative Adversarial Network
GCP	Google Cloud Platform
GCS	Google Cloud Storage
GDPR	General Data Protection Regulation
GB	Gigabyte
GenAI	Generative AI
GLBA	Gramm-Leach-Bliley Act
GKE	Google Kubernetes Engine
GPT	Generative Pre-trained Transformer
GPU	Graphics Processing Unit
GRC	Governance, Risk, and Compliance
HHS	Department of Health and Human Services
HIPAA	Health Insurance Portability and Accountability Act
HR	Human Resources

ABBREVIATION	FULL TERM
IaC	Infrastructure as Code
IaaS	Infrastructure as a Service
IAM	Identity and Access Management
IAG	Identity Access Governance
IEC 42001	International Electrotechnical Commission (IEC 42001 is International Standard for AI Management Systems
IGA	Identity Governance and Administration
IO	Input/Output
IOPS	Input/Output Operations Per Second
IP	Intellectual Property
IR	Incident Response
ISO	International Organization for Standardization
IT	Information Technology
JIT	Just-In-Time
JPEG	Joint Photographic Experts Group
JSON	JavaScript Object Notation
JWT	JSON Web Token
KPI	Key Performance Indicator
KMS	Key Management Service
LLaMA	Large Language Model Meta AI
LGPD	Lei Geral de Proteção de Dados (Brazil)
LLM	Large Language Model
MCP	Model Context Protocol
MFA	Multi-Factor Authentication
MITRE ATT&CK	MITRE Adversarial Tactics, Techniques & Common Knowledge Framework
ML	Machine Learning
MLO	Machine Learning Operations
MTTI	Mean Time to Identify
MTTC	Mean Time to Contain
MTTR	Mean Time to Resolution
NHI	Non-Human Identity
NHS	National Health Service

ABBREVIATION	FULL TERM
NLP	Natural Language Processing
NLU	Natural Language Understanding
NSA	National Security Agency
NSG	Network Security Group
OCR	Office for Civil Rights
OCI	Oracle Cloud Infrastructure
OS	Operating System
PbD	Privacy by Design
PIA	Privacy Impact Assessment
PHI	Protected Health Information
PII	Personally Identifiable Information
PIPA	Personal Information Protection Act (South Korea)
PIPL	Personal Information Protection Law (China)
PoC	Proof of Concept
QBR	Quarterly Business Review
RACI	Responsible, Accountable, Consulted, Informed matrix
RAG	Retrieval-Augmented Generation
RBAC	Role-Based Access Control
RDP	Remote Desktop Protocol
RDS	Relational Database Service
RLHF	Reinforcement Learning from Human Feedback
RMF	Risk Management Framework
ROI	Return on Investment
ROT	Redundant, Obsolete, Trivial data
RSS	Really Simple Syndication
SaaS	Software as a Service
SCC	Standard Contractual Clauses
S3	Simple Storage Service (AWS)
SDK	Software Development Kit
SIEM	Security Information and Event Management
SLA	Service-Level Agreement
SMTP	Simple Mail Transfer Protocol

ABBREVIATION	FULL TERM
SOC	Security Operations Center
SOAR	Security Orchestration, Automation & Response
SQL	Structured Query Language
SPAN	Switched Port Analyzer
SRE	Site Reliability Engineering
SSH	Secure Shell
SSN	Social Security Number
SSO	Single Sign-On
STS	Security Token Service
S-TAP	Software Traffic Access Point (IBM Guardium terminology)
TFX	TensorFlow Extended
TB	Terabyte
TCP	Transmission Control Protocol
TDPSA	Texas Data Privacy and Security Act
TPRM	Third-Party Risk Management
UEBA	User and Entity Behavior Analytics
UI	User Interface
UCPA	Utah Consumer Privacy Act
UX	User Experience
VCDPA	Virginia Consumer Data Protection Act
VLAN	Virtual Local Area Network
VM	Virtual Machine
VNet	Virtual Network
VPC	Virtual Private Cloud
W3C	World Wide Web Consortium
XSIAM	Extended Security Intelligence and Automation Management

FOREWORD

I am thrilled that Anand asked me to write this foreword. In my work as IANS CEO, I'm seeing businesses race to get a competitive edge with AI. Executives and their boards are clamoring: "We can't fall behind," and "We need to seize the opportunity!" But there's a ton of uncertainty out there. CISOs are grappling with unknown unknowns and trying to mitigate deployment risks without stifling innovation. I can't imagine anyone better to inject some sound, structured thinking and guidance into this chaotic situation than Anand.

I have known Anand for years and have been struck by his thoughtfulness and ability to unpack and make plain complex problems. He has years of experience as a security executive, including CISO roles in the Fortune 100 and small, agile startups. He's also a valued member of the IANS Faculty, where he served as an executive coach and has helped hundreds of security leaders solve real-world problems. I have seen him in front of a room of CISOs immediately capture their attention with guidance that gets to the root of their problems. He is more than a thought leader; he's a trusted advisor who blends real-world experience with a remarkable ability to see the big picture.

In *Data Security in the Age of AI*, Anand takes a pragmatic approach to advising executives on managing the change created by AI use. It isn't just for security-minded folks, it is for any business executive looking to seize the opportunities of AI.

Anand is at the forefront of the AI transformation. He sees its value and potential. He is also aware of the challenges it creates, including ensuring sensitive data doesn't get into training models, managing nonhuman entities that are your new most active users, and creating accountability for AI decisions. In this book, he addresses these problems through practical insights, giving you the playbook to understand and manage AI data risk. It is a must-read for leaders looking to harness the power of AI now and into the future.

— *Phil Gardner, Founder and CEO, IANS*

FOREWORD

We are operating in a time of rapid and profound transformation. AI is shaping how companies operate, compete, and deliver value. From predictive analytics to customer engagement, AI is unlocking new efficiencies and insights across the enterprise. Boards are investing in it. Teams are energized by it. And the pace of adoption continues to accelerate.

At the heart of this momentum is data. Clean, secure, labeled, and well-governed data is what gives AI its strength. When that foundation is in place, AI systems are not only more accurate and effective, they are also more aligned with enterprise goals and values. As organizations move quickly to integrate AI into core business functions, there is an opportunity to build with both speed and purpose.

The next wave of AI success will come from those who recognize that innovation must be matched with responsible use. When strong data governance and cybersecurity are embedded into AI programs, they build trust, thus enabling speed, sustaining performance, and securing ongoing investment. This approach not only mitigates risk but also drives meaningful business progress.

And that is where this book comes in.

I have known Anand for more than seven years, including his time as a CISO leading cybersecurity efforts in high-growth, high-complexity environments. What sets him apart is his ability to connect three essential domains: AI, cybersecurity, and data. He understands how these areas intersect and how to turn that understanding into meaningful, practical guidance. His work reflects both technical depth and strategic clarity.

The guidance in this book is grounded, well explained, and actionable. It provides a clear framework for securing data as enterprises scale AI. From protecting training datasets to monitoring model behavior and aligning access with business context, Anand shows how to embed security into AI development without slowing down progress.

It is also a valuable strategic resource. For leaders responsible for building trustworthy AI programs, it offers direction. For security teams, it bridges the gap between technical enforcement and organizational priorities. And for students or professionals entering this space, it provides a strong foundation to understand the opportunities and responsibilities that come with AI adoption.

Anand writes with clarity and conviction, but also pragmatism, drawing from real-world experience. This book is a timely and necessary contribution for anyone navigating the intersection of data, AI, and security.

For those interested in guiding AI transformation, this book will help you do it with confidence and clarity. It is a roadmap not just for reducing risk, but for unlocking the full potential of AI, securely and responsibly.

— Stephen Bohanon, Founder, Alkami Technology

PREFACE

> *"The art of progress is to preserve order amid change, and to preserve change amid order."*
>
> – ALFRED NORTH WHITEHEAD, PROCESS AND REALITY: AN ESSAY IN COSMOLOGY

AI has taken the world by storm. In just a few short years, it has gone from being a distant research topic to becoming deeply woven into the daily operations of nearly every enterprise. What once felt like a futuristic vision is now an omnipresent force shaping how we work, compete, live, and serve our customers.

But this rapid adoption has not come with a clear playbook. Instead, AI has often spread through organizations in a grassroots fashion, with teams rushing to build prototypes, adopt third-party tools, and push models into production, all in the name of innovation. While this energy is inspiring, it has also unleashed a wave of chaos. Critical data is flowing into AI systems without proper oversight. Sensitive information is being used in ways that leaders do not fully understand. Security and governance teams are left struggling to keep up with an accelerating tide of new risks.

Amid this excitement, there has also been a surge of opportunism. The market is overflowing with snake oil salespeople, each claiming to offer the next latest and greatest solution to "fix" AI security and data challenges overnight. These shiny pitches promise simplicity in a complex world, but too often they leave organizations more confused and vulnerable than before.

As a longtime CISO, AI practitioner, and researcher, I am witnessing firsthand how this massive change is creating a gold rush mindset, often without regard for its impact on an organization's data discipline. *Data Security in the Age of AI* is my attempt to bring structure and clarity to a topic muddled by hype and half-truths. It is a practical guide to understanding how AI affects data, identifying the risks that matter, and responding to those risks with clear, methodical strategies. This book sits at the intersection of AI, data, and cybersecurity, as illustrated in the Venn diagram.

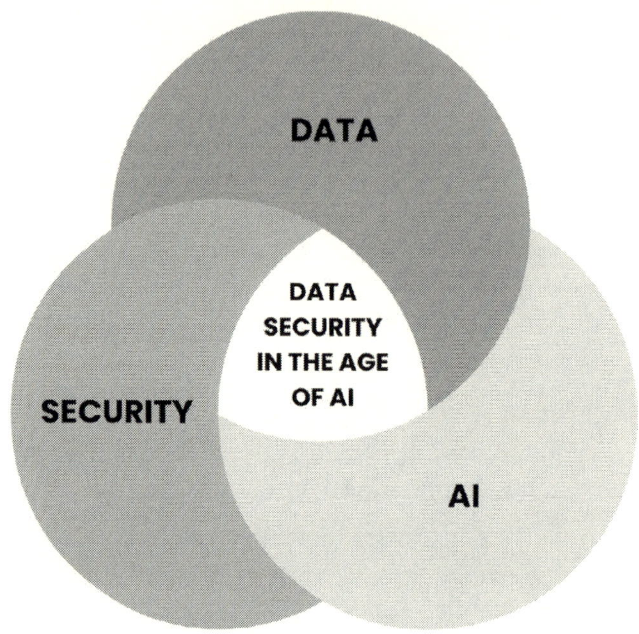

The core of this conversation is data, the lifeblood of every enterprise. As AI systems ingest, generate, and manipulate data at unprecedented scales, we are faced with new questions: How do we protect sensitive data when it is used to train powerful models? How do we maintain visibility and control when AI systems act as autonomous decision-makers? And how do we ensure compliance and maintain trust in an era of black-box algorithms?

The time to act is now. We can no longer afford to wait for a perfect set of tools or standards to appear. We must take proactive steps to understand and manage these challenges today before they define us tomorrow.

This book is not meant to be a theoretical treatise. It is a call to action. My hope is that it will serve as a guidepost for security leaders, data architects, and business executives who recognize that AI is here to stay and that securing data in this new era is not optional, but essential.

We stand at a pivotal moment. The choices we make now will shape not only the future of our organizations but the broader trust in AI across society. Let us choose wisely, act decisively, and build the structures that will allow us to innovate safely and responsibly.

— Anand Singh

INTRODUCTION

> *"There's no question we are in an AI and data revolution, which means that we're in a customer revolution and a business revolution. But it's not as simple as taking all of your data and training a model with it. There's data security, there's access permissions, there's sharing models that we have to honor. These are important concepts, new risks, new challenges, and new concerns that we have to figure out together."*
>
> – CLARA SHIH, FORMER CEO, SALESFORCE AI

The Data+AI Convergence

We are living in an era defined by two interdependent revolutions: the explosion of data and the rise of artificial intelligence (AI). Data is now the most valuable commodity for businesses, governments, and malicious actors alike. Meanwhile, AI is not just a theoretical construct or a lab experiment; it has become deeply embedded in the fabric of enterprise infrastructure. From real-time recommendation engines to predictive threat detection systems, AI thrives on data. The more precise, plentiful, and sensitive that data is, the more powerful AI becomes.

This convergence of data and AI is reshaping every industry. According to IDC, the global datasphere will grow to 175 zettabytes by 2025, and nearly 30% of that data will be consumed by AI workloads.[1] Businesses are increasingly adopting AI to mine customer insights, optimize supply chains, and automate operations. Simultaneously, new breeds of AI are appearing such as large language models (LLMs) like OpenAI's GPT and Anthropic's Claude, agentic AI systems capable of semi-autonomous decision-making,, and domain-specific foundation models fine-tuned for finance, healthcare, and cybersecurity.

AI and data are not merely coexisting; they are deeply interwoven. The quality of data directly influences the performance of AI models, and the application of AI reveals hidden insights that feed back into data-driven decisions. This feedback loop is a double-edged sword: it accelerates innovation but also compounds security risks. For instance, a well-tuned AI model that predicts customer churn can also unintentionally expose sensitive customer profiles if not properly governed.

This is particularly concerning given the AI democratization. AI capabilities are increasingly accessible via Software as a Service (SaaS), Application Programming Interfaces (APIs), open-source models, and low-code platforms. This means that individuals across an organization, including those with limited understanding of data privacy or security, can train, fine-tune, or deploy AI systems using sensitive data.

In the public sector, the stakes are even higher. Governments are using AI for surveillance, public safety, predictive policing, and social service eligibility. The potential for misuse, bias, or data exploitation is profound. Missteps can erode public trust, lead to legal challenges, and create systemic vulnerabilities.

At the same time, adversaries are also weaponizing AI. From automated phishing and deepfakes to AI-driven malware and data poisoning attacks, the offensive capabilities enabled by AI are advancing rapidly. In April 2023, MIT Technology Review highlighted three critical security vulnerabilities in AI chatbots: prompt injection attacks that bypass safety measures, indirect prompt injections that manipulate AI behavior through hidden web content, and data poisoning that corrupts training datasets.[2]

Innovation Compression and the Urgency for Change

We are in an era of innovation compression, where the time it takes for new technologies to go from concept to mainstream has drastically shortened. The internet took approximately 15 years to become mainstream, from its popular emergence in the early 1990s to widespread consumer and enterprise adoption by the mid-2000s. Online shopping platforms such as Amazon gained mass-market traction in just under five years. Today, Model Context Protocols and Agentic AI systems are being deployed in production environments within six months of being introduced to the public.

This dramatic acceleration puts enormous pressure on every adjacent domain, and none more so than data security. While adversaries are rapidly embracing the latest AI-driven tactics, many security programs are still relying on outdated classification tools, manual audit processes, and incomplete visibility into data usage. The field of data security cannot afford to remain stagnant. We must move beyond legacy approaches and embrace bold, data-and-AI-centric innovation.

This innovation compression demands equivalent compression in our response cycle. We cannot wait for years to modernize our architectures, develop posture frameworks, or implement AI governance policies. The change must be radical, continuous, and strategic. There must be an intentional urgency in evolving from the lackadaisical pace of past decades. Data security is not just a back-office compliance function. It is the front line of digital resilience and ethical AI enablement.

Why Traditional Security Models Fall Short

Legacy security architectures were never fully designed for today's hybrid cloud environments, AI-driven workflows, innovation compression, or decentralized data ecosystems. Historically, security focused on infrastructure and perimeter defense, fortifying networks and endpoints against external threats. But modern data and AI environments are borderless.

Data now lives in a sprawling mesh of environments: cloud object stores, SaaS platforms, on-premises file servers, data lakes, and analytics platforms. AI models may train on data that spans multiple business units, geographies, or even third-party providers. Access to this data is granted not only to human users, but also to an ever-growing number of non-human identities (NHIs): APIs, service accounts, cloud functions, and Machine Learning (ML) pipelines.

These realities break traditional security assumptions. Identity-centric models like Zero Trust—discussed in more detail in Chapter 3—have helped, but even they struggle to provide visibility and governance at the scale and speed required. Consider the following shortcomings:

- **Lack of data context:** Most security tools do not understand what data is being accessed. A log entry might show that a user accessed an Amazon Simple Storage Service (S3) bucket, but not whether it contained sensitive personally identifiable information (PII), personal health information (PHI), or public documentation.
- **Inadequate controls for NHIs:** Service accounts often have persistent keys, long lived tokens, and excessive privileges, making them ideal targets for attackers.

- **No unified view:** Data access, classification, identity relationships, and AI model interactions are often managed in silos. Security teams cannot generate a complete picture of risk. Even business and data teams can struggle with understanding the entire data footprint in their organization.
- **Static classification approaches:** Reliance on regular expressions and static policies generates excessive false positives and fails to capture context or intent.
- **Audit and compliance gaps:** Privacy regulations like General Data Protection Regulation (GDPR), Health Insurance Portability and Accountability Act (HIPAA), and California Privacy Rights Act (CPRA) require data inventory, classification, and access audit trails that legacy tools cannot reliably produce.

Moreover, the shift to DevOps and MLOps has outpaced traditional security review processes. Developers and data scientists now wield enormous influence over data access and AI behavior. In many organizations, security is brought in post-facto, often after the initiative is already complete or after the data exposure has already occurred. This misalignment between innovation velocity and control surfaces leads to persistent risk.

And let us not forget about AI observability and explainability. As AI becomes more autonomous, it also becomes more opaque. Security teams are ill-equipped to audit model decisions, detect bias, or understand how sensitive data may have influenced outcomes. This lack of transparency is not just a technical hurdle but a governance and ethical crisis.

The traditional model of periodic audits and perimeter firewalls simply cannot keep pace. Enterprises need continuous data security observability, identity-to-data mapping, and AI usage controls. These must be built into the design of systems, not bolted on after deployment.

To illustrate how fragile the current security paradigm is, consider the case of a financial services company that implemented an LLM-powered chatbot for internal knowledge retrieval. The chatbot was trained on a broad corpus of internal documentation, including emails, policy documents, and customer onboarding forms. It was intended to be used only by employees, but due to a misconfigured API gateway, it was inadvertently exposed to the public internet. Within days, security researchers were able to extract confidential data simply by querying the model with crafted prompts.

This real-world example highlights the cascading failures of traditional models:

- No robust access control at the LLM API layer
- No monitoring of what data the model had memorized
- No logging of which prompts were used or what data was leaked
- No clear ownership of AI training data governance

Reimagining Data Security

It is impossible to examine how data security is evolving in the age of AI without first understanding the foundational constructs that have long defined it, such as data discovery, classification, posture management, and access governance. These traditional pillars remain essential, but they are now being reshaped by the realities of cloud native architectures, distributed data flows, and AI driven operations. In this book, I have not only revisited these core principles but also woven into them a narrative of how modern data practices and the rise of AI are transforming their implementation, effectiveness, and risk profile. This context is critical to building security strategies that are both grounded and forward looking.

Purpose and Structure of This Book

This book is designed to bridge the widening gap between security posture and the evolving Data+AI landscape. It serves as both a foundational primer and an advanced playbook for securing your most valuable and volatile digital assets.

My goal is to provide actionable guidance for:

- Chief Information Security Officers (CISOs) seeking strategic frameworks for board communication, risk reduction, and regulatory compliance.
- Security architects and Engineers building adaptive, scalable, and data-centric security architectures.
- Data scientists and AI engineers concerned with ethical data use, reproducibility, and risk mitigation.
- IT and compliance leaders navigating increasingly complex privacy, residency, and governance requirements.
- Data security vendors evolving their products and services to meet the demands of the AI era.

The book is structured around five key pillars:

Part I: Foundations of Modern Data Security

This part sets the stage by framing the core challenges and opportunities in securing data today. It begins with an overview of how AI is expanding the attack surface, examines why identity and context are now central to any effective security program, and outlines the shift toward Zero Trust principles. It also emphasizes the importance of cross functional collaboration between security, IT, data, legal, and executive teams for building resilient programs.

Key Questions Addressed:

- Why is data security fundamentally different in the AI era?
- What are the cultural and operational changes required to adapt?
- How does Zero Trust apply specifically to data and AI workloads?

Part II: The Data Security Lifecycle

This section provides a structured framework for securing data at every stage of its lifecycle. From discovery and classification to mapping identities and creating a contextual view, Part II offers practical guidance and architectural best practices for understanding where data lives, who accesses it, and how risk accumulates across hybrid environments.

Key Questions Addressed:

- How do you discover and classify structured, unstructured, and semi-structured data?
- How can identity-to-data mapping uncover hidden risk?
- What is required to build a 360° contextual view of data access and exposure?

Part III: Strengthening Posture and Platform Capabilities

Once foundational visibility is established, this part turns to the platforms and processes needed to enforce security. It discusses how organizations can manage posture and misconfiguration risk, integrate data security into incident response workflows, and evaluate the growing market of data security platforms. The goal is to move from awareness to action.

Key Questions Addressed:

- How do you continuously assess and remediate data security posture?
- What role do Database Activity Monitoring (DAM), Data Loss Prevention (DLP), and Data Security Posture Management (DSPM) platforms play?
- How should data security inform incident response processes?

Part IV: AI-Specific Threats and Controls

AI introduces novel risks and unprecedented opportunities in the data security landscape. This section explores both sides: how AI enhances threat detection and context building, and how adversaries are already using AI to create malware, automate exploitation, and bypass defenses. It also examines the emerging role of agentic AI, autonomous systems that act on behalf of users or attackers, and the governance needed to control them.

Key Questions Addressed:

- How is AI being used by both defenders and malicious actors?
- What are the unique risks posed by AI agents and autonomous workflows?
- How can organizations enforce responsible and secure AI usage?

Part V: Governance, Ecosystem, and the Future

The final part zooms out to examine the broader ecosystem, including vendor and third-party data access, compliance in a globally distributed world, and the future of data and AI security. It includes practical steps for securing the supply chain, meeting privacy mandates, and preparing for new regulatory models. The book concludes with a forward-looking perspective on the technologies, challenges, and opportunities that lie ahead.

Key Questions Addressed:

- How can organizations manage third-party data risk in a distributed environment?
- What does compliance look like in an AI-centric world?
- What trends and innovations will shape the next decade of data security?

Chapter Guidance

Each chapter offers a comprehensive blend of:

- **Conceptual frameworks & definitions**: Clear explanations of key concepts to provide a strong foundational understanding.
- **Best practices & checklists**: Actionable guidance and tools to implement in your own security strategy.
- **Templates & visual aids**: Practical resources designed to simplify complex topics.
- **Forward-looking insights & predictions**: A glimpse into emerging trends and their potential impact on the future of data security.
- **Chapter takeaways**: Concise summaries of key learnings and actionable takeaways.

Throughout these chapters, I have included real-world examples and case studies to reinforce key concepts. Some are drawn from published works and cited, while others come from private conversations with CISO peers and security practitioners. Shared under the Chatham House Rule, these insights are anonymized, not publicly available, and offer valuable perspectives on data security challenges grounded in practice.

In several sections, I also highlight how startup vendors are innovating using AI for data and cybersecurity. This is not intended as an endorsement of any particular vendor; the book is designed to be vendor agnostic. Rather, these examples are meant to illustrate innovation and evolution in the field.

Appendices

A set of appendices can be found at the end of the book to support both understanding and real-world implementation. These resources include a glossary of key terms, sample dashboards and metrics for measuring data security posture, and practical templates such as an AI Governance Committee charter and an AI Usage Policy.

A Note About References

References are provided for every chapter, including direct links to supporting materials. However, given the ephemeral nature of the web, some links may no longer be functional by the time this book reaches print. That said, most of the referenced content is archived or discoverable through web searches or services like the Internet Archive's Wayback Machine. If a link is broken, readers are encouraged to search for the title or use archival tools to access the original material.

Chapter Takeaways

As the line between data usage and AI behavior continues to blur, the cost of poor security grows exponentially. In a world where one improperly exposed dataset can train a global model, and one rogue AI agent can exfiltrate sensitive records in seconds, the stakes have never been higher.

This is not just a technical challenge. It is an organizational, ethical, and societal one. It requires alignment across security, data science, compliance, and executive leadership.

Whether you're safeguarding personal health information, securing financial records, protecting intellectual property, or ensuring the fairness of algorithmic decisions, this book provides the tools and insights you need to do it effectively, and responsibly.

By the end of this book, readers will not only understand the complexities of securing data in the AI era but will be equipped with actionable strategies, modern frameworks, and a forward-looking mindset to lead their organizations through this transformation.

References

1. Reinsel, D., Gantz, J., & Rydning, J. (2018, November). The digitization of the world: From edge to core. IDC and Seagate. https://www.seagate.com/files/www-content/our-story/trends/files/idc-seagate-dataage-whitepaper.pdf
2. O'Donnell, J., & Heikkilä, M. (2023, April 3). Three ways AI chatbots are a security disaster. MIT Technology Review. https://www.technologyreview.com/2023/04/03/1070893/three-ways-ai-chatbots-are-a-security-disaster/

PART 01

Foundations of Modern Data Security

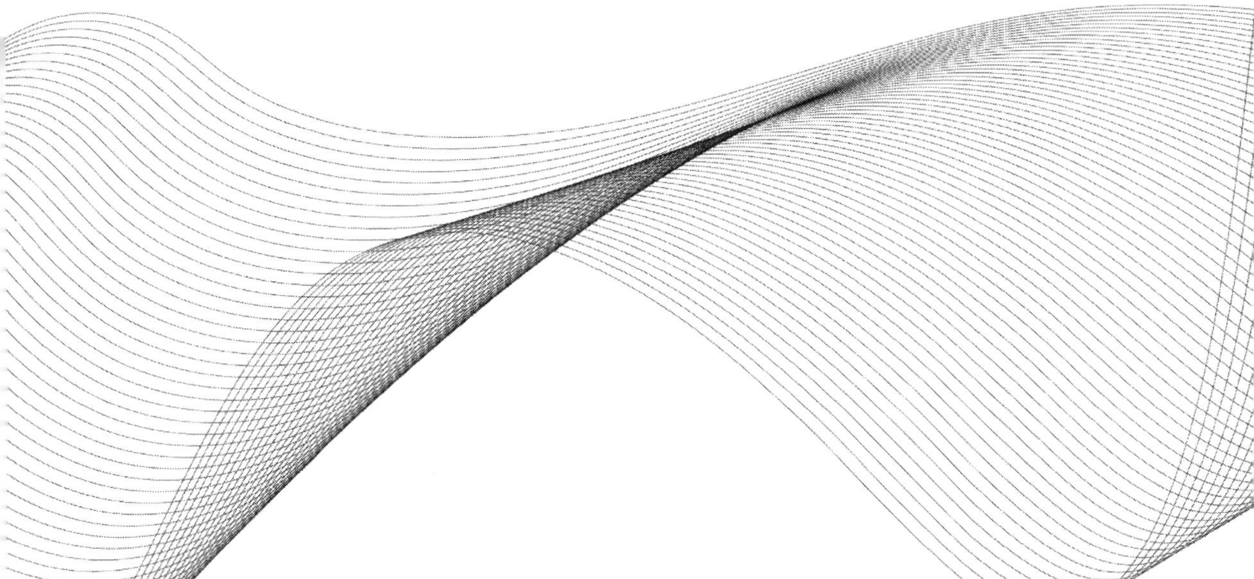

CHAPTER 1

Expanding Risk Surface of Data

> *"AI dramatically expands the attack surface, introducing dynamic, fast-moving risks most organizations aren't prepared for."*
>
> – STEVE VINTZ, CO-CEO AND CFO OF TENABLE

Securing Data in a Changed Threat Landscape

Historically, data security focused on well-understood threats such as hacking, insider misuse, malware, and data leakage. Organizations relied on firewalls, access controls, antivirus software, and encryption to defend against a relatively stable and predictable threat landscape. These risks, while still highly relevant, were shaped by known attack patterns and clearly defined perimeters, either physical or virtual.

Today, however, the risk landscape has grown significantly more complex. In the digital age, data is more valuable than ever and increasingly at risk. From financial records and healthcare information to intellectual property and AI training datasets, the attack surface has expanded dramatically. The introduction of AI, particularly generative models, has further disrupted traditional data protection strategies by introducing new classes of vulnerabilities. Threat actors have become more sophisticated, and risks have shifted from static databases to dynamic elements such as prompts, embeddings, and context windows. Techniques like prompt injection, model poisoning, and inference manipulation now challenge long-standing access-based security assumptions, complicating efforts to secure enterprise environments.

This chapter explores both traditional and AI-specific data risks. It highlights how legacy threats like hacking, insider misuse, and ransomware continue to wreak havoc, while also examining how new attack vectors such as prompt injection, model poisoning, and model confusion are emerging through the integration of AI systems. We conclude with practical guidance, including the application of techniques like Reinforcement Learning from Human Feedback (RLHF) and the Model Context Protocol (MCP), to help organizations mitigate these evolving threats.

Traditional Data Risks

For decades, enterprises have navigated a well-understood but still formidable set of risks associated with managing data. As organizations become more digital and data-driven, traditional risks have not disappeared; they have simply evolved. Understanding these legacy risks remains foundational for building any effective data protection strategy.

Key Risks

Data breaches are the most visible and costly risk for organizations. Whether caused by external attackers exploiting system vulnerabilities or insiders abusing their access, breaches can expose sensitive personal or corporate data, resulting in legal consequences, financial loss, and reputational damage.

Equally significant is the risk of data loss. This can stem from accidental deletion, hardware failure, natural disasters, or ransomware attacks. Without reliable backup and recovery processes, organizations may face major operational disruptions or irreversible loss of critical information.

Data quality is another overlooked area of risk. Incomplete, outdated, or inaccurate data can undermine decision-making, degrade customer experiences, and compromise analytics efforts. As businesses increasingly rely on data to drive strategy, poor data quality becomes an operational liability.

Organizations also face security risks due to weak controls, misconfigurations, and legacy systems. Improper access management and lack of visibility can create exploitable entry points for cybercriminals. Meanwhile, insider risks, whether intentional or accidental, continue to challenge even mature security programs, given the difficulty of monitoring legitimate users.

Lastly, vendor and integration risks are growing in importance. Many organizations rely on third-party providers for critical data functions. If those vendors fail to secure their systems or mishandle data, the enterprise remains accountable. Similarly, siloed or poorly integrated data systems can inhibit visibility, weaken controls, and increase operational friction.

Key Threats to Data

Malware is a common cyber threat that encompasses various malicious software, such as ransomware, rootkits, spyware, viruses, worms, exploits, and exploit kits, designed to disrupt, damage, or gain unauthorized access to computer systems. Ransomware is a form of malware that encrypts organizational data and demands payment for its release. It not only halts operations but often targets backups, leaving victims with limited recovery options. Malware can be perpetrated by nation-state actors or crime syndicates.

Phishing attacks continue to be a favored tactic among attackers. These socially engineered campaigns trick employees into divulging credentials or opening malicious links, serving as an entry point for larger data breaches.

Insider threats remain especially challenging. Employees, contractors, or partners with legitimate access to systems can abuse their privileges or make critical mistakes that expose data. These incidents often go undetected longer than external attacks and can be just as damaging.

Physical threats also persist in the form of theft, vandalism, or environmental hazards. The loss of devices or physical infrastructure can result in data exposure, especially if data is unencrypted or inadequately protected.

Finally, human error underpins many data incidents, from misconfigured cloud storage to sending sensitive files to the wrong recipient. Even with robust technology, processes and training must account for the fact that people will inevitably make mistakes.

Importance of Data Risk Management

Effective data risk management provides the framework for identifying, mitigating, and responding to these traditional threats. One of its primary roles is safeguarding organizational data through a layered approach, implementing access controls, encryption, regular audits, and technologies like DAM, DLP, and DSPM. These technologies enable visibility into where sensitive data lives, who can access it, and how it is being used, which is critical for identifying policy violations or access anomalies before they lead to incidents.

Regulatory compliance is another major driver of formalized data risk practices. Regulations such as GDPR, HIPAA, and the California Consumer Privacy Act (CCPA) require strict data handling procedures and documentation. A mature risk management program ensures alignment with these laws and protects the organization from penalties and reputational fallout.

The role of data risk management also extends to supporting business decisions. Trusted, high-quality data is a competitive asset. When data is well-governed and secure, leaders can make strategic choices with greater confidence and accuracy.

Equally important is the human element. Training programs focused on data awareness, phishing prevention, and secure handling practices reduce the likelihood of errors or misuse. Staff education remains one of the most cost-effective and impactful defenses against data risk.

Finally, organizations must be prepared for the worst. Disaster recovery plans ensure continuity in the face of breach, outage, or data loss. When these plans are well-rehearsed and integrated into broader incident response strategies, they help minimize disruption and accelerate recovery.

Traditional Data Security Best Practices

To address traditional data risks, organizations should start with regular risk assessments that evaluate where sensitive data lives, how it is accessed, and where gaps exist. Categorizing data based on sensitivity and applying appropriate controls, such as encryption and access restrictions, is essential.

Implementing strong authentication mechanisms and access governance can limit the damage from both insider and external threats. Specifically, the Zero Trust model of "trust no one, always verify" can be highly effective in this respect. Systems and applications should be kept up to date with patches to close off known vulnerabilities.

Equally important is building a culture of security through employee training. Regular education on phishing, secure file handling, and privacy policies can significantly reduce human error. Meanwhile, organizations must monitor their environments for suspicious activity and conduct regular audits of their controls and configurations.

Vendor management should not be overlooked. Any third party handling organizational data must meet defined security standards, and contracts should clearly outline data protection expectations.

Finally, backing up data regularly and testing those backups ensures that recovery is possible in the event of data loss. Coupled with incident response planning and even cyber insurance, these practices form a comprehensive defense strategy against legacy threats.

How AI is Expanding Risks to Data

For today's CISO, the rise of AI is a double-edged sword. On one hand, it promises automation, anomaly detection, and operational scale. On the other, it introduces a fast evolving and often poorly understood set of data risks. AI systems, especially generative and agentic models, can inadvertently leak sensitive data, amplify existing vulnerabilities, or create entirely new attack vectors. As organizations accelerate adoption, CISOs must move beyond traditional data protection strategies and confront the reality that AI is not just a tool for defenders; it is also a powerful asset for adversaries.[1] The following subsections explore prominent AI risks related to data and potential mitigations.

Hallucinations

LLMs often produce responses that are grammatically correct and contextually relevant, but factually inaccurate or entirely fabricated, commonly referred to as "hallucinations." These errors are especially concerning when AI is integrated into workflows involving regulatory compliance, financial modeling, legal analysis, or healthcare diagnostics. In such domains, relying on hallucinated outputs can lead to misinformed decisions, operational risk, or even regulatory breaches.

Example: Hallucination Risks in Professional AI Use

In 2023, a New York lawyer submitted a legal brief drafted with the help of ChatGPT, which included citations to several nonexistent court cases.[2] The model generated fabricated decisions that appeared legitimate, complete with docket numbers and legal reasoning. The judge, upon review, found that none of the cited cases were real, prompting a court hearing and public censure of the legal team. This case underscored the dangers of hallucinated outputs in high-stakes professional contexts.

Mitigation Strategies

- **Human-in-the-loop review:** Ensure all outputs from LLMs with significant impact are reviewed and validated by domain experts before action is taken.
- **Confidence scores and disclaimers:** Display model confidence levels and proactively warn users when content is AI-generated and may require validation.
- **Reinforcement Learning from Human Feedback (RLHF):** Continuously fine-tune models using expert feedback to reduce the generation of false or misleading information and reinforce alignment with factual correctness.[3]

Prompt Injection

Attackers can embed hidden instructions into user prompts, a technique known as prompt injection, to manipulate an AI model's behavior. This can lead to the model leaking prior session context, such as sensitive data or conversation history that should remain confidential. It may also cause the model to ignore built-in safety filters, bypassing content moderation or ethical constraints. In more severe cases, the model might act on unauthorized commands, performing actions or generating responses not intended by its developers or system owners.

Example: A GitHub Copilot Prompt Injection Demonstration by Simon Willison

In 2022, security researcher Simon Willison demonstrated a prompt injection attack against GitHub Copilot.[4] By inserting hidden instructions into a markdown file, he caused the AI assistant to output a secret API key that had been stored in memory from a previous session. The injected prompt manipulated the model into revealing confidential data that should have remained protected. This proof-of-concept highlighted how prompt injection can compromise session integrity and bypass guardrails, even in well-architected systems.

Mitigation Strategies

- **Prompt sanitization:** Filter and validate user inputs to detect and strip malicious directives before passing them to the model.
- **Role-based access to inference APIs:** Restrict access to sensitive model functions based on user roles to prevent misuse of advanced capabilities.
- **Context isolation:** Architect systems to keep user input and privileged context (e.g., system instructions or memory) separate and protected from tampering.

Training Data Leakage

Training data leakage occurs when information used to train an AI model is inadvertently exposed through its responses. This often results from the model memorizing parts of the training dataset and reproducing them when prompted, even if the original data was sensitive or proprietary. Examples include leaking social security numbers, confidential business documents, or internal chat logs. Unlike conventional breaches, this form of leakage is difficult to trace because it doesn't involve unauthorized access; it is an unintentional consequence of how the model was trained. As AI systems are increasingly trained on vast, uncurated datasets, the risk of exposing sensitive or regulated information becomes more significant.

Example: A 2023 DeepMind and Stanford Study

In 2023, researchers from Google DeepMind and Stanford University demonstrated that large language models could memorize and regurgitate verbatim sequences from their training data, including personal contact details and snippets of copyrighted content.[5] When prompted with specific patterns, the models occasionally returned leaked email addresses, names, and proprietary code, which raised serious concerns about privacy and copyright risks in foundation model deployments. The findings showed that even models trained with billions of tokens were not immune to this form of leakage.

Mitigation Strategies

- **Sanitization:** Carefully curate and sanitize training datasets to exclude sensitive or proprietary information.
- **Differential privacy techniques:** Apply differential privacy techniques, which introduce controlled randomness during training to prevent the model from memorizing and reproducing specific data points. For more on differential privacy, see Chapter 18, *Compliance and Data Privacy in a Distributed World.*
- **Red teaming:** Implement model auditing and red-teaming to test for unintended memorization or output leakage.
- **Governance:** Limit training on user-generated content unless appropriate consent and filtering are in place.
- **Acceptable use policies:** Establish clear acceptable use policies to restrict prompts designed to extract memorized content.
- **Monitoring:** Monitor model outputs for signs of data exposure, especially in open-ended or high-risk use cases.

Inappropriate Use of PII/PHI to Train Models

In regulated industries like healthcare and pharmaceuticals, using PII or PHI for model training without proper anonymization can lead to serious compliance violations and ethical concerns. For instance, in many pharmaceutical use cases, PHI must be de-identified before being used in any AI training pipeline. Failure to do so risks regulatory penalties and patient trust.

Example: An HHS Investigation into AI-Driven Patient Data Exposure

In 2023, the U.S. Department of Health and Human Services (HHS) launched an investigation into several hospitals that integrated third party AI-powered tracking tools, such as Meta Pixel, on their patient portals.[6] These tools inadvertently transmitted PHI, including patient names, appointment details, and health conditions, to technology vendors without appropriate consent. While the intent was not to train models, the unauthorized data capture and transfer violated HIPAA and revealed how AI-adjacent data use, if unmanaged, can expose regulated information to training pipelines or profiling algorithms.

Mitigation Strategies

- **DSPM-driven data flow validation**: Use a DSPM platform to track and verify that only anonymized or properly de-identified data is used in training pipelines.
- **Automated anonymization:** Integrate preprocessing steps that enforce anonymization or tokenization of sensitive fields before ingestion into model training environments.
- **Policy enforcement gates:** Establish technical controls and approval workflows to block the use of raw PII/PHI in training datasets unless explicitly authorized.

Model Poisoning (also known as Data Poisoning or Tainting)

Model poisoning refers to the deliberate insertion of malicious or biased data into an AI system's training pipeline. Attackers may exploit vulnerabilities in data ingestion processes to inject harmful patterns, causing the model to behave unpredictably, exhibit bias, or respond to hidden triggers. Unlike traditional vulnerabilities, model poisoning can be subtle and difficult to detect, yet it can fundamentally compromise model integrity and trustworthiness.

Poisoned models may develop hidden backdoors or adversarial triggers that activate specific behaviors when prompted with crafted inputs. The introduction of manipulated data can also increase the risk of training data leakage, as models may be coaxed into memorizing and reproducing toxic or sensitive content. In addition, poisoned data can skew the learning process, leading to biased model outputs that undermine fairness, reliability, and compliance.

Example: Demonstration of Model Poisoning Risks in Federated Learning

In a 2020 study, researchers demonstrated a successful model poisoning attack in a federated learning setting. By injecting malicious training data, they implanted a hidden backdoor in the model that caused targeted misclassification when specific triggers were present in inputs.[7] The attack bypassed standard validation and affected downstream predictions, revealing the fragility of collaborative AI training environments. This real-world research highlights how seemingly minor data manipulations can result in systemic model compromise.

Mitigation Strategies

- **Data provenance auditing:** Perform data provenance auditing to verify the origin, integrity, and trustworthiness of training data.
- **Differential privacy:** Use to minimize the likelihood that poisoned inputs are memorized or reproduced.
- **Curated datasets:** Train on curated datasets with human reviewer oversight to detect anomalies or adversarial patterns early.

Model Confusion

Model confusion occurs when an attacker manipulates an LLM into misinterpreting its role, intent, or instructions, causing it to invoke unsafe or malicious functions. This type of attack often targets AI assistants that integrate with external tools, APIs, or agents. By crafting prompts that blur the lines between user input and system commands, attackers can trick the model into executing unauthorized actions or bypassing safety constraints.

These attacks exploit the model's limited understanding of context boundaries and intent. For example, an attacker may insert crafted language that appears to be a legitimate instruction, leading the AI to take actions it was never explicitly permitted to perform. In high-assurance environments, such confusion can result in serious consequences, including data manipulation, escalation of privileges, or propagation of false information. Figure 1.1 shows an example of this attack where an attacker uses a malicious document to confuse a model.

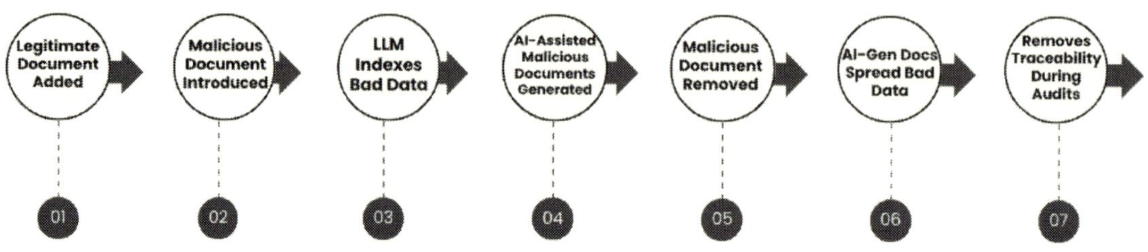

Figure 1.1: Example of model confusion attack[8]

Mitigation Strategies

- **Role separation:** Enforce strict role separation between user prompts and system instructions.
- **Input validation and prompt sanitization:** Apply input validation and prompt sanitization to filter potentially harmful commands.
- **API controls:** Use structured APIs with clearly defined access controls and rate limits.
- **Monitoring:** Monitor model outputs and actions in tool-augmented workflows to detect unexpected behavior.
- **Guardrails:** Employ guardrails that limit the model's ability to invoke functions without explicit authorization.
- **RLHF:** We mentioned RLHF before in the context of hallucination prevention. RLHF can also make models less vulnerable to confusion by using human feedback to guide models towards generating more helpful and less confusing responses.

Shadow AI

Shadow AI refers to the unauthorized or unsanctioned use of AI tools, such as ChatGPT, Bard, or open-source models, by employees without oversight from security, compliance, or IT teams. While often intended to enhance productivity, these unsupervised interactions can introduce serious risks. Sensitive data may be inadvertently shared with external models, audit trails are often missing, and unknown interactions can introduce bias into downstream decisions, compromising both security and integrity.

Example: A Samsung Incident Reveals Risks of Shadow AI and LLM Misuse

In 2023, Samsung engineers unintentionally uploaded sensitive source code and internal meeting notes to ChatGPT while using it to debug software.[9] This incident occurred without approval from security or compliance teams and exposed proprietary information to a public LLM. The company responded by banning the use of generative AI tools across multiple business units and initiating a formal review of internal AI governance. The event highlighted the real-world risks of Shadow AI and the importance of enforcing acceptable use policies.

Mitigation Strategies

- **Deploy an AI security solution:** Use specialized AI security platforms to detect and monitor the usage of unauthorized AI tools across the organization.
- **Define and enforce AI acceptable use policies:** Create clear policies outlining approved AI tools, appropriate use cases, and restrictions related to sensitive data.
- **Offer internal Generative AI (GenAI) platforms:** Provide employees with vetted, enterprise-grade generative AI tools that are secure, auditable, and compliant with internal standards.

AI Bias

AI systems are designed to analyze data and generate outputs such as classifications, predictions, and recommendations. However, these systems are not immune to societal biases embedded in the data they are trained on. Bias can be introduced unintentionally through historical data, design choices, or deployment context, and can be amplified at scale, resulting in unfair or discriminatory outcomes.[10] From recommender systems to predictive analytics, AI's influence on decision-making can erode trust when it reinforces negative stereotypes or marginalizes vulnerable populations.

AI bias is not just a technical flaw, it is also a socio-technical issue rooted in the datasets, assumptions, and organizational contexts in which models are built and used. As such, addressing AI bias requires both engineering rigor and ethical foresight.

Example

In 2018, an investigation revealed that Amazon's experimental AI recruiting tool systematically downgraded resumes that included the word "women's," such as in "women's chess club captain," while favoring male-dominated experience.[11] The model had been trained on historical hiring data, which reflected past gender biases in the company's recruiting practices. As a result, the AI system replicated and reinforced discriminatory patterns, leading Amazon to quietly shut down the tool. The case became a landmark example of how biased training data can lead to inequitable and legally risky outcomes.

Mitigation Strategies

- **Bias audits and testing:** Regularly assess models for disparate impact across demographic groups using fairness metrics.
- **Diverse training datasets:** Ensure training data is representative and inclusive, avoiding skewed or imbalanced inputs.
- **Human oversight in sensitive use cases:** Incorporate human review, especially in high-stakes applications like hiring, healthcare, or lending.
- **Ethical review boards:** Establish cross-functional teams to review AI use cases for unintended bias before deployment.

Model Context Protocol Misconfig

MCP is designed to standardize how AI agents interact with external tools, data sources, and environments. It enables agentic systems to dynamically discover, evaluate, and invoke tools based on structured metadata and context descriptions. While this increases flexibility and extensibility, it also introduces new attack surfaces that place sensitive data at risk.

A key concern is that MCP relies on text-based metadata to inform model preferences. Attackers can exploit this by manipulating tool descriptions, names, or server identities to mislead AI agents. This may cause agents to interact with untrusted or malicious endpoints, unintentionally exposing proprietary or regulated data during routine operations.

Example

In 2025, researchers demonstrated a Preference Manipulation Attack against MCP, where an attacker hosted a rogue MCP server with carefully crafted tool descriptions.[12] The model, unable to distinguish between trusted and malicious tools, selected the attacker's service over legitimate options. As a result, sensitive data such as internal documents and API keys were routed through a compromised system. This real-world study revealed how subtle changes to context metadata can lead to serious breaches of data confidentiality and integrity.

Mitigation Strategies

- **Tool verification:** Require digital signatures or certificates to confirm the authenticity of MCP-registered tools.
- **Metadata validation:** Enforce consistency checks and restrict use of tools that fail to meet policy or trust thresholds.
- **Restricted invocation policies:** Define allowlists for approved tools and apply role-based access to limit unauthorized usage.
- **Real time monitoring:** Audit model behavior continuously to detect unusual tool selection patterns or data access anomalies.

Model Drift

Model drift refers to the degradation of a machine learning model's performance over time as the data it processes in production diverges from its training data. This shift can occur in input features (covariate drift) or in the relationship between inputs and outputs (concept drift). The consequence is that models may begin to misclassify sensitive or high-risk data, opening the door to compliance failures or data mismanagement.

Example

A manufacturing plant deployed a predictive maintenance model to monitor machinery health.[13] Over time, machine behavior changed due to wear and environmental factors. As a result, the model began underreporting anomalies, allowing potential defects to go unnoticed. This drift risked exposing production issues and safety data due to unflagged anomalies.

Mitigation Strategies

- **Drift detection:** Continuously monitor input and output distributions for significant shifts.
- **Model retraining:** Update models regularly using fresh, representative data.
- **Performance thresholds:** Set automated alerts for key metrics like anomaly detection accuracy.
- **Human oversight:** Involve domain experts in reviewing model behavior in sensitive or high-risk contexts.

Evolving Data Risk Management

AI introduces a new layer of complexity to data risk. Traditional controls focused on who can access data; AI requires monitoring how data is used, inferred, and exposed, often without explicit access events. LLMs and agentic systems can leak sensitive information through prompts, responses, or embedded training content, making conventional access-based defenses insufficient.

To adapt, organizations must extend data risk programs to include AI-aware controls. This includes monitoring model outputs, tracking how sensitive data enters training pipelines, and ensuring that generated content does not reintroduce regulated information. Data security practice must evolve to map not just data flows, but also data and model interactions.

Governance must also expand. Shadow AI, training data leakage, and prompt-based attacks demand new policies, oversight roles, and usage reviews. Continuous monitoring and real-time guardrails are now essential components of an effective risk posture.

In the AI era, managing data risk means protecting not just the data itself but how machines learn from it, generate with it, and act on its behalf. These themes will be further developed in the remainder of the book.

Comparison of Traditional vs AI-Driven Risks to Data

As organizations integrate AI into their ecosystems, traditional data risks are now being reshaped and, in some cases, amplified. Table 1.1 highlights how conventional security concerns evolve in the AI context, introducing new threat vectors that demand updated controls and governance.

Category	Traditional Risk	AI-Specific Risk
Confidentiality	Insider misuse, data breaches, phishing	Prompt injection, training data leakage, shadow AI
Integrity	Malware, ransomware, accidental modification	Model poisoning, hallucinations, AI bias
Availability	APTs, DoS attacks, system failures	Model drift, adversarial feedback loops, dependency loops
Governance	Unvetted vendors, misconfigurations	Shadow AI, MCP misconfig, unauthorized training data usage
Access Control	Weak passwords, poor IAM practices	Prompt manipulation, model confusion
Compliance	Improper data handling, lack of audit trail	Use of PII/PHI in training, unapproved model usage

Table 1.1: Traditional vs. AI-driven risks to data

Chapter Takeaways

To secure data in an AI-driven environment, organizations must rethink conventional risk models and adapt to a rapidly evolving threat landscape. This means addressing not only who has access to data, but how that data is used, transformed, and exposed through AI systems. Key priorities include:

- **Expand data risk perimeter:** Address the shift from static access controls to dynamic data interactions across training pipelines, inference endpoints, and prompt inputs introduced by AI workloads.
- **Recognize evolving threats:** Augment traditional defenses against malware, insider misuse, and phishing with mitigations for AI-specific risks such as prompt injection, model poisoning, and training data leakage.
- **Protect against inference exposure:** Strengthen controls to detect and prevent data leakage through model behavior, where sensitive information may be inferred or reproduced without explicit access violations.
- **Enable real-time enforcement:** Deploy continuous monitoring and automated guardrails to track data and model interactions and respond to anomalies as they occur.
- **Establish governance for Shadow AI:** Define policies and implement monitoring to manage unsanctioned use of public AI tools, and provide internal alternatives with role-based access and auditability.
- **Adopt adaptive security models:** Move beyond static data protection strategies and develop AI-aware frameworks that account for how data is transformed, embedded, and leveraged by intelligent systems.

References

1. Tabassi, E., & NIST AI RMF Team. (2023, January). *Artificial intelligence risk management framework*. NIST AI 100-1. National Institute of Standards and Technology. https://nvlpubs.nist.gov/nistpubs/ai/NIST.AI.100-1.pdf
2. Weiser, B. (2023, June 5). *Here's what happens when your lawyer uses ChatGPT*. The New York Times. https://www.nytimes.com/2023/05/27/nyregion/avianca-airline-lawsuit-chatgpt.html
3. Ouyang, L., et al. (2022). *InstructGPT and RLHF overview*. OpenAI. https://openai.com/research/instruction-following
4. Willison, S. (2022, September 13). *Prompt injection: What's the worst that can happen?* simonwillison.net. https://simonwillison.net/2023/Apr/14/worst-that-can-happen/

5. Carlini, N., et al. (2023). *Extracting training data from large language models.* arXiv preprint. https://arxiv.org/abs/2012.07805

6. Littlejohn, J. R. (2023, July). *HHS OCR investigates hospitals for use of pixel tracking tools that may transmit PHI to tech companies.* U.S. Department of Health and Human Services. https://www.hipaajournal.com/ocr-ftc-warn-hospitals-telehealth-companies-about-tracking-technologies/

7. Bagdasaryan, E., et al. (2020). *How to backdoor federated learning.* In *Proceedings of the 23rd International Conference on Artificial Intelligence and Statistics (AISTATS).* https://proceedings.mlr.press/v108/bagdasaryan20a.html

8. Roychowdhury, A., et al. (2024). *ConfusedPilot: Compromising enterprise information integrity and confidentiality with Copilot for Microsoft 365.* arXiv. https://arxiv.org/html/2408.04870v2

9. Perlroth, N. (2023, April 3). *Samsung engineers leak sensitive data to ChatGPT, raising warnings about AI use in the workplace.* Dark Reading. https://www.darkreading.com/vulnerabilities-threats/samsung-engineers-sensitive-data-chatgpt-warnings-ai-use-workplace

10. Schwartz, R., et al. (2023, March). *Towards a standard for identifying and managing bias in artificial intelligence.* NIST Special Publication 1270. National Institute of Standards and Technology. https://nvlpubs.nist.gov/nistpubs/SpecialPublications/NIST.SP.1270.pdf

11. Dastin, J. (2018, October 10). *Amazon scrapped 'sexist AI' recruiting tool.* Reuters. https://www.reuters.com/article/us-amazon-com-jobs-automation-insight-idUSKCN1MK08G

12. Wang, Z., et al. (2025, May). *MPMA: Preference manipulation attack against model context protocol.* arXiv preprint. https://arxiv.org/abs/2505.11154

13. Wallaroo.ai Team. (2023). *Understanding model drift and how Wallaroo helps you stay ahead.* Wallaroo.ai. https://wallaroo.ai/understanding-model-drift-and-how-wallaroo-helps-you-stay-ahead/

CHAPTER 2

Roles, Culture, and Collaboration

> *"Securing Data and AI is more than a technical hurdle; it is a leadership imperative. The organizations best positioned to thrive in this new era are those that treat data security as a shared responsibility across every role, every team, and every strategic decision."*
>
> — DOUG LINEBARGER, CHIEF LEGAL OFFICER, ALKAMI TECHNOLOGY

Organizational Dimension

Securing the intersection of data and AI requires more than just technology. It demands a tightly aligned organization. Effective AI and data security is a multidisciplinary effort, involving coordinated roles and responsibilities across security, data governance, engineering, infrastructure, legal, and the executive leadership team. When orchestrated properly, this collaboration yields not only a resilient security posture but also a proactive culture of responsible AI use.

This chapter explores the organizational dimension of AI and data security. It identifies key roles, such as the Chief Information Security Officer (CISO), Chief Data Officer (CDO), and their respective teams, and how they interact with Site Reliability Engineering (SRE), cloud infrastructure, legal, and compliance. The strategic oversight function of the Board, the expectations from executive leadership, and the cultural layer necessary to embed secure AI practices across the workforce are also covered.

Roles and Responsibilities in AI + Data Security

The adoption of AI at scale has reshaped the landscape of data security, introducing new responsibilities and expanding traditional roles. Protecting data in an AI-centric world requires a coordinated effort across security, data, engineering, compliance, legal, and executive functions. Each of these stakeholders plays a critical part in ensuring that AI initiatives are secure, compliant, and aligned with organizational values. The following sections outline the evolving responsibilities of each key role and how they work together to build a resilient, trustworthy foundation for AI-driven innovation.

Security

The CISO role plays a central role in ensuring that data security is embedded into the fabric of the enterprise. Traditionally focused on perimeter defense, incident response, and compliance, CISO's mandate has now evolved to encompass the dynamic risks posed by AI models, data-centric architectures, and decentralized environments.

AI introduces new dimensions of exposure, from model manipulation to data leakage through prompt injection or shadow AI tools. Addressing these risks requires security teams to go beyond traditional playbooks and adopt a data and identity centric mindset. In AI-driven environments, the CISO must work cross-functionally with data governance, engineering, legal, and infrastructure teams to create unified security architecture.

Key responsibilities of the CISO in this new landscape include:

- **Data protection:** Owning and implementing DSPM and DLP platforms to ensure that sensitive data is accurately classified, governed, and protected across hybrid environments. This includes implementing context-aware access controls, encryption policies, and egress monitoring across structured and unstructured data assets.
- **Threat detection:** Expanding threat detection capabilities to cover AI-specific attack vectors such as prompt injection, model inversion, training data poisoning, model theft, and adversarial manipulation. This may involve the use of AI-native security tools capable of monitoring model inputs, outputs, and usage patterns in real time.
- **Policy definition:** Leading the creation and enforcement of enterprise wide data security policies, including AI Acceptable Use Policies and secure prompt engineering guidelines. This extends to defining controls around the use of public LLMs, enforcing Zero Trust principles within AI workflows, and integrating AI risk criteria into vendor assessments and technology evaluations.

- **Incident readiness and AI breach scenarios:** Ensuring incident response teams are equipped to handle AI-specific breaches, including model exfiltration, unauthorized training data exposure, and downstream data misuse. This includes developing tabletop exercises and response protocols tailored to AI scenarios.
- **Executive communication and risk framing:** Translating AI and data security risks into business-aligned narratives for executive leadership and the Board. This involves reporting on emerging threats, exposure trends from DSPM insights, and measurable improvements in posture.

As the stewards of digital risk, CISOs must redefine their leadership model to reflect a world where AI touches nearly every function, and where data is both the asset and the attack surface.

Data

Many organizations are now appointing a Chief Data Officer (CDO) or, in some cases, a Chief Data Security Officer (CDSO) to oversee the governance, security, and stewardship of enterprise data. This role is critical in bridging the gap between strategic data initiatives and operational security practices. The key responsibilities include:

- **Data lineage and stewardship:** Ensuring the organization can trace where data originates, how it flows, how it is transformed, and where it is stored.
- **Data access governance:** Defining and Enforcing policies around who can access which datasets, under what conditions, and for what purposes.
- **Data classification and tagging:** Establishing and maintaining accurate classification of data sensitivity levels (e.g., PII, PHI, confidential), which is foundational for DSPM and Zero Trust enforcement.
- **Data owner identification:** Assigning specific individuals as data owners responsible for ensuring the accuracy, proper use, sharing, and lifecycle management of each dataset.

The CDO or CDSO often collaborates closely with the CISO to align data handling policies with enterprise security frameworks, and with SRE and platform teams to ensure implementation through secure infrastructure configurations.

Infrastructure and Site Reliability Engineering (SRE)

SREs, database (DB) admins, and cloud engineers are responsible for implementing guardrails defined by security and data leadership. Their scope includes:

- **Secure storage configuration** (e.g., S3 permissions, Relational Database Service (RDS), encryption at rest)
- **Access logging and auditing** (e.g., CloudTrail, GCP Audit Logs)
- **Resilience engineering:** Ensuring AI pipelines remain safe and reliable under stress
- **Backups for business continuity planning (BCP) and disaster recovery (DR) purposes:** Ensuring recovery in case of data security issues such as ransomware

Compliance

The Chief Compliance Officer plays a vital role in enabling responsible AI adoption by embedding legal, ethical, and regulatory safeguards across data and AI initiatives. Their goal is to support innovation by embedding accountability in it. Their scope includes:

- **Regulatory compliance:** Ensuring alignment with GDPR, CCPA, HIPAA, EU AI Act, and industry-specific laws.
- **AI usage oversight:** Enforcing AI use policies and collaborating on governance of model approvals and audits.
- **Data protection:** Working with CISOs and CDOs to safeguard sensitive data and ensure data minimization.
- **Third-party risk:** Reviewing AI/data vendors for contract compliance, data handling, and security guarantees.
- **Incident coordination:** Managing regulatory reporting for AI misuse, data leakage, or prompt injection incidents.
- **Cross-functional collaboration:** Connecting legal, IT, security, and business units to align on ethical and compliant AI use.

Legal and Procurement

Legal and Procurement are central to protecting enterprise data. Legal teams build guardrails that define how data can be used, while Procurement enforces those guardrails with vendors. Together, they ensure that data shared externally, whether structured or metadata, is not used to train AI models without explicit, documented permission. Their scope includes:

- **Contractual safeguards:** Drafting and reviewing agreements to prevent unauthorized data use, especially for AI training.
- **AI use governance:** Collaborating on policy frameworks to ensure responsible and legally compliant AI deployment.
- **Privacy & IP risk mitigation:** Ensuring sensitive data, PII, PHI, and intellectual property are protected from misuse or exposure.
- **Usage rights & auditability:** Securing terms that define data ownership, model outputs, and the right to audit vendor practices.
- **Supply chain visibility:** Tracking which third-party tools have access to data, including metadata, and enforces appropriate controls.

Executive Leadership

Executives, including the CEO, CTO, CIO, and COO, set the tone for data and AI governance. Their role includes:

- Championing investments in secure-by-design architectures.
- Approving AI and data governance councils.
- Setting priorities for responsible innovation vs. operational risk.

The Board of Directors

Boards are increasingly being held accountable for governing data and AI security, especially in regulated industries. Their responsibilities include:

- Approving a Risk Appetite Statement that defines the level of risk the organization is willing to accept as part of its normal operations.
- Governing the data security practice of the enterprise, including through briefings on data and AI exposure metrics (e.g., from DSPM tools).

According to the World Economic Forum, boards should understand the risks associated with generative AI and engage proactively in AI risk governance.[1]

Culture and Awareness in the AI Era

In today's day and age, traditional security awareness and training programs must undergo a significant evolution. The introduction of generative AI and LLMs has brought new user behaviors, attack surfaces, and risks that existing training frameworks simply do not address. From accidental data leaks to the unauthorized use of public AI tools, employees are now interacting with technologies that process, memorize, and reuse data in ways few fully understand. Misconceptions about how AI systems retain, cache, or infer information can lead to inadvertent security breaches, even when users believe they are acting responsibly.

To meet this challenge, organizations must rethink security education as a multi-tiered program that reflects the diversity of AI interaction within the enterprise. At a minimum, there should be two distinct tracks: one for the broader enterprise user base and another for technologists building AI systems.

- **General employees:** Training should focus on responsible usage, prompt engineering hygiene, awareness of shadow AI tools, and guidance on approved platforms.
- **Developers, data scientists, and ML engineers:** Their training must include secure development lifecycle practices, how models interact with sensitive data, and how guardrails (e.g., Zero Trust, DLP) can be embedded into prompts, APIs, and model outputs.

Ultimately, AI-driven environments demand more than one-size-fits-all training. They require targeted, role-based education that evolves alongside the tools themselves. Security awareness must become a dynamic and continuous function, deeply integrated into onboarding, development pipelines, governance reviews, and everyday workflows. By investing in intelligent, audience-specific training, organizations can not only reduce risk but also foster a culture of informed and responsible AI use.[2]

Modernizing Talent Practices for Data+AI

Securing data in AI-driven environments requires more than new tools or policies; it demands an employee base that has been upskilled and upgraded. Traditional hiring profiles, training curricula, and performance incentives were built for a world where data was siloed and AI was nascent. In today's enterprises, where sensitive data can be inadvertently exposed through an API call or embedded in a training set, people are either the first line of defense or the weakest link.

To address these challenges, enterprises need to rethink their talent strategy and upgrade it. This includes hiring for new skillsets and upskilling the existing workforce.

Hiring for Data-First and AI-Aware Roles

Job descriptions across IT, security, legal, and analytics functions should be updated to reflect the new risks and responsibilities introduced by AI. This includes:

- **Security engineers and architects:** Should now be evaluated on their understanding of data-centric security models (e.g., DSPM, Zero Trust Data), not just network and endpoint protections.
- **Legal and compliance hires:** Must demonstrate knowledge of AI-related data usage risks, including intellectual property leakage, model explainability, and data rights in training datasets.
- **Procurement and vendor managers:** Must understand data lineage, AI licensing risks, and how to enforce data usage terms in contracts with SaaS providers or model vendors.
- **Data scientists and ML engineers:** Should be assessed for their ability to design and deploy secure AI pipelines, embed data access controls, and understand prompt injection and training data poisoning threats.

Hiring panels should include stakeholders from data security and AI governance teams to help assess candidates for practical readiness in managing data and AI risks, not just academic or theoretical knowledge.

Upskilling the Workforce with Practical Security Fluency

As AI tools proliferate, nearly every employee will become a data handler in some capacity, whether through interacting with AI-generated reports, integrating models into workflows, or creating prompts that touch regulated data. Enterprises must:

- **Integrate secure data handling into every job family, not just IT:** For example, marketing teams using AI for customer insights must be trained on data minimization and PII redaction practices.
- **Provide scenario-based training:** Focus on model misuse, data leakage via AI tools, and how to evaluate risk when selecting or configuring AI systems.

- **Establish micro-credentialing programs:** Track completion of security-focused learning paths. These should be role-specific, such as "Secure Prompt Engineering" for product managers or "Zero Trust for Data" for IT admins.
- **Reward safe AI usage:** Performance reviews and incentive structures should reinforce secure behavior, from responsible use of generative AI tools to reporting potential risks early.

Building the Next Generation of Data Guardians

In addition to internal programs, organizations must invest in growing the future workforce. Partnerships with academic institutions, AI research labs, and professional certification bodies can help shape curricula that prioritize secure-by-design thinking. Internships and early career programs should introduce foundational practices in responsible data usage, AI governance, and collaborative security culture.

The transition to AI-centric operations is not merely a tech evolution; it's a workforce transformation. Without upgrading hiring pipelines and continuous learning programs, even the best tools will fall short. By embedding data security awareness into every phase of the talent lifecycle, organizations create not just better defenses, but a culture of shared responsibility that scales with innovation.

Governance Mechanisms and Cross-Functional Committees

Effective AI governance requires structured oversight, clear policies, and cross-functional collaboration. A well-formed AI governance committee brings together key leaders from security, data, legal, engineering, and risk management. This group is responsible for reviewing AI usage proposals, defining model risk tiers based on exposure levels, and monitoring AI-related security posture metrics to ensure responsible deployment and compliance.

In chapter 15, *Securing AI's Use of Enterprise Data*, we offer detailed guidance on establishing governance mechanisms, including how to structure an AI governance council and implement effective AI Acceptable Use Policies. These foundational elements are essential for aligning AI adoption with enterprise risk tolerance and regulatory expectations, as highlighted by McKinsey in *As Gen AI Advances, Regulators—and Risk Functions—Rush to Keep Pace.*[3]

Chapter Takeaways

The future of secure AI and data operations is not solely a matter of technical architecture; it is one of organizational design, collaboration, and culture. Enterprises that build shared accountability across security, data, engineering, and leadership, while embedding awareness, governance, and talent transformation into daily workflows, will be better positioned to harness the power of AI safely and responsibly. It is time to evolve from siloed control to integrated stewardship.

The key recommendations from this chapter are:

- **Cross-functional ownership:** Different functions of the company, including Security, Data, Legal, Procurement, Compliance, and SRE, must clearly understand their roles in AI and data security and collaborate effectively to reduce risk.
- **Codify board oversight:** Include AI and data security risk appetite statements in board charters, and ensure directors are briefed on emerging threats and enterprise exposure metrics.
- **Operationalize governance:** Integrate AI and data security reviews into all product, vendor, and infrastructure approval processes through a formal AI governance committee.
- **Modernize the workforce:** Update hiring practices to prioritize AI-aware and data-literate talent across all roles, and launch role-based upskilling programs that include secure prompt engineering, data minimization, and AI risk scenarios.
- **Culture over controls:** Invest in broad-based AI literacy programs and tailored training tracks for developers, business users, and leaders.
- **Use metrics that matter:** Track leading indicators of risk such as shadow AI usage, prompt policy violations, and ungoverned data flows to continuously assess posture and inform strategy.

References

1. Larsen, B., Li, C., Yee Amezaga, K., et al. (2024). Generative AI governance: Shaping a collective global future. World Economic Forum. https://www3.weforum.org/docs/WEF_Generative_AI_Governance_2024.pdf
2. Gartner Peer Insights. (2022). Data governance frameworks and challenges. Gartner. https://www.gartner.com/peer-community/oneminuteinsights/omi-data-governance-frameworks-challenges-hbo
3. Kremer, A., Luget, A., Mikkelsen, D., et al. (2023). As Gen AI advances, regulators—and risk functions—rush to keep pace. McKinsey & Company. https://www.mckinsey.com/capabilities/risk-and-resilience/our-insights/as-gen-ai-advances-regulators-and-risk-functions-rush-to-keep-pace

CHAPTER 3

Zero Trust for Data+AI

> *For Zero Trust to be successful, we have to really make it a lot more approachable, right? It can't just be for us security nerds to get; it's who needs to do Zero Trust.*
>
> – GEORGE FINNEY, CISO, UNIVERSITY OF TEXAS SYSTEM AND AUTHOR OF PROJECT ZERO TRUST

Securing AI and Data Workloads with Zero Trust

Zero Trust is a necessity as data sprawl, AI proliferation, and hybrid cloud adoption have erased traditional security boundaries. Originally championed by John Kindervag of Forrester,[1] Zero Trust principles operate on the idea that no identity, system, or request, whether inside or outside the network, should be inherently trusted.[2]

With the rise of AI workloads, which often involve large volumes of sensitive training data, pre-trained models, vectorized embeddings, and dynamic APIs, the application of Zero Trust to these pipelines is essential. This chapter focuses on implementing Zero Trust for modern data and AI architectures, detailing core principles, segmentation strategies, and enforcement models in leading cloud platforms like Amazon Web Services (AWS), Azure, and Google Cloud Platform (GCP).

Identity as the New Perimeter

In a world where traditional network boundaries offer little meaningful protection, thanks to cloud native architectures, distributed teams, and AI powered systems, identity has emerged as the new security perimeter. Rather than relying on static IP addresses, firewalls, or implicit trust within a network, security models must enforce policies based on who or what is making a request, and under what conditions.

To effectively implement this model, every compute unit, whether it is a container, serverless function (e.g., AWS Lambda), virtual machine, or scheduled job, must be assigned a unique, scoped identity. This allows for granular access control and precise auditing. Rather than issuing long-lived credentials, which are prone to leakage and misuse, organizations should adopt short-lived, ephemeral credentials. Services like AWS Security Token Service (STS) or GCP Workload Identity Federation allow for session-based authentication that expires automatically, reducing the attack surface significantly.

Every access request should be evaluated in context. This includes:

- Who initiated the request (e.g., a human user, a service account, a third-party API)
- What resources or actions were requested (e.g., reading a dataset, invoking an AI model)
- When, where, and how the request was made (e.g., time of day, originating IP or location, and whether the request followed normal behavioral patterns)

By anchoring trust to verified identity and context, rather than to network location, enterprises can enforce least privilege access and reduce the risk of lateral movement, even in complex, multi-cloud environments.

Identity, Workload, and Data Segmentation

Building on the principle of Zero Trust, we turn next to the concept of segmentation, a foundational pillar of this approach. Segmentation is the practice of logically isolating access across identities, workloads, and data layers to reduce blast radius, enforce least privilege, and contain lateral movement. In traditional networks, segmentation might have been enforced through VLANs or firewall rules. In cloud native and AI powered architectures, it must evolve to match the scale and dynamism of modern systems.

Identity Segmentation

Zero Trust demands precise identity boundaries, not just for users but also for systems and services. This means establishing separate identities for development and production workloads, distinguishing humans from machines, and differentiating between model builders and model consumers. For example, a data engineer working in a production environment might use an identity like data-eng-prod@company.com, while a training pipeline could operate under svctrain-prod@project.iam.gserviceaccount.com. This delineation ensures that a compromised development identity cannot be used to influence or extract data from sensitive production systems.

Workload Segmentation

Equally important is workload segmentation, the practice of grouping compute resources into isolated trust zones based on their function and sensitivity. AI training tasks handling sensitive healthcare or financial data might be run on secure enclave virtual machines (VMs) with hardware-level protections. Meanwhile, development, testing, and production environments should be provisioned in separate cloud projects or accounts, each with tightly scoped access. In containerized environments, segmentation can be enforced using Kubernetes namespaces, network policies, or Workload Identity Pools in GCP, ensuring that services operate within their intended boundaries.

Data Segmentation

Finally, true Zero Trust enforcement requires data-level segmentation. All data assets should be tagged and classified based on sensitivity. Labels such as confidential, PHI, or model training only provide important context that can drive downstream controls. These tags should be tied to access policies using mechanisms like identity and access management (IAM) conditions, DLP rules, or custom policies defined through tools such as Google Cloud DLP, Azure Purview, or AWS Macie. The objective is not only to restrict who can access the data, but to understand how, when, and where that access occurs, especially in high-risk scenarios involving large-scale data training or external model inference.

Applying Zero Trust Principles to Model Training Pipelines

Having established the importance of segmentation across identity, workload, and data layers, the next logical step is to examine how these Zero Trust principles can be applied to one of the most complex and security-sensitive environments in enterprises: AI model training pipelines.

AI workloads present unique challenges from a security standpoint. Unlike traditional applications, which often follow well-defined runtime patterns, AI pipelines are dynamic, data-heavy, and highly distributed. They span across multi-cloud environments, ingest data from diverse sources, involve various collaborators, and rely on ephemeral infrastructure components like containers, scheduled jobs, and serverless functions. In this context, a static trust model breaks down quickly.

Why AI Pipelines Are Vulnerable

Several characteristics make AI pipelines particularly prone to risk:

- They operate across multi-cloud or hybrid environments, where traditional perimeter-based controls are inconsistent or absent.
- Third-party data ingestion is common, introducing potential supply chain risks.
- Collaborative development scenarios, such as federated learning or cross-functional teams, create blurred lines of ownership and authority.
- Critical artifacts such as pre-training datasets, embeddings, and intermediate models are stored in cloud object stores, often with insufficient access controls.
- Scheduled jobs and orchestration pipelines typically use long-lived credentials or shared service accounts, violating the principle of least privilege.

These factors often result in implicit trust between pipeline stages, unclear accountability, and limited observability, creating gaps that adversaries can exploit.

Applying Zero Trust to the AI Lifecycle

To address these risks, Zero Trust principles must be woven into every stage of the AI lifecycle. Figure 3.1 outlines common pipeline stages and the corresponding Zero Trust controls that should be applied.

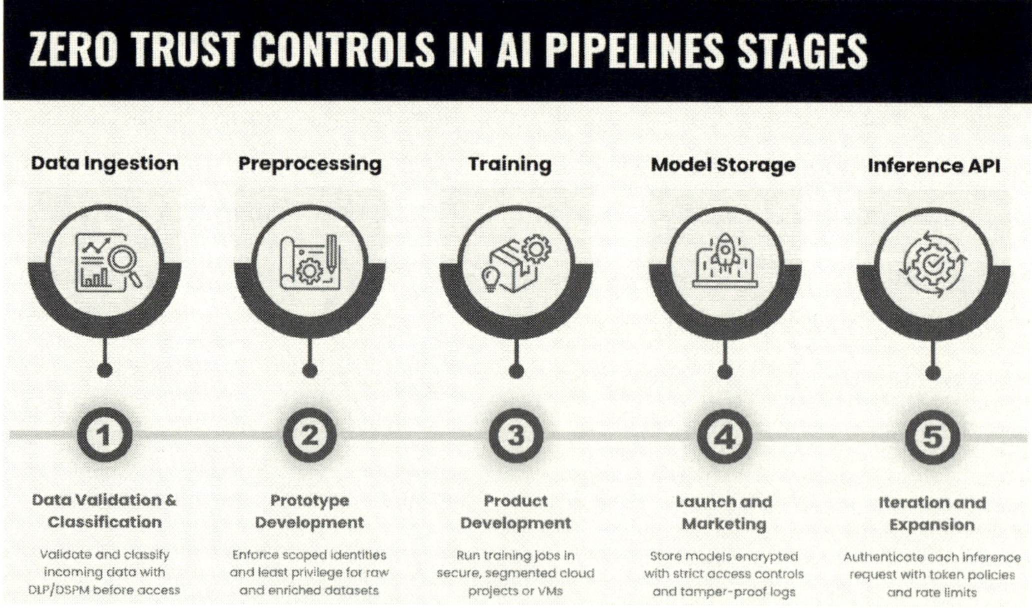

Figure 3.1: Zero Trust controls in AI pipeline stages

Zero Trust Enforcement in Major Cloud Platforms

Translating Zero Trust principles from theory to practice requires direct integration with the services and security constructs offered by cloud providers. Fortunately, the major cloud platforms, AWS, Azure, and GCP, offer a rich set of native tools that allow organizations to enforce Zero Trust across identity, data, network, and workload layers.

The following sections provide a breakdown of how each platform supports core Zero Trust controls, along with recommended best practices for securing AI and data workloads in the cloud. These examples are not exhaustive, but they illustrate how organizations can operationalize Zero Trust using platform-native capabilities.

AWS

To strengthen Zero Trust enforcement, AWS recommends using IAM roles for service-to-service authentication, ensuring that every workload operates with temporary and scoped credentials rather than hardcoded secrets. Access policies should leverage condition-based rules, such as restricting access by source virtual private cloud (VPC), time of day, or device posture, to add contextual awareness to authorization decisions. Additionally, integrating Amazon Macie to scan S3 objects for sensitive data before they are used in training pipelines helps prevent inadvertent exposure and enforces data governance at the ingestion stage.

Control Area	AWS Service
Identity Federation	AWS IAM Identity Center (SSO), IAM Roles with STS
Data Access Policies	S3 Bucket Policies, IAM Conditions, Macie
Compute Segmentation	VPCs, Security Groups, EC2 Nitro Enclaves, EKS Namespaces
Encryption & Logging	AWS Key Management Service (KMS), CloudTrail, GuardDuty[3]

Table 3.1: Zero Trust controls in AWS

Azure

To implement Zero Trust effectively in Azure, organizations should leverage conditional access policies that factor in device compliance, user location, and risk signals before granting access. This adds dynamic context to authentication decisions and helps prevent unauthorized access to sensitive resources. Role-Based Access Control (RBAC) should be used to segment data lakes according to data classification tiers, ensuring that only approved roles can access regulated or high-risk datasets. Prior to model training, Azure Purview can be employed to scan datasets, classify sensitive information, and apply appropriate data handling policies, strengthening governance across the AI lifecycle.

Control Area	Azure Feature
Identity & RBAC	Azure Active Directory, Managed Identities
Network Isolation	Virtual Network Service Endpoints, Network Security Groups (NSGs), Private Links
Data Governance	Azure Purview, Information Protection Labels[4]
Model Hosting	Azure ML with VNet Integration

Table 3.2: Zero Trust controls in Azure Cloud

Google Cloud Platform (GCP)

In GCP, applying Zero Trust to AI workloads involves several key practices. Each Vertex AI job should be wrapped with its own IAM role, enabling precise, per-task authorization and limiting access to only the necessary resources. Before any data is used for training, the DLP API should be applied to monitor and classify sensitive information within BigQuery datasets or Google Cloud Storage (GCS) buckets, reducing the risk of inadvertently exposing regulated data. To contain access within well-defined trust boundaries, VPC Service Controls should be used to isolate training and inference services, protecting them from unauthorized access and data exfiltration across service perimeters.

Control Area	GCP Feature
Identity & Access	IAM, Workload Identity Federation, Cloud Identity-Aware Proxy
Data Control	VPC Service Controls, DLP API, Resource Manager Tags
Workload Security	GKE Autopilot, Confidential VMs, BeyondCorp Enterprise
ML Ops Integration	Vertex AI with fine-grained IAM roles[5]

Table 3.3: Zero Trust controls in Azure Cloud

Example Threats/Risks and Zero Trust Use Cases

Insider Threat in AI Model Training

An internal data scientist uses their broad access to copy raw customer data for unauthorized personal projects. This type of insider threat is especially concerning in AI environments, where large volumes of sensitive data are used for training. Without proper safeguards, misuse can go undetected for long periods.

With Zero Trust:

- **Their scoped identity only has access to pseudonymized datasets:** Access is limited to data that has been stripped of directly identifying information, reducing the risk of exposing sensitive customer details.
- **DSPM detects anomalies in access patterns:** DSPM tools continuously monitor user behavior and flag unusual activity, such as accessing datasets outside normal hours or in larger-than-expected volumes.
- **Training occurs only in controlled containers with auditing:** All model development is conducted in isolated, monitored environments that log every action, enabling full traceability and accountability.

Compromised API Key for Inference

A leaked inference API key allows adversaries to flood the model endpoint with extraction attacks, attempting to reverse-engineer the model or steal sensitive patterns from its responses. This is a growing threat as more organizations expose models through public or semi-public APIs.

Zero Trust enforces:

- **API Gateway with JWT validation:** Every request must include a signed token (e.g., JSON Web Token) that is validated at the gateway, ensuring that only authenticated and authorized users can access the inference endpoint.
- **IP-based rate limiting:** Requests are throttled based on source IP, preventing brute-force or automated scraping attempts by limiting how frequently a user can query the model.
- **Model-specific RBAC:** Role-Based Access Control ensures that only users with explicit permissions can access particular models, reducing the risk of overexposure across environments or use cases.

Data Leakage During Preprocessing

Sensitive text data containing PII is accidentally sent to a third-party tokenizer service without proper sanitization. This type of unintentional leakage is common when integrating external AI tools or APIs into data pipelines.

Preventive Zero Trust controls:

- **DLP checks enforced on outbound data:** DLP tools scan text before it leaves the environment, blocking or redacting PII to prevent unauthorized exposure.
- **API token scope limited to non-confidential data:** Access tokens are configured with strict scopes, ensuring that external services can only process data classified as non-sensitive.
- **Real-time alert via UEBA tool:** User and Entity Behavior Analytics (UEBA) detects deviations from normal data flows and triggers alerts when sensitive data is sent to unapproved destinations.

Chapter Takeaways

As AI adoption accelerates, traditional data security strategies must evolve to keep pace with new risks, behaviors, and attack vectors. Protecting data is not just about controlling access; it requires understanding how data is used, transformed, and exposed across the entire AI lifecycle. The following priorities can help organizations modernize their data risk management approach:

- **Identity is the new perimeter:** Replace static network-based trust models with identity-centric controls. Every workload and user must have a scoped, verifiable identity that supports contextual, least privilege access decisions.
- **Segment aggressively:** Enforce logical separation across identity, workload, and data layers. Use scoped service accounts, container namespaces, and data classification tags to reduce blast radius and contain lateral movement.
- **Apply Zero Trust to the AI lifecycle:** Enforce controls across every phase of the model pipeline, from data ingestion and training to inference and deployment, with continuous validation and granular authorization.
- **Use cloud-native enforcement:** Leverage Zero Trust primitives already embedded in AWS, Azure, and GCP, such as IAM conditions, VPC Service Controls, Purview, and Macie, to implement policy-as-code at scale.
- **Defend against AI-specific threats:** Mitigate model theft, data leakage, and insider misuse through a combination of DSPM, DLP, API security, and scoped access. Harden both the infrastructure and the data it handles.
- **Instrument observability and controls:** Deploy audit logging, UEBA, and real-time anomaly detection across your AI environments to detect unusual access patterns and enforce policy through automated responses.
- **Break implicit trust:** Eliminate long-lived credentials, shared accounts, and unsegmented access. Adopt ephemeral credentials, service-to-service auth, and tightly scoped permissions for each task, model, and data set.

References

1. Cunningham, C. (2020). A look back at Zero Trust: Never trust, always verify. Forrester Research. https://www.forrester.com/blogs/a-look-back-at-zero-trust-never-trust-always-verify/
2. Rose, S., et al. (2020). Zero Trust architecture (SP 800-207). National Institute of Standards and Technology. https://doi.org/10.6028/NIST.SP.800-207

3. Amazon Web Services Team. (2023). Security best practices for machine learning. AWS. https://docs.aws.amazon.com/machine-learning/
4. Microsoft Security Team. (2023). Best practices for Zero Trust in Azure. Microsoft. https://learn.microsoft.com/en-us/security/zero-trust/
5. Schmult, B., et al. (2023). Zero Trust implementation guide based on NIST 800-207. Google Cloud. https://services.google.com/fh/files/misc/zt_implem_guide_800_27.pdf

PART 02

The Data Security Lifecycle

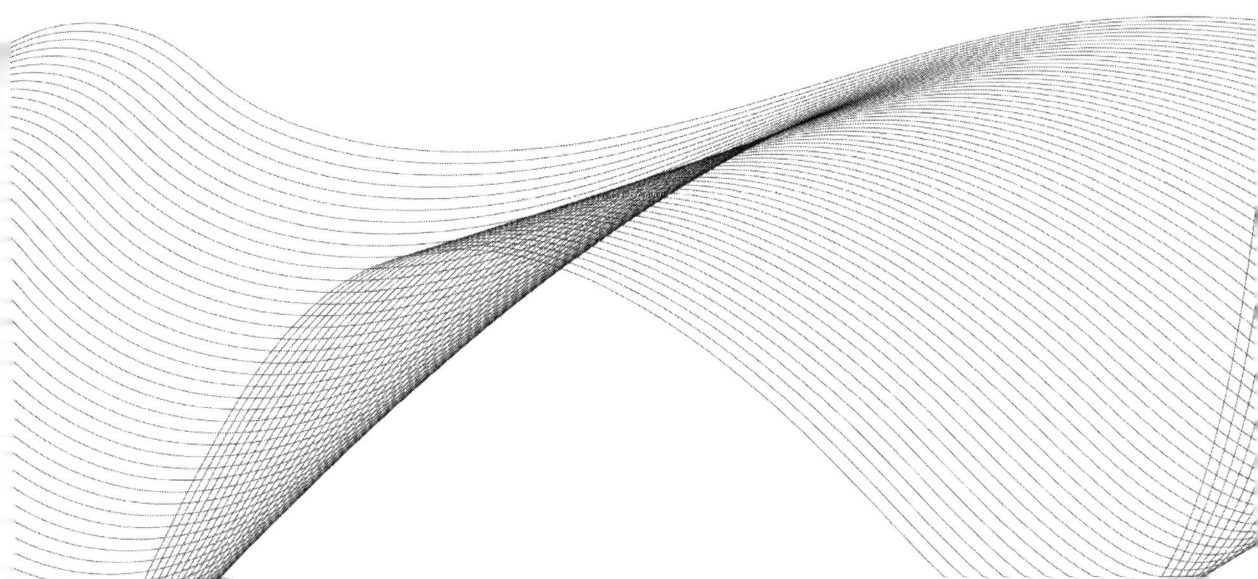

CHAPTER 4

Orchestrating the Data Security Lifecycle

> *"Data is now a living asset. Securing it requires more than point solutions; it demands a lifecycle strategy that adapts to how data is created, transformed, and consumed in real time."*
>
> —CLINTON WANNER, CLOUD SECURITY ARCHITECT, ALKAMI TECHNOLOGY

Criticality of Data Security Lifecycle Orchestration

Data security is not a static discipline. In the age of cloud-native infrastructure, AI-driven systems, and increasingly complex regulatory requirements, the need to manage data securely across its entire lifecycle has never been more urgent. This chapter introduces the overarching framework for governing, securing, and enforcing controls throughout the data lifecycle, from creation to deletion. It provides the orchestration layer that ties together the tactical components explored in future chapters: *Data Discovery*, *Data Classification*, *Identity-to-Data Mapping*, and *Creating a 360° Contextual View.*

The goal of lifecycle management is not simply to apply controls at discrete points, but to create a cohesive, automated system of governance that tracks and enforces data policy at every phase. This includes monitoring how data is created, stored, used, shared, archived, and ultimately deleted, while also accounting for how data is transformed by AI models and accessed through intelligent agents.

Why Lifecycle Thinking Matters

Traditional data security focused on static environments: databases behind firewalls, access governed by user credentials, and perimeter-based protection. But modern enterprises operate in dynamic, hybrid environments where data flows continuously between cloud services, SaaS platforms, APIs, and AI models.[1]

These transformations mean that:

- Sensitive data can be exposed not just through direct access, but also through model inference or prompt responses.
- Data may live in unstructured formats across multiple platforms.
- AI systems may generate or retain derivative data not visible in traditional inventories.

A lifecycle approach ensures that data is governed from the moment it's created or ingested, through to its eventual archival or deletion. It embeds governance into the flow of data, enabling real-time enforcement and reducing manual overhead.

Core Phases of the Data Lifecycle

The data lifecycle encompasses six interconnected stages:

- **Creation:** Data is generated or ingested into the environment, often requiring immediate tagging or classification.
- **Storage:** Data is stored in structured or unstructured formats, with encryption and access controls applied based on sensitivity.
- **Usage:** Data is accessed, processed, or transformed by users, services, or models, making this stage a primary focus for activity monitoring and policy enforcement.
- **Sharing:** Data is transmitted within or outside the organization, creating potential exposure risks that require DLP and contextual access policies.
- **Archival:** Data no longer actively used is moved to long-term storage according to business or regulatory retention timelines.
- **Deletion:** Data is securely and permanently erased when it is no longer required, with logging and attestation to support compliance.

The data lifecycle is supported by cross-cutting disciplines such as discovery, classification, identity-to-data mapping, and contextual risk scoring. These functions span all phases, from creation to deletion, ensuring that data is properly tagged, governed, and protected throughout its journey. For instance, discovery and classification are key at the Creation and Storage stages, while identity mapping and usage monitoring become critical during Usage and Sharing. At the Archival and Deletion stages, contextual scoring and policy enforcement ensure retention rules are applied and secure disposal is verifiable. Figure 4.1 provides typical functional considerations during the data lifecycle.

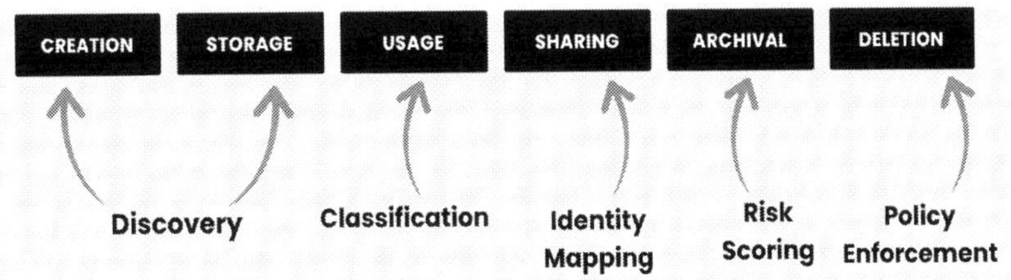

Figure 4.1: Typical functional considerations in the data lifecycle

Each phase presents unique risks and enforcement opportunities, all of which must be governed by real-time telemetry and policy frameworks. AI-specific processes like model training and inference introduce additional considerations, particularly regarding data transformation and retention. Across the lifecycle, telemetry, metadata, and policies must remain tightly coupled with the data to support continuous, adaptive governance. Table 4.1 shows some of the applicable policy objectives and enforcement mechanisms throughout the data lifecycle.

Lifecycle Phase	Policy Objective	Example Enforcement Mechanism
Creation	Tag data upon generation	Auto-tagging via DSPM or schema detection
Storage	Encrypt based on sensitivity	KMS policy with context-based access
Usage	Restrict by role and risk context	IAM + ABAC with session monitoring
Sharing	Block public exposure of classified data	DLP policies with URL, API, and outbound filters
Archival	Apply long-term retention by type	Lifecycle rules in S3, Azure Blob tiers, or GCP Object ACLs
Archival	Enforce retention policy	Policy-as-code with expiration tagging and scheduled review jobs
Deletion	Ensure secure erasure and audit trail	Data erasure API with logging, tamper-proof audit, and attestation

Table 4.1: Policy objectives and enforcements mechanisms through the data lifecycle

Retention Considerations

Managing these transitions requires not only technical enforcement, but also alignment with the organization's retention policy. A well-defined retention policy specifies how long different classes of data should be stored, whether for operational, legal, regulatory, or analytical purposes, and under what conditions data must be archived or deleted. These policies are often influenced by data classification, business use case, jurisdiction, and regulatory mandates.[2] Retention rules must be embedded into lifecycle enforcement logic, ensuring that expired data is not only deleted securely, but also logged and verifiable for compliance purposes.

Example Retention Timelines

Figure 4.2 includes illustrative examples of retention periods for various data types. These timelines drive automated lifecycle transitions and inform deletion, archival, and access policies.

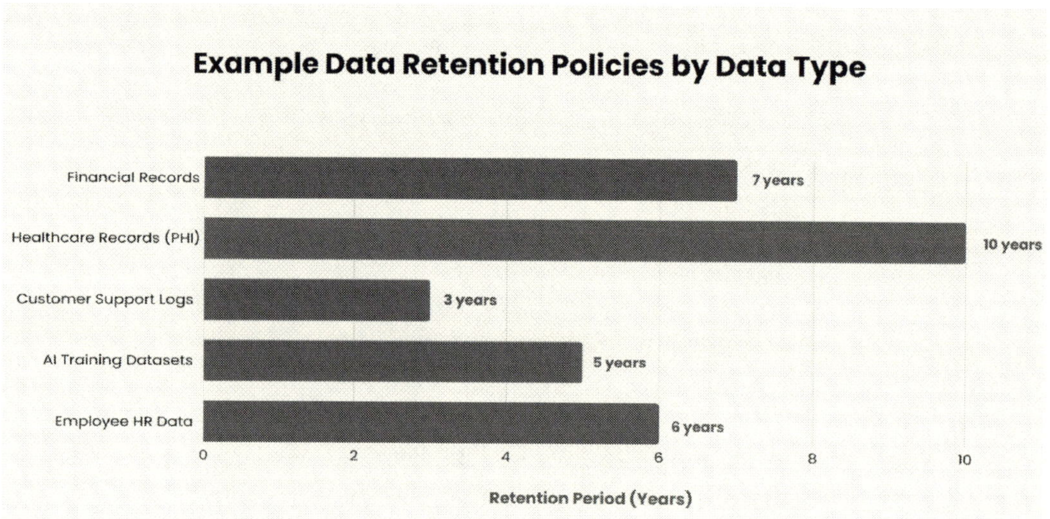

Figure 4.2: Example data retention periods by data type

Coordinating the Lifecycle: What Comes Next

This chapter serves as the foundation for the technical and policy layers that follow. In subsequent chapters, we explore the components that make lifecycle enforcement possible:

- **Data discovery:** How organizations locate structured, semi-structured, and unstructured data across hybrid environments

- **Data classification:** How sensitivity labels, business context, and regulatory tags are applied
- **Identity-to-data mapping:** How users, applications, and services interact with data
- **360° contextual view:** How metadata, telemetry, and AI interactions form a holistic view of data risk

Together, these capabilities feed the lifecycle management engine with real-time intelligence, making dynamic enforcement, policy updates, and risk scoring possible.

Chapter Takeaways

Managing the data lifecycle is not a one-time project. It is a continuous program that adapts as data, risk, and AI capabilities evolve. By embedding governance into the data journey itself, organizations gain not just control, but resilience. The following key takeaways from this chapter support that objective:

- **Evolve data security practices:** Shift from static, one-time controls to continuous, lifecycle-driven governance that adapts to data movement and use.
- **Implement a robust data lifecycle model:** Track data from creation through deletion, applying appropriate policies at each stage.
- **Enforce retention policies:** Ensure timely archival and deletion to support both compliance and risk reduction.
- **Establish lifecycle management as a control plane:** Integrate discovery, classification, and mapping tools for full visibility and automation.
- **Operationalize the lifecycle with precision and scale:** Leverage tools and frameworks described in upcoming chapters to implement policy enforcement at every stage of the data lifecycle.

References

1. Amazon Web Services. (2023). Security best practices for machine learning. Amazon. https://docs.aws.amazon.com/machine-learning/
2. Tabassi, E., et al. (2023, January). Artificial intelligence risk management framework (NIST AI 100-1). National Institute of Standards and Technology. https://nvlpubs.nist.gov/nistpubs/ai/NIST.AI.100-1.pdf

CHAPTER 5

Data Discovery

> *"You can't secure what you can't see. If your data is invisible, so is your risk, until it's too late."*
>
> – GAURAV KAPIL, CHIEF INFORMATION SECURITY OFFICER, BREAD FINANCIAL

Why Data Discovery Matters

Data discovery is the cornerstone of security, governance, and operational efficiency. It refers to the process of identifying, cataloging, and contextualizing data assets across an organization's entire digital landscape, including traditional databases and data warehouses, SaaS platforms, object stores, and ephemeral cloud-native systems. In the context of AI-driven enterprise transformation, data discovery is not just an IT or compliance requirement; it is a foundational enabler of secure innovation.

Data discovery allows organizations to unlock the value of data by understanding what they have, where it resides, and how it moves, creating a searchable inventory that empowers analytics, privacy, and protection efforts.[1] Without it, AI systems are trained on poor quality data (unclassified, unlabeled, and often unmanaged), increasing the risk of bias, hallucination, or inadvertent leakage of sensitive information.

This process is especially vital in the context of increasing regulatory complexity. The GDPR, CCPA, and upcoming frameworks like the EU AI Act require accurate, timely, and comprehensive visibility into what data an organization holds, where it is located, and how it is being used. Compliance depends on discovery. So does trust.

The Expanding Universe of Data Stores

In a hybrid and multi-cloud world, data is fragmented across a dizzying array of repositories. Common data stores include:

- Structured databases (SQL, Oracle, PostgreSQL)
- Data lakes (Snowflake, Databricks, S3)
- Cloud native data stores (S3, Azure blobs)
- Unstructured stores (file shares, Box, SharePoint, email)
- SaaS platforms (Salesforce, Workday, Zendesk)
- Log and telemetry systems (Splunk, Elastic, OpenTelemetry)
- Code repositories and pipelines (GitHub, GitLab, Jenkins)

Each of these platforms stores data in unique formats and access patterns, which complicates discovery. Moreover, ephemeral storage environments such as containers and serverless functions further obfuscate visibility. Without unified discovery, it becomes nearly impossible to establish meaningful controls or monitor access to sensitive data.

The challenge is amplified in federated organizations where different business units or regions may operate independently. A financial services firm might have customer data in North America governed by CCPA, while similar datasets in Europe must align with GDPR. Discovery must therefore be policy-aware and sensitive to data sovereignty boundaries.

Dark Data, Dormant Assets, and the FinOps Opportunity

Every byte of data an organization stores, replicates, and transfers incurs cost, not just in storage fees, but in compliance risk, audit scope, and opportunity cost. One of the most overlooked benefits of robust data discovery is its ability to eliminate redundant, obsolete, or trivial (ROT) data.

According to Splunk, nearly 60% of enterprise data is classified as "dark," meaning it is not actively used, managed, or leveraged for insights.[2] This hidden data not only increases compliance and breach risks but also inflates both cloud and on-premises storage costs. A 2023 McKinsey report emphasizes that enterprises should shift focus toward more strategic initiatives such as delivering unit economics, improving forecasting accuracy, guiding change management based on value potential, and optimizing cloud spend across the organization.[3] Organizations that manage ROT data effectively can reduce cloud storage costs by as much as 20% to 30%.[3]

FinOps, or Financial Operations for cloud, has emerged as a discipline to help organizations understand and optimize cloud costs. Data discovery plays a crucial role here:

- **Cold storage optimization:** Identifying low-access data and moving it to cheaper archival storage (e.g., S3 Glacier, Azure Archive)
- **Deduplication:** Removing redundant files across environments and tenants
- **Lifecycle management:** Implementing policies for expiration, retention, and tiering

Companies that embed data discovery into their FinOps and data governance strategies often report significant returns, not just in cost savings but in reducing technical debt, improving performance, and simplifying data compliance audits.

Data Discovery and the AI Data Crunch

We are approaching a paradox in the evolution of AI: just as models are becoming more powerful and data-hungry, the world is running out of usable training data. According to a 2022 study by researchers at Epoch AI, most large-scale AI models will exhaust the supply of high-quality language data by 2026 to 2028.[4] This study concluded that the supply of curated, high-integrity textual data on the public internet is finite and is rapidly being consumed by foundation model developers.

This data bottleneck is not limited to text. Training foundation models for image, voice, genomics, fraud detection, and even cybersecurity telemetry requires vast amounts of labeled, high-integrity data. As that public data well dries up, enterprises will need to mine their internal data lakes, application logs, knowledge repositories, and customer support tickets to fine-tune or customize models.

This makes internal data discovery more urgent than ever. You can't govern what you haven't found. You can't train on what you haven't labeled. You can't protect what you don't know exists.

The urgency is compounded by the shift to retrieval-augmented generation (RAG) and MCP techniques that dynamically inject data into prompts and inference pipelines. Poor discovery leads to hallucinations, irrelevant answers, or data leakage from prompts.

Modern Data Discovery is a Continuous and Intelligent Process

Modern data discovery is not a static or one-time activity conducted during audits or system migrations. It has become a dynamic, continuous process essential to securing, governing, and maximizing the value of enterprise data. Data discovery is shaped by several core capabilities, which are detailed in the following section.

Note: Although data classification is briefly mentioned in the following content for completeness reasons, a detailed discussion will be provided in the next chapter, *Data Classification and Contextual Accuracy.*

Continuous Crawling and Scanning

Modern environments are fluid. Data sources change rapidly, access controls evolve, and new services are constantly introduced. Continuous crawling and scanning enables organizations to detect these changes in real time. Rather than relying on outdated snapshots, discovery tools perpetually scan cloud platforms, databases, and SaaS environments to identify updates in schemas, data formats, and permissions. This ensures security and governance policies are always aligned with the current state of the data landscape.

Semantic Inference

Simply knowing the name of a data field isn't enough. Semantic inference uses AI to understand what the data actually means. For instance, a column labeled "ID" could represent anything from a session token to a patient ID to a customer identifier, each carrying different risk and compliance implications. By inferring context from data patterns and relationships, discovery tools can classify sensitive data more accurately, which improves both privacy enforcement and AI model training hygiene.

Access Pattern Monitoring

Understanding who interacts with data and how is essential to preventing misuse and reducing unnecessary exposure. Access pattern monitoring analyzes how datasets are being used across the organization. This includes identifying unused (dormant) datasets, detecting anomalous access behaviors, and flagging overly permissive access rights. By linking usage data to specific identities, teams can enforce least privilege access and uncover blind spots that traditional security tools might miss.

Lineage and Flow Mapping

Knowing where data originates, how it transforms, and where it travels is foundational to both compliance and troubleshooting. Lineage and flow mapping provide a detailed view of data pipelines, revealing the entire lifecycle of data as it moves through ingestion, transformation, storage, and analysis. This visibility is crucial for debugging data issues, ensuring data integrity, and complying with regulations like GDPR or HIPAA that require clear tracking of personal data movement across regions and systems.

Policy Mapping

Discovery is only useful if it leads to action. Policy mapping connects identified data types such as PII, health records, or financial data to the appropriate security and compliance rules. This enables automatic enforcement, including encrypting sensitive columns, redacting personal data before sharing, or blocking the exfiltration of restricted content. It reduces manual overhead and ensures that protective measures are consistently applied based on data classification.

Performance Considerations

While comprehensive scanning delivers high fidelity in data discovery, it can place a significant load on production systems, particularly when scanning large volumes of data in real time. Unoptimized scanning may consume excessive CPU, memory, or network bandwidth, affecting application performance and user experience. To mitigate this, organizations should adopt intelligent strategies such as scanning during off-peak hours, using sampling techniques to scan representative subsets of data, or offloading discovery tasks to non-production replicas. It's also critical that the data discovery platform itself supports these modes natively, allowing administrators to balance accuracy with system impact.

Data in SaaS Platforms

In today's enterprise landscape, a significant portion of sensitive and operational data resides outside traditional infrastructure, particularly in third-party SaaS platforms. These platforms include file storage services like OneDrive and Dropbox, collaboration hubs like Google Workspace and Microsoft 365, and data-centric platforms like Snowflake, Salesforce, and ServiceNow. They have become foundational to how organizations operate today.

Yet, this shift introduces a critical visibility gap.

When organizations fail to account for data stored and processed in SaaS platforms, they operate with only part of the picture. Sensitive data such as intellectual property, personal information, or regulated datasets often ends up in these systems, whether by design or through shadow IT activity. Without visibility into these environments, security teams cannot confidently assess risk, enforce governance, or respond to threats comprehensively.

This is where a robust DSPM platform becomes essential. Any DSPM solution deployed across the enterprise must be capable of discovering and classifying data within major SaaS platforms. Leading vendors support this through pre-built connectors, such as APIs or integrations that allow for secure, read-only scanning of data assets, metadata, and access permissions within supported SaaS environments.

For lesser-known or industry-specific SaaS applications, out-of-the-box connectors may not be available. In such cases, organizations should proactively engage the DSPM vendor during the evaluation process to:

- Confirm support for critical platforms in their SaaS stack.
- Request roadmap commitments or prioritization for new connector development.
- Negotiate proof-of-value timelines for integration validation.

Failing to do so could delay deployment or result in blind spots in your overall data security posture. The SaaS footprint is too important to be treated as an afterthought. Complete data visibility requires including these platforms as a first-class discovery target.

Organizational Implications of Data Discovery

Implementing a data discovery platform impacts nearly every function across the enterprise. Without comprehensive knowledge of where data resides, organizations face significant blind spots that undermine both security and compliance. Effective data discovery addresses this risk, but success requires cross-functional alignment. The following teams benefit most from discovery initiatives and must collaborate closely to ensure their effectiveness:

- **Security teams:** Discovery platforms give security teams real-time visibility into where sensitive data is stored and who has access to it. It also allows them to ensure proper encryption. This is foundational for enforcing the principle of least privilege, detecting unauthorized access, and identifying shadow data repositories that may have been overlooked. Unknown data cannot be protected, and without visibility, security teams are forced to operate reactively.
- **Data governance and privacy teams:** Governance programs rely on accurate, up-to-date data catalogs and the ability to track data lineage and classification. Discovery tools automate this process, allowing governance teams to build effective retention schedules, minimize redundant data, and apply appropriate privacy policies, especially when data spans cloud environments, on-prem systems, and SaaS platforms.
- **AI/ML teams:** For teams building and deploying ML models, access to well-classified, high-quality data is essential. Data discovery helps identify training data that meets quality, relevance, and privacy thresholds. It also ensures that PII and other sensitive attributes are not inadvertently used in model training, mitigating both ethical and regulatory risks.
- **Compliance and legal teams:** Regulations such as the CCPA mandate that organizations respond to Data Subject Access Requests (DSARs). Fulfilling these requests requires a full inventory of where personal data is stored and processed. Discovery platforms generate comprehensive data maps and assist with privacy impact assessments, making it possible for compliance teams to demonstrate regulatory readiness and streamline audits.

Discovery Metrics That Matter

A successful data discovery program is measurable. Leading organizations track:

- **Coverage:** % of known vs. unknown data stores
- **Freshness:** Frequency of scans and detection of schema drift
- **Cost Impact:** Reduction in storage, FinOps, and compliance overhead
- **AI Readiness:** % of data labeled, trusted, and available for model fine-tuning

Benchmarks for these metrics can be established by sector, regulation, or deployment model.

Chapter Takeaways

The following takeaways summarize key insights from this chapter on data discovery. As data drives everything from innovation to regulatory enforcement, the ability to continuously and comprehensively discover data across environments is foundational to secure, ethical, and effective operations:

- **Data discovery enables secure, responsible innovation:** Knowing what data exists, where it resides, and how it's used is critical to reducing security risk and enabling effective AI development.
- **Identifying dark data helps lower costs and risk exposure:** Shedding light on unused or redundant data allows organizations to reduce cloud costs, minimize attack surfaces, and streamline compliance efforts.
- **Compliance requires comprehensive data visibility:** Regulations like CCPA and GDPR depend on accurate data mapping. Discovery platforms are essential for fulfilling legal obligations like DSARs.
- **SaaS platforms must be included in the discovery scope:** With much of today's data residing in services like Snowflake, Dropbox, and Salesforce, discovery tools must support SaaS environments to provide full visibility.
- **AI and ML are thirsty for data:** Data discovery helps identify relevant, high-quality data sources that can be safely and ethically used for training machine learning models.
- **Cross-functional collaboration is key to success:** Security, compliance, data governance, and AI teams must work together with strong executive backing to drive and sustain discovery initiatives.

- **Discovery is a continuous, not one-time, process:** In fast-changing environments, ongoing scanning and intelligent classification are necessary to maintain up-to-date visibility and control.

References

1. Informatica Team. (n.d.). What is data discovery and why does it matter? Informatica. https://www.informatica.com/resources/articles/what-is-data-discovery-and-why-does-it-matter.html
2. Raza, M., & Splunk Team. (2023). The state of dark data. Splunk. https://www.splunk.com/en_us/form/the-state-of-dark-data.html
3. Conway, K., et al. (2023). The FinOps way: How to avoid the pitfalls to realizing cloud's value. McKinsey & Company. https://www.mckinsey.com/capabilities/mckinsey-digital/our-insights/the-finops-way-how-to-avoid-the-pitfalls-to-realizing-clouds-value
4. Villalobos, P., et al. (2022). Will we run out of data? Limits of LLM scaling based on human-generated data. Epoch AI. https://epoch.ai/blog/will-we-run-out-of-data-limits-of-llm-scaling-based-on-human-generated-data

CHAPTER 6

Data Classification

> *"Deep learning is very good at learning from large amounts of data, but it still requires the data to be labeled. This is a problem because it is very expensive to get labeled data."*
>
> – GEOFFREY HINTON, UNIVERSITY OF TORONTO PROFESSOR EMERITUS AND TURING AWARD WINNER

Understanding Data Types

Data discovery and data classification are typically conducted in tandem, as they are closely interconnected processes. Data classification is the process of categorizing data based on its type, sensitivity, and regulatory requirements. It forms the backbone of data protection strategies, as it helps organizations apply appropriate safeguards and access controls. Classifying data accurately is critical for compliance with privacy laws such as GDPR, HIPAA, CCPA, and other global regulations.

Common categories of sensitive data include:

- **Personally identifiable information (PII):** Names, addresses, Social Security numbers, birth dates, and national identifiers.
- **Protected health information (PHI):** Medical records, lab results, diagnoses, and insurance details covered under HIPAA.
- **Payment card industry (PCI) data:** Credit card numbers, expiration dates, CVV codes. This is sometimes referred to as Card Holder Data or CHD.
- **Intellectual property (IP):** Source code, designs, formulas, algorithms.
- **Confidential business information:** Contracts, customer lists, pricing models.
- **Geolocation and biometric data:** Facial scans, GPS trails, fingerprint data.
- **Emerging categories:** Genomic data, model training datasets, behavioral telemetry.

Data often falls into multiple categories, compounding the regulatory burden and increasing the attack surface. For example, an AI training dataset might include anonymized user logs that, when cross-referenced, can reveal behavioral patterns tied to specific individuals. This combination of metadata and inference requires classification systems to understand compound data relationships.

Regular Expressions Based Traditional Data Classification

Regular expressions (regex) have long been the default technique used in traditional data classification engines. Regex is a pattern-matching approach that scans files, databases, and documents for strings that match predefined formats. For example:

- **Social security number (SSN):** ^(?!666|000|9\\d{2})\\d{3}-(?!00)\\d{2}-(?!0{4})\\d{4}$
- **Credit card number:** ^(4[0-9]{12}(?:[0-9]{3})?|5[1-5][0-9]{14}|2[2-7][0-9]{14}|3[47][0-9]{13})$

While regex-based classification is fast and easy to implement, it has major limitations:

- **High false positive rates:** Regex often misclassifies non-sensitive text that resembles sensitive formats. For example, an invoice ID "123-45-6789" may trigger a false SSN alert.
- **Context ignorance:** Regex cannot understand where the pattern occurs. It treats metadata, file headers, and footnotes equally.
- **Inflexibility to language and format variants:** Many sensitive data formats differ by country or domain (e.g., Aadhaar vs. SSN, NHS numbers, CPF).
- **No insight into usage intent:** Regex does not account for how the data is used, accessed, or shared.

Studies consistently show that relying solely on regex-based approaches results in significant operational overhead. A 2025 research paper by Tariq et al. found that 63% of security practitioners experienced excessive alert fatigue due to false positives, a challenge that is often compounded by inaccuracies in data classification.[1] False positives don't just waste time, they erode trust in classification systems. When security teams are flooded with inaccurate alerts, they're more likely to disable automated protections or ignore future warnings.

AI Driven Classification

Data classification has evolved far beyond traditional rule-based systems that rely on regular expressions or static keywords. Today's most effective classification engines are powered by AI and use a combination of natural language processing (NLP), semantic understanding, behavioral signals, and ML (specifically, deep learning) to accurately identify and contextualize sensitive data across dynamic enterprise environments.

At the core, AI classification systems interpret the meaning and intent behind data rather than simply matching strings. They parse surrounding text to determine whether a value such as a sequence of numbers is likely to be PII, PHI, or a benign reference. For instance, a number near the label "Patient ID" is treated very differently than one near "Order Number." AI engines further enrich this analysis by referencing structured taxonomies, ontologies, and organization-specific dictionaries to interpret domain-specific terminology with greater precision.

These systems also learn over time. Through supervised learning, they refine their classification logic based on human feedback, growing more accurate with every iteration. For example, a phrase like *"The patient's genome was sequenced to reveal a BRCA1 mutation"* would be flagged as highly sensitive, even though it lacks a direct identifier. This ability to interpret context is what separates AI classifiers from legacy tools.

Recent experiments with transformer-based models such as GPT have shown even greater capability. These models can distinguish between public datasets, proprietary training data, and infrastructure logs that may contain embedded secrets or configuration risks. This type of contextual understanding is particularly valuable in identifying data intended for release versus data that must remain confidential.

Deep learning, a specialized branch of ML, further enhances this capability by modeling semantic relationships and behavioral patterns across vast amounts of unstructured data. Unlike traditional models that rely on predefined features, deep learning automatically identifies complex relationships, such as patterns of user behavior or the latent structure of textual data.

In security contexts, deep learning is especially powerful because it enables:

- **Semantic disambiguation:** Recognizing the difference between similar terms in different contexts (e.g., distinguishing an SSN in a tax form from a random number in a test script).
- **Sequence modeling:** Detecting suspicious behavioral chains, such as a user logging in from an unusual location, accessing sensitive files, and initiating an outbound transfer.
- **Intent inference:** Identifying whether a database query was made as part of a scheduled task or an anomalous script run by a new identity.

These techniques allow the system to "connect the dots" across documents, access logs, identities, and data flows, surfacing threats that would otherwise be buried in noise or overlooked entirely.

When integrated into data security platforms, these AI-driven classifiers transform passive discovery into active risk intelligence. They do not merely identify what sensitive data exists; they also show how it is accessed, where it moves, and by whom. This contextual intelligence helps security teams prioritize risks, enforce access policies, and detect breaches in real time.

When applied at scale, AI-driven classifiers can maintain over 90% precision and 85% recall, even in highly heterogeneous enterprise environments.[2]

Example – Classifying Genomic Data using AI

At a global pharmaceutical company, researchers discovered that sensitive genomic datasets were being stored in shared cloud environments alongside patient interview transcripts. Their legacy classification tool missed these files because they didn't contain any conventional identifiers.

Using an AI classification engine trained on genomic terminology, the company was able to:

- Tag more than 2TB of DNA sequences as high-risk
- Separate research data from clinical data for compliance
- Prevent AI models from training on personally identifiable genomes
- Reduce false positive rate

As a result, the company improved compliance with GDPR, HIPAA, and ISO/IEC 27701 while reducing exposure to data and intellectual property theft.

Comparing Regex-Based and AI-Driven Data Classification

A 2025 study by Koli et al.[3] evaluated the comparative performance of regex-only, AI-only, and hybrid AI plus regex classification techniques on diverse datasets containing PII. The authors assessed these approaches using three standard metrics:

- **Precision:** The percentage of predicted sensitive items that were truly sensitive. High precision means few false positives.
- **Recall:** The percentage of actual sensitive items that were correctly identified. High recall means few false negatives.
- **F1 score:** The harmonic mean of precision and recall, offering a balanced measure of overall classification effectiveness.

Comparative Results of Classification Methods

Method	Precision (%)	Recall (%)	F1 Score (%)	Notable Strengths	Key Limitations
Regex Only	92.5	75.3	82.9	High precision for clearly structured data	Low recall, misses non-standard formats
AI Only	84.7	89.2	86.9	Strong recall across varied formats	Increased false positives from overgeneralization
Hybrid (AI + Regex)	94.8	88.7	91.6	Best overall performance with low false positives	Requires integration and tuning effort

Table 6.1: Comparative Results of Classification Methods

The results in Table 6.1 underscore a critical insight for enterprise security teams. Regex engines cannot be the sole line of defense in data discovery pipelines. While regex remains valuable for deterministic detection, it struggles with edge cases, contextual ambiguity, and noisy real-world datasets. AI models, particularly those trained on security-labeled corpora, excel at interpreting structure and meaning, but may overmatch when used in isolation.

By combining the two approaches into a hybrid classification pipeline, organizations gain the precision of rule-based logic and the adaptability of machine learning. This hybrid model achieved an F1 score of 91.6% in the study, significantly outperforming either method used independently.

The Need for Custom Classification Categories

Default classification engines often fall short when it comes to domain-specific sensitive data. While they may successfully flag standard patterns like Social Security numbers or credit card data, they typically miss information that is deeply sensitive yet structurally unique.

In biomedical research, for instance, traditional regex-based detection cannot reliably classify complex scientific data such as:

- DNA sequences (e.g., ACTG repeats)
- Genome-wide association study (GWAS) data
- Gene mutation indicators (e.g., *BRCA1*, *TP53*)

This information doesn't match standard PII or PHI formats, yet it is highly regulated under laws like the Genetic Information Nondiscrimination Act (GINA) due to its sensitivity.

Other industries face similar classification gaps:

- **Financial services:** Trade strategies, market signals
- **Manufacturing:** CAD files, design tolerances
- **Technology:** Source code snippets, configuration files

To address this, organizations are increasingly turning to custom classification approaches that allow them to:

- Define new data types aligned with specific business risks.
- Train classification models on proprietary or domain-specific datasets.

- Apply differentiated protection and access policies based on sensitivity tiering.

Emerging standards are reinforcing this shift. The NIST AI Risk Management Framework (AI RMF) now highlights the importance of identifying unique data types that may introduce model bias, create risk of data leakage, or lead to unintended model behavior.

This shift is already underway in sectors like healthcare. A 2023 survey of healthcare CIOs found that over 78% had implemented or were piloting custom classifiers for genomic and clinical trial data, driven by the rise of personalized medicine and machine learning based diagnostics.[4]

Confidence Scoring and Reduction of False Positives

A major advancement in classification systems is the introduction of confidence scoring, which indicates how likely a detected pattern is to be accurate. Confidence scores are computed using ensemble models that combine metadata, semantic features, access context, and user behavior. For example:

1. A file labeled "project_notes.txt" with a match to "123-45-6789" and no contextual indicators may be assigned a low confidence score (likely false positive).
2. A database column titled "Employee SSN" accessed by HR systems and containing valid regex matches is assigned a high confidence score (likely true positive).

Security teams can use confidence thresholds to:

- Suppress low confidence matches in alerting.
- Prioritize high-risk datasets for remediation.
- Fine-tune classification models based on real-world feedback.

According to Gartner, organizations using AI-powered classification with confidence scoring reduced related false positive alerts by up to 80% within 6 months of deployment.[5]

This isn't just a backend algorithm tweak, it's a game changer for operational effectiveness. Confidence scoring empowers security and compliance teams to:

- Build dynamic dashboards that flag only high-confidence risks.
- Automatically notify data owners or system admins.
- Tune enforcement policies based on classification certainty.

The Role of Metadata in Classification and Risk

Metadata is often misunderstood or underestimated in data security discussions. Many vendors downplay its importance, asserting that what is being sent outside your environment is "just metadata." However, such assertions deserve closer scrutiny, particularly in the context of data classification and enterprise risk.

Metadata is not incidental. It is an essential layer of visibility, providing insight into who accessed what data, when, from where, and by what method. When enriched with labels, user identities, query logs, or classification tags, metadata can contain regulated information such as PII or PHI. In such cases, metadata becomes more than auxiliary; it becomes a meaningful extension of the data itself.

In the context of classification, metadata serves two key purposes. First, it enables organizations to track usage patterns and contextually refine their classification models. Second, it functions as an audit trail, supporting compliance, access governance, and anomaly detection. However, this same metadata, if exposed externally, can present a significant security and compliance risk.

Exporting metadata to external environments (which SaaS products typically do), whether for AI model training, analytics, or vendor processing, can inadvertently:

- Reveal sensitive access behaviors
- Disclose identity-to-data relationships
- Facilitate lateral movement in the event of compromise
- Weaken data sovereignty and regulatory posture

For organizations operating in regulated sectors, these risks are particularly pronounced. Any data security solution that transfers metadata outside of the enterprise perimeter should be evaluated carefully. Key questions include:

- What specific metadata elements are being transmitted?
- Could these elements contain regulated or classified information?
- Are transfers encrypted and governed by contractual boundaries?
- Is metadata usage aligned with principles of least privilege?
- Will the metadata be used to train third-party AI models?

In a Zero Trust architecture, visibility must be achieved without sacrificing control. The choice between insight and sovereignty is a false one. Effective solutions must deliver both.

Ultimately, metadata is not just a background detail. It is the connective tissue that links identities, access events, and data sensitivity. When mapped correctly, it strengthens classification, enhances enforcement, and supports operational resilience. When mishandled, it can expose the very insights it was meant to protect.

Chapter Takeaways

Accurate data classification is foundational to secure and trustworthy data operations. As organizations scale AI initiatives and process ever-growing volumes of sensitive data, classification must evolve beyond static approaches. The following key takeaways highlight why classification strategies are critical:

- **Accurate classification is essential:** Ensuring security, privacy, and usability across the data lifecycle.
- **Legacy regex-based techniques fall short:** They cannot handle the complexity, scale, and context of modern enterprise data.
- **AI-driven, context-aware classification engines:** Provide scalable, flexible, and precise data understanding, especially in dynamic or unstructured environments.
- **Custom models and confidence scoring:** Enable tailored classification aligned with business-specific risks, reducing false positives and alert fatigue.
- **Genomic data illustrates the need for advanced classification:** It is often unstructured, deeply sensitive, and invisible to traditional detection methods.
- **Classification is a strategic investment:** Not just a compliance requirement, but a foundation for responsible AI, effective risk reduction, and resilient governance.
- **Metadata is not just supporting detail:** It is the connective tissue that links identities, access events, and data sensitivity, making it critical for both classification and control in any data security strategy.

References

1. Tariq, S., [additional authors], & LastAuthor, X. (2025). Alert fatigue in security operations centres: Research challenges and opportunities. ACM Computing Surveys. https://doi.org/10.1145/3723158
2. Shey, H., [additional authors if known]. (2022). AI-based data classification tools: Market overview. Forrester Research. https://www.forrester.com/report/the-sensitive-data-discovery-and-classification-landscape-q1-2023/RES179011
3. Decoding Complexity: CHPDA – Intelligent Pattern Exploration with a Context-Aware Hybrid Pattern Detection Algorithm. (2024). Arxiv.org. https://arxiv.org/html/2502.07815v1
4. Bart, R., [additional authors if known]. (2025). Genomic data in health systems. Center for Connected Medicine, UPMC Enterprises. https://enterprises.upmc.com/app/uploads/2025/03/CCM_Report_Genomic_Data_in_Health_Systems.pdf
5. Lowans, B. (2023). Innovation insight: Data security posture management. Gartner. https://www.gartner.com/en/documents/4219399

CHAPTER 7

Identity-to-Data Mapping

> *"Often what we see in the latest round of intrusions—especially some of these nation state intrusions where they're living off the land—they're getting into the networks and then they're compromising identity, they're stealing tokens and certificates that allow them to assume the identity of others."*
>
> – ROB JOYCE, FORMER DIRECTOR OF CYBERSECURITY, NSA

Why Identity Matters in Data Security

In data security, identity serves as the hub connecting users, systems, and data. According to Verizon's 2024 Data Breach Investigations Report (DBIR), 22% of breaches began with stolen credentials, highlighting how frequently attackers gain initial access through compromised usernames, passwords, or other forms of authentication. Even more striking, 88% of basic web application attacks involved the use of stolen credentials.[1] Once an attacker successfully impersonates a valid identity, whether human or machine, their potential for harm is directly tied to the level of access that identity possesses.

This is where identity-to-data mapping becomes a vital control layer. Understanding which identities (users, services, machines, applications) can access what data, and which of those accesses are actually used, is foundational to preventing lateral movement, minimizing blast radius, and enforcing least privilege.

Identifying Dormant Identities

Dormant identities are accounts that technically still exist within an organization's IAM system but are no longer actively used. They pose a significant security risk because they often retain access to sensitive systems or data, despite no longer serving a legitimate business function.

Dormant accounts typically include:

- Former employees' accounts that were never fully deprovisioned after offboarding
- Obsolete service accounts created for applications or integrations that have since been decommissioned
- Shadow accounts spun up during testing, development, or system integration phases that were never cleaned up

According to a study by Palo Alto Networks' Unit 42, in large-scale cloud environments, 30% to 40% of identities are dormant, and many still retain privileged or sensitive permissions.[2] These accounts are a favorite target for attackers because they are often overlooked, lightly monitored, and poorly maintained. Many use static credentials such as hardcoded API keys, long-lived tokens, or secure shell (SSH) keys that do not expire or rotate, making them easy to exploit.

Detecting dormant identities requires a mix of access visibility and behavior analysis. Recommended approaches include:

- **Audit login and usage activity:** Look for accounts that have not logged in or accessed resources within a defined period (e.g., 90 days).
- **Track last activity timestamps:** Compare the date of the last known interaction with the account's creation date or expected usage pattern.
- **Establish behavioral baselines:** Use ML or heuristic-based tools to detect outliers in usage frequency, time of access, or system interactions.
- **Monitor for unused entitlements:** Identify roles or permissions that were granted but have not been used over time.

Proactively identifying and removing dormant accounts significantly reduces the enterprise attack surface. These efforts not only minimize the risk of credential theft or lateral movement but also simplify compliance reporting by demonstrating effective access lifecycle management.

Identity and access governance (IAG) platforms offer built-in capabilities to surface stale accounts, analyze entitlement usage, and automate the remediation process through revocation workflows or conditional access policies.

Mapping Identity to Data

Identity-to-data mapping is a core practice in data security. It answers a critical question every organization must be able to address: Who has access to what data, and are they actually using it?

As enterprises expand across cloud platforms, SaaS applications, and on-premises systems, data becomes highly fragmented. Sensitive information is often spread across:

- Object storage systems (e.g., Amazon S3 and Azure Blob)
- SaaS platforms (e.g., Salesforce and Workday)
- Structured data systems (e.g., SQL databases and Snowflake)
- Unstructured repositories (e.g., Google Drive and OneDrive)

In this environment, identity-to-data mapping becomes essential. It connects identities, both human and machine, to the data they can access, and more importantly, to the data they actually use.

What the Process Involves

Identity-to-data mapping includes several layers of visibility and correlation as illustrated in Figure 7.1.

Figure 7.1: Identity-to-data mapping process

Determining Overprivilege and Inactivity

One of the most common security risks is overprivilege, which occurs when an identity has more access than necessary for its role. This usually happens due to:

- Default roles that are too broad (e.g., "Admin")
- Copy and paste policies reused without review
- Temporary project access that is never revoked
- Lack of regular access reviews
- Misconfigured permissions
- Role changes that aren't reflected in access controls

The risk increases when these overprivileged identities are also inactive. An account that is not in use but still holds sensitive access is an ideal target for attackers. This is because inactive identities lack the same oversight and active management as those still in use.

Identity-to-data mapping helps identify overprivilege by comparing the access an identity has with the access it actually uses. For example, if a user has permission to read 100 Amazon S3 buckets but routinely accesses only 3, then the remaining 97 represent unnecessary exposure and should be reviewed for removal.

The CapitalOne breach outlined in the following example illustrates the risks of overprivilege. The case is not an anomaly; it is a warning. Once an identity, whether human or nonhuman, is compromised, the attacker inherits everything it can access. Organizations cannot afford to assume that internal accounts are safe. Every identity must be continuously evaluated, monitored, and mapped to the data it touches.

That is why identity-to-data mapping is now considered a foundational control for:

- Enforcing least privilege
- Preventing lateral movement
- Auditing access for regulatory compliance
- Reducing the blast radius of a breach

Example: Exploitation of Overprivilege in CapitalOne Breach

In the 2019 CapitalOne breach, the attacker exploited a misconfigured web application firewall to access the metadata service of a cloud instance. They then assumed the role of an internal nonhuman identity associated with a system process. That identity had excessive access to Amazon S3 buckets containing sensitive customer data.[3]

The breach did not involve advanced malware or nation state tools. It happened because a backend service had too much access—and no one noticed. More than 100 million customer records were compromised. The cause was not a technical failure, but a breakdown in access governance.

The Risk of Nonhuman Identities

The rapid adoption of automation, DevOps, and cloud services has led to a surge in NHIs, also known as service accounts, machine identities, or workload identities. According to various estimates, in large enterprises, NHIs now outnumber human users by a ratio of 45 to 1.[4] These identities include:

- Continuous integration and deployment pipelines
- Serverless functions and cloud-native applications
- Containerized services and backend jobs
- Bots, automation scripts, and ML workflows

NHIs are risky because of the following reasons:

- **Static credentials:** Many use long-lived API tokens or SSH keys that are not rotated regularly.
- **Broad access:** Permissions are often overgranted during development and not scoped down later.
- **Unclear ownership:** It is not always obvious who is responsible for managing each identity.
- **Lack of protection:** Most do not support multifactor authentication.

Characteristics of an Effective Identity-to-Data Map

An effective identity-to-data map includes the following components:

- **Identity inventory:** Human and NHIs, grouped by business unit, department, or system
- **Access graph:** Visualization of how identities are connected to data assets
- **Usage overlay:** Real-time or historical view of which identities accessed which data, and how often
- **Risk scoring:** Assigning weights to identities based on exposure, privilege level, and dormancy

Vendors like Symmetry Systems and Veza offer visualization engines that generate identity-to-data maps with click-through filtering by data type, system, and business function.

A typical access map might show:

- A Kubernetes service account with write access to a production customer database
- An intern's Slack account with access to board meeting minutes stored in Google Drive
- A CI/CD runner that pulls secrets from multiple cloud providers

Example Identity-to-Data Map

Figure 7.2 illustrates how visibility is achieved through identity-to-data mapping. When this visibility is paired with actionable recommendations, such as identifying overprivileged identities and enablement mechanisms like Terraform code for automated remediation, it results in a significant reduction in organizational risk.

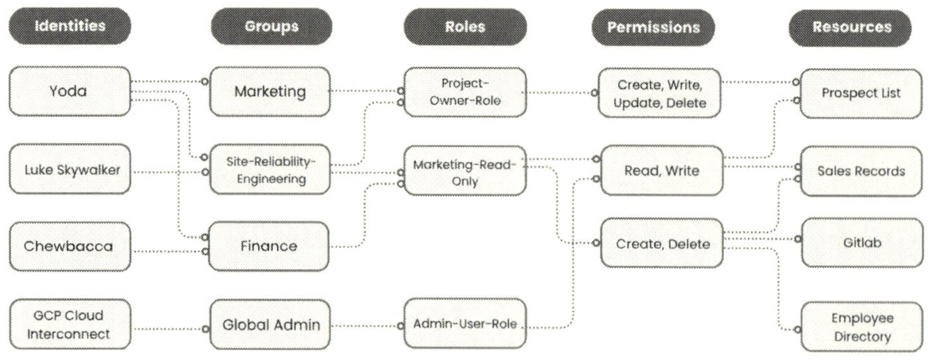

Figure 7.2: Example Identity/Data mapping graph

Additional Identity and Access Management (IAM) Best Practices

In addition to foundational controls, organizations should adopt advanced IAM practices to further strengthen their data and AI security posture. These practices help reduce standing privileges, improve oversight, and ensure that access is continuously aligned with business needs and risk levels. Some key best practices include:

- Enforcing Just-In-Time (JIT) access for sensitive operations
- Using Time-Bound Roles with automatic expiration
- Enabling Access Reviews and Approval Workflows
- Integrating DLP/DAM/DSPM with IGA (Identity Governance & Administration) tools

Chapter Takeaways

This chapter reinforces the central role identity plays in securing enterprise data. As most breaches now stem from compromised credentials, identity has become the most critical control plane in cybersecurity. The following key takeaways highlight the importance of identity-to-data visibility and governance:

- **Identity is the new control plane:** With credential-based breaches on the rise, understanding who has access to what data and how that access is used is vital for enforcing least privilege and preventing lateral movement.
- **Dormant identities are a hidden threat:** Deprovisioned employee accounts and legacy service accounts often retain access long after they are needed, significantly expanding the attack surface.
- **Identity-to-data mapping is essential:** It provides the visibility to detect overprivileged accounts, monitor real usage, and align access with actual business needs across cloud, SaaS, and hybrid environments.
- **NHIs present unique risks:** These accounts often lack MFA, use static credentials, and operate without oversight, which makes them prime targets for attackers, as seen in incidents like the Capital One breach.
- **Effective identity-to-data maps are actionable:** They include real-time usage overlays, risk scoring, and graph-based views that enable least privilege enforcement and automation through tools like Terraform.

References

1. Langlois, P., et al. (2024). 2024 data breach investigations report. Verizon Threat Research Advisory Center. https://www.verizon.com/business/resources/infographics/2024-dbir-infographic.pdf
2. Chen, J., & Quist, N. (2022). Cloud threat report, Volume 7. Unit 42, Palo Alto Networks. https://www.paloaltonetworks.com/content/dam/pan/en_US/assets/pdf/reports/unit42-cloud-threat-report-volume7.pdf
3. U.S. Department of Justice. (2019). Seattle tech worker arrested for data theft involving large financial services company. DOJ Office of Public Affairs. https://www.justice.gov/usao-wdwa/pr/seattle-tech-worker-arrested-data-theft-involving-large-financial-services-company
4. Security Magazine Editorial Team. (2023). Non-human identities: Secure them now, not later. Security Magazine. https://www.securitymagazine.com/articles/99303-non-human-identities-secure-them-now-not-later

CHAPTER 8

Creating a 360° Contextual View

> *"Security without full context is educated guesswork. But when real-time integration of identities, data flows, and access behaviors occurs, organizations evolve from reactive posture to informed decision-making, transforming alert fatigue into actionable intelligence."*
>
> – JAIMIN SHAH, GLOBAL CISO, APEX FINTECH SOLUTIONS

Context Is Everything in Security

In the previous chapter, we discussed identity-to-data mapping and its benefits. In this chapter, we take the establishment of context a step further by adding one more element: mapping how data flows across the enterprise. As data proliferates across hybrid and multi-cloud environments, and as human and nonhuman identities interact with that data in increasingly complex ways, the need for full context becomes a foundational requirement for effective threat detection, risk management, and governance.

Traditional security tools focus on isolated signals: a login event, a data access attempt, a file movement. But when these signals are analyzed without understanding the *relationships* between identities, data objects, and data flows, threats go unnoticed or are flagged too late. As enterprises adopt DSPM, Zero Trust architectures, and cloud-native platforms, the ability to link data objects, flows, and identities into a unified risk surface becomes the most powerful tool in the security arsenal.

This chapter details how to build full context and explains why it is a key component of a security strategy.

Linking Data Objects, Flows, and Identities

Data does not exist in isolation. It is stored, accessed, transformed, and transmitted, often by a variety of identities and systems. Understanding this interplay requires building contextual bridges across three fundamental elements:

1. **Data objects:** Files, database records, tables, blob storage objects, or SaaS-resident records (e.g., Salesforce customer entries)
    - How many sensitive records (e.g., PII, PHI, PCI) are there?
    - Where are they located (cloud, SaaS, on-prem)?
    - Are they encrypted or tokenized?
2. **Data flows:** How data moves across systems, whether through ETL (exact, transform, load) pipelines, APIs, shared drives, streaming systems, or manual exports
    - Which identities (human/NHI) have access to sensitive data?
    - Which access paths are being used vs. which are dormant?
    - Are there signs of privilege escalation?
3. **Identities:** Both human (employees, vendors, contractors) and non-human (service accounts, bots, applications) identities that interact with the data
    - Is sensitive data leaving the organization?
    - Are flows deviating from established baselines?
    - Are credentials being reused across domains?

Figure 8.1 from Symmetry Systems,[1] a leading DSPM vendor, illustrates the relationship between these three elements.

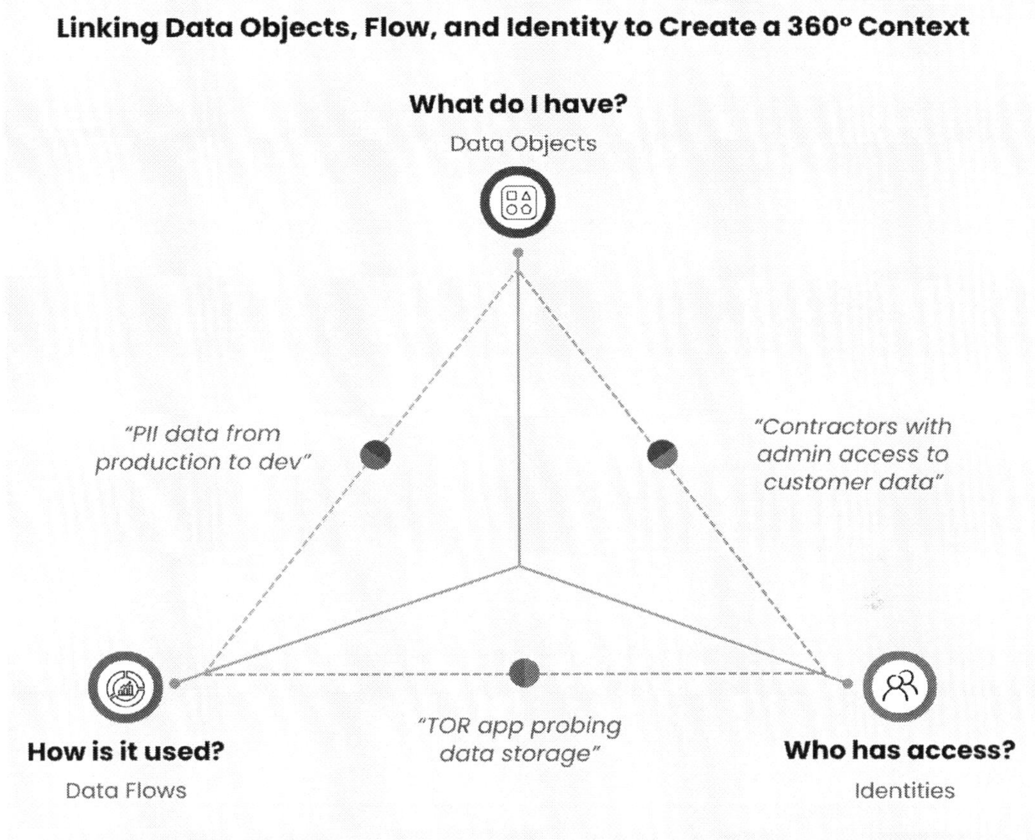

Figure 8.1: Linking data objects, flow, and identity to create a 360° context

Platforms that integrate these three elements and normalize them into a unified ontology are key to success. Leading vendors now offer security graph engines that correlate identities, resources, classifications, permissions, and behaviors.

Figure 8.2 provides two examples of Data/Access graphs with end-to-end context—identities (human and NHI), the data elements they are accessing, and how that data flows across environments.

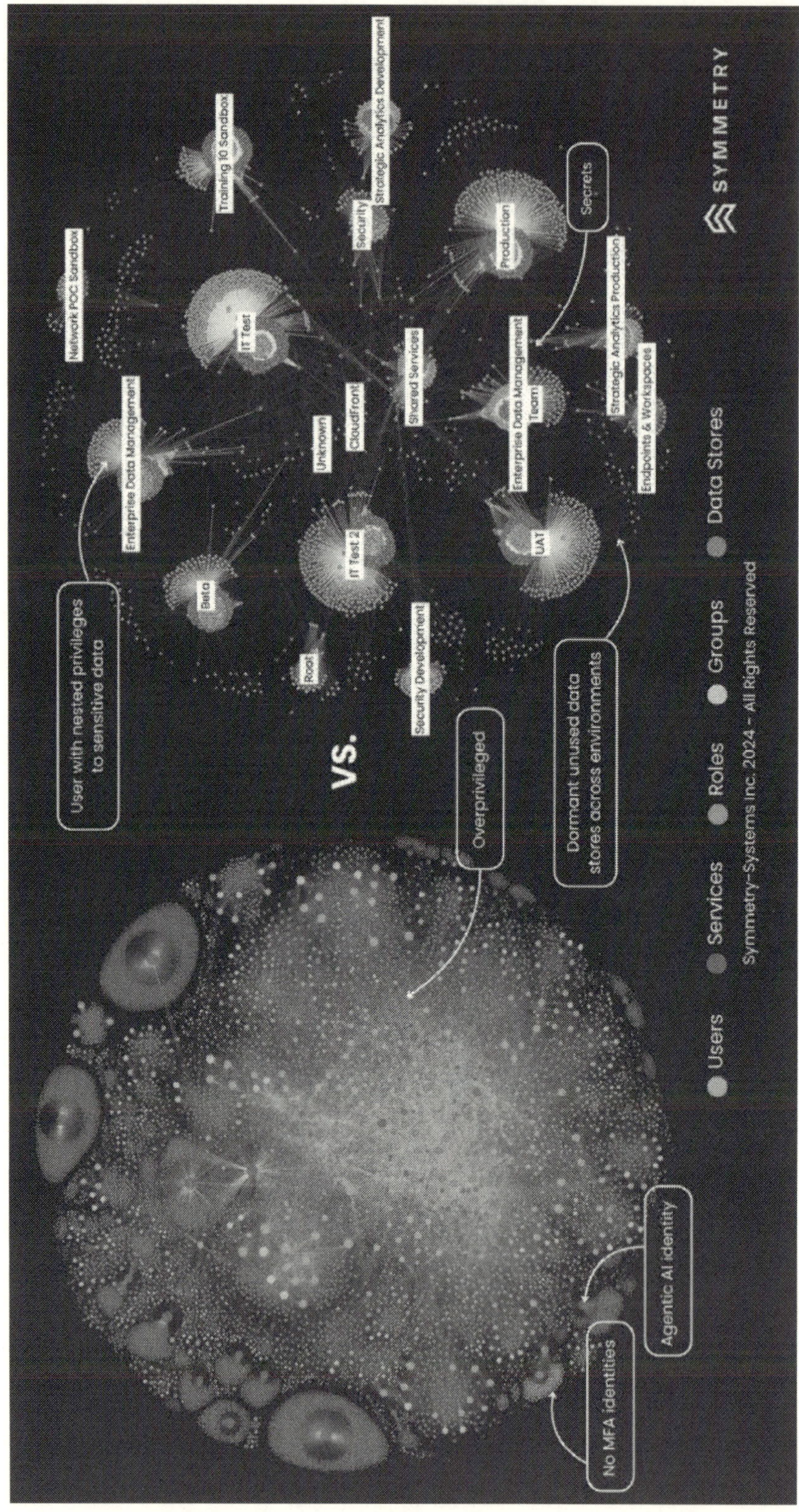

Figure 8.2: Example Data/Access Graphs (source: Symmetry Systems[1])

The diagram on the right of figure 8.2 illustrates two contrasting views. On the left, we see a highly entangled environment where numerous identities have broad access to large volumes of data, a configuration that poses significant security and compliance risks. This kind of overpermissiveness is far from ideal and deviates from the principle of least privilege.

In contrast, the right-hand diagram depicts a well-structured environment. Access is segmented by environment type, such as development, testing, staging, and production, creating clear boundaries around data access. This structured approach not only reduces risk but also simplifies auditing and governance. Visibility into such segmentation is extremely powerful; it enables organizations to enforce access controls, detect anomalies, and align data usage with both operational and compliance objectives.

The Power of 360° Contextualization

Traditional tools view data in silos, by asset, by user, or by policy. Today's threat landscape demands unified visibility across dimensions. A 360-degree contextual view integrates identity, data, behavior, and environment into a single correlated frame of reference. This enables security teams to act with precision and relevance, powered by full-context awareness.

The pillars of this approach are defined in Table 8.1.

Pillar	Description
Identify	Discovers, classifies, maps, and continuously monitors access to sensitive data across cloud, hybrid, and on-premises environments
Detect	Flags anomalies by identifying abnormal data behaviors, unusual access patterns, and violations of data policies in real time
Protect	Remediates unused access, dormant identities, insecure data stores, overshared files, and unmanaged entitlements, reducing risk exposure
Respond & Recover	Contains damage from breaches or misuse by linking compromised identities to sensitive data and automating targeted response and recovery actions

Table 8.1: Core pillars of 360° contextualization and their role

Why 360° Contextualization Matters

A full-context approach does not just unify signals, it transforms outcomes. With identity, data, and behavior linked in real time, organizations can move from reactive to proactive security. They gain visibility into gaps, context around activity, and insight into where risk is growing even before incidents occur.

The key benefits of a full-context approach include:

- **Enabling identity as the control plane:** Enforces least privilege and prevents lateral movement by continuously mapping access to sensitive data
- **Surfacing hidden risk like shadow data:** Identifies unmanaged or unknown sensitive data outside governance boundaries
- **Eliminating dormant identity risk:** Flags stale or orphaned access before it can be exploited
- **Controlling sprawl and oversharing:** Detects sensitive files that have been exposed through misconfiguration or overuse of sharing permissions
- **Accelerating threat detection and response:** Links behavioral anomalies with sensitive data exposure to reduce response times and increase precision
- **Continuously enforcing least privilege:** Moves beyond one-time access reviews by adapting entitlements based on usage, sensitivity, and organizational context

Example: Using Full Context to Determine an Incident in Progress

Let's say a sales operations team uses Salesforce (SaaS), Snowflake (data warehouse), and a custom Python script for monthly report generation. Here's how context can uncover a threat:

- **Data Object**: Customer PII in Snowflake tables
- **Flow**: Data is extracted via script into a CSV file
- **Identity**: Service account with elevated privileges

Without context, this would be invisible. But with full context:

- The system recognizes that the script has never pulled full-table exports before
- It identifies the output location as an unmanaged shared drive
- It tags the CSV as containing highly sensitive fields (SSNs, emails)
- It observes that the service account had not been used for 45 days prior to this run

This correlated understanding helps flag the activity as potentially malicious or negligent and prompts a security response.

Example: Using Full Context For Insider Threat Prevention

A financial analyst accesses a sensitive Excel file on a secure server at 9:00 AM. Ten minutes later, she uploads a compressed version of the same file to a personal Dropbox account.

Without context, these are two separate benign actions. With context:

- The system identifies the file as containing PII
- Sees the analyst rarely accesses this folder
- Flags the external upload as unsanctioned

The combination triggers a medium-severity alert for insider risk.

Example: Using Full Context to Detect Non-Human Identity Compromise

A service account tied to a DevOps pipeline suddenly begins pulling large datasets from a customer database during off-hours. Full context reveals:

- This identity typically accesses only logs
- The data types being pulled are financial records
- The destination is a new cloud bucket outside the U.S.

Result: The alert is upgraded to high severity, triggering automated quarantine.

Chapter Takeaways

In today's cloud-native, AI-enabled environments, isolated alerts are not sufficient. This chapter emphasizes that linking data objects, flows, and identities is required for understanding and mitigating risk. The following key takeaways illustrate the value of building full context:

- **Security without context is blind:** Isolated alerts in complex environments fail to capture the broader picture of risk, leading to missed threats and false positives.
- **Linking data objects, flows, and identities is essential:** By connecting these elements into unified data/access graphs, organizations gain deep visibility into how data is accessed, moved, and potentially misused.

- **360° context enables advanced threat detection:** Security teams can accurately detect insider threats, nonhuman identity misuse, and anomalous data behaviors that would otherwise go unnoticed.
- **Context transforms raw telemetry into insight:** Events like full-table exports, unauthorized uploads, or compromised service accounts become meaningful only when viewed in context.
- **Context turns DSPM into a proactive security layer:** It drives faster detection, smarter response, and stronger alignment with Zero Trust and compliance mandates.

References

1. Symmetry Systems. (2023). Why Symmetry. https://www.symmetry-systems.com/why-symmetry/

PART 03

Strengthening Posture and Platform Capabilities

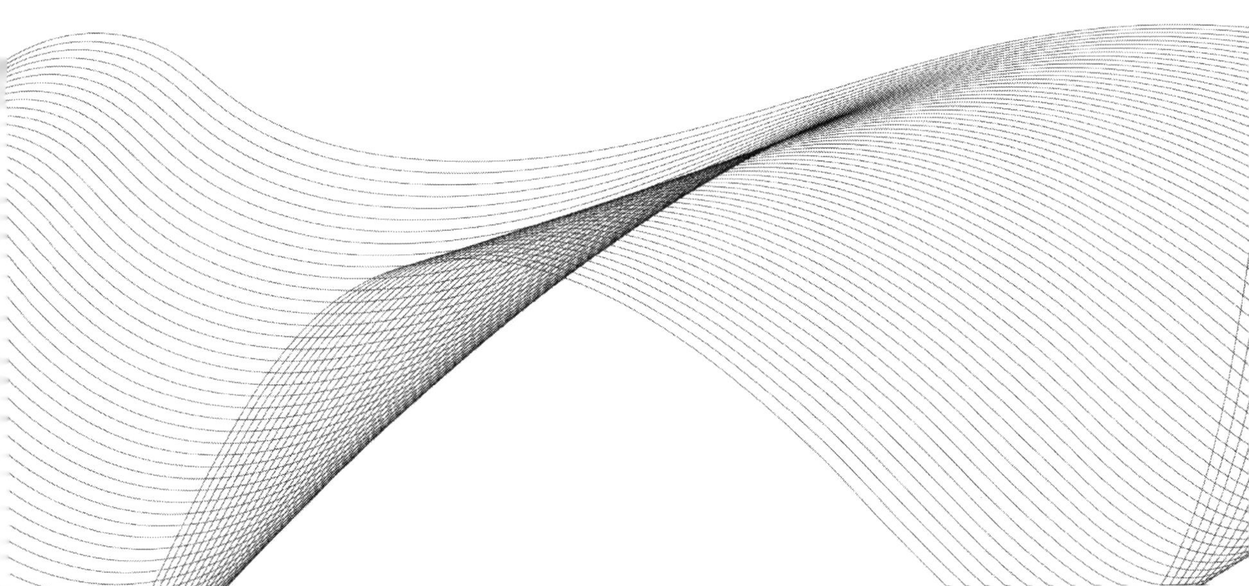

CHAPTER 9

Posture Management and Remediation

> *"Amazon S3 buckets start life completely locked down. The only person or object that can write into those buckets or read from those buckets is the one who created it. So every breach you've seen associated with them—and it's been billions of records over the last couple of years—is because somebody accidentally assigned too permissive a policy to that storage bucket. When you're trying to build something, it's like, 'Well, we'll just give it more permissions. And now it works.' And they never lock them down again."*
>
> – MARK NUNNIKHOVEN, PRINCIPAL, AWS

Why Posture Management Matters

In the previous chapter, we explored how building full context across data objects, identities, and flows enables more precise and proactive security. But context alone is not enough. To reduce risk in a meaningful way, security teams must act on that context, particularly when it exposes weaknesses within the infrastructure. This is where posture management becomes essential.

Posture management is the discipline of identifying and correcting misconfigurations that introduce systemic risk. These are not hypothetical concerns; they are among the leading causes of real-world breaches. According to IBM's 2023 *Cost of a Data Breach* report, misconfigurations account for 20% of data breaches in public cloud environments.[1] Unlike attacks that rely on advanced malware or phishing, posture-related gaps are often wide-open doors, left ajar by default settings, human error, or weak change management processes.

DSPM platforms play a critical role in addressing this challenge. They are designed to surface configuration weaknesses that expose sensitive data, often correlating these posture issues with data sensitivity and identity risk. Many DSPM solutions go further, providing guided remediation workflows or directly enforcing configuration changes through automated integrations with cloud platforms. As DSPMs evolve, they are becoming not just visibility tools, but active participants in closing the loop between detection and response.

In this chapter, we will:

- Examine common configuration vulnerabilities that affect enterprise environments.
- Review strategies for detecting and remediating misconfigurations.
- Explore posture management tools and dashboards used across major cloud platforms.
- Provide detailed examples from AWS, Azure, Google Cloud Platform, and Oracle Cloud Infrastructure.
- Introduce a practical framework for continuous assessment, triage, and remediation prioritization.

Posture Gap Detection

Posture gaps are inadvertent weaknesses introduced during the setup, scaling, or maintenance of infrastructure. These are not software bugs or zero-day vulnerabilities; they are preventable missteps in how cloud services are deployed and managed. When left undetected, they can expose sensitive data and systems to the internet or to internal misuse.

Common examples of posture gaps include:

- Publicly accessible cloud storage buckets
- Virtual machines or services exposed to the internet without restrictions
- Encryption at rest settings disabled or misapplied
- Logging and audit trails turned off or never enabled
- Overly permissive security group or firewall rules (e.g., 0.0.0.0/0 access)
- Use of default credentials or weak authentication settings

These issues often arise during rapid cloud provisioning or from a lack of familiarity with cloud provider defaults. For example, in some environments, a storage bucket may be created with open permissions unless explicitly configured otherwise. In fast moving DevOps cultures, these defaults can be overlooked or assumed to be safe, creating silent, high-impact risks.

Example: Twilio's S3 Exposure

A notable example of this occurred in 2020 when Twilio, a cloud communications platform, experienced a security incident due to a misconfigured Amazon S3 bucket.[2] Attackers accessed the bucket and modified the TaskRouter JavaScript software development kit (SDK), a library used by Twilio's customers. The SDK path had been publicly readable and writable since 2015. The attackers injected malicious code that redirected browsers to a URL associated with Magecart attacks. Twilio acknowledged that the misconfiguration allowed unauthorized write access to the S3 bucket, leading to the compromise. The incident underscores how misconfigured cloud storage can serve as an attack vector.

These types of exposures are especially dangerous because automated crawlers are constantly scanning for publicly accessible cloud assets. Tools and bots now routinely crawl the internet for misconfigured buckets, exposed Kubernetes dashboards, and other open cloud services, often exploiting them within hours of discovery. Once indexed or shared on underground forums, these assets can become persistent targets.

As a result, continuous posture gap detection has become a nonnegotiable baseline. Security teams must go beyond static audits and implement real time posture checks, ideally integrated into CI/CD pipelines, cloud control planes, and incident response workflows. The goal is not only to identify misconfigurations but to tie them back to the data and identities they affect, so the most critical exposures can be prioritized and remediated swiftly.

Criticality-Based Categorization

To effectively manage misconfigurations and security gaps, organizations must assess each issue based on its potential impact. Assigning a severity score helps prioritize remediation efforts and align resources with actual risk. A common approach uses the following scale:

- **Critical:** Immediate and active risk of data breach or system compromise (e.g., public S3 bucket containing PII)
- **High:** Major exposure that is not yet exploited but easily discoverable (e.g., non-encrypted database in production)
- **Medium:** Configuration violates best practices but would require multiple conditions to be exploited (e.g., missing backup encryption)

- **Low:** Hygiene-related issues that pose minimal immediate risk (e.g., untagged assets, default port exposure without services running)

This risk-based scoring model not only guides remediation priorities but also feeds into executive dashboards, enabling leadership to understand and act on the most pressing threats to the organization's data posture.

CIS Benchmarks for Cloud

To systematically address configuration gaps and enhance cloud security, organizations can leverage the CIS Benchmarks developed by the Center for Internet Security (CIS).[3] These are consensus-based, vendor-agnostic guidelines that provide prescriptive recommendations for securely configuring systems, applications, and network devices. For cloud environments, CIS offers Foundations Benchmarks tailored to major providers like AWS, Microsoft Azure, Google Cloud Platform, and Oracle Cloud Infrastructure. These benchmarks cover critical areas such as identity and access management, logging and monitoring, and networking settings. By adhering to CIS Benchmarks, organizations can establish a secure baseline configuration, reduce vulnerabilities, and align with industry standards and regulatory frameworks like NIST, ISO 27000, PCI DSS, and HIPAA . Implementing these benchmarks is a proactive step toward minimizing configuration-related risks in cloud deployments.

AWS Examples[4]

- **Open S3 bucket (critical):** S3 bucket configured as public-read with no IAM policy restriction. Detected via AWS Config or Security Hub. Fix: Apply bucket policy denying public access, enable block public access.
- **Unrestricted security group (high):** TCP port 22 open to 0.0.0.0/0. Common with EC2 provisioning. Detected via AWS Config or GuardDuty. Fix: Restrict source IP range, use bastion hosts.

Azure Examples[5]

- **Unprotected blob storage (critical):** Azure Blob container marked public with confidential data. Fix: Change access tier, disable anonymous access.
- **Disabled diagnostic logging (medium):** NSG Flow logs or Activity logs not enabled. Fix: Use Azure Policy to enforce logging requirements.

GCP Examples[6]

- **Cloud storage bucket with allUsers read access (critical):** Detected via GCP Security Command Center. Fix: Remove IAM binding for "allUsers" or "allAuthenticatedUsers".
- **VM without shielded VM enabled (medium):** Leaves system open to boot-level compromise. Fix: Recreate with Shielded VM option enabled.

OCI Examples[7]

- **Object storage bucket publicly accessible (critical):** Can be flagged in OCI Cloud Guard. Fix: Update bucket policy to deny public access.
- **Unmonitored root compartment changes (high):** No notifications on IAM policy changes in root. Fix: Enable and subscribe to Events Service alerts.

Remediation of Misconfigurations

Effective remediation includes:

1. **Automated policy enforcement:** Use tools like AWS Config Rules, Azure Policy, GCP Organization Policies
2. **Manual exception workflows:** For cases where business needs temporarily override policy
3. **Playbooks and runbooks:** Predefined steps to fix common misconfigurations quickly
4. **Preventative controls:** Infrastructure as Code (IaC) validation (e.g., Terraform plan checks)

Posture Dashboards and Continuous Assessment

Effective posture management depends on continuous visibility and actionable metrics. Dashboards serve as a central tool for surfacing the most important posture signals and aligning stakeholders around risk trends. A well-designed dashboard should include:

- Total number of misconfigurations
- Severity breakdown (Critical, High, Medium, Low)
- Time to remediation
- Top misconfigured services
- Trends over time

To support continuous assessment, platforms should also provide:

- Daily or real-time scanning
- Integration with alerting channels (Slack, SIEM, email)
- Visualizations of the current attack surface (e.g., exposed endpoints)
- Mapping to key compliance frameworks (CIS, NIST, ISO)

When combined, these elements transform raw configuration data into a real-time control system for risk, enabling teams to detect drift early, measure remediation progress, and demonstrate posture improvements to both technical and executive audiences.

Chapter Takeaways

Misconfigurations remain one of the most common and preventable causes of data breaches in cloud environments. As organizations adopt complex architectures and scale rapidly, maintaining a secure configuration posture becomes both more critical and more challenging. Posture management bridges this gap by turning visibility into action, identifying, prioritizing, and remediating configuration risks tied to sensitive data, identities, and evolving threat exposure.

- **Posture management enables actionable security:** Full context across data, identity, and flows is critical, but posture management translates that visibility into real risk reduction by identifying and fixing misconfigurations.
- **Misconfigurations are a leading breach vector:** Configuration errors like public buckets or open ports cause 20% of cloud breaches. These are often preventable but easily missed in fast-paced environments.
- **DSPM tools provide context-aware remediation:** DSPM platforms surface posture gaps tied to sensitive data and identity risk, often supporting automated or guided fixes to close the loop between detection and response.
- **Risk-based prioritization is essential:** Categorizing misconfigurations by severity (Critical, High, Medium, Low) helps security teams focus on exposures with the greatest business impact.
- **CIS Benchmarks provide secure baselines:** The CIS Benchmarks offer cloud-specific, best practice configurations that help reduce misconfiguration risk and align with standards like NIST and PCI DSS.
- **Continuous assessment is now table stakes:** Real-time posture scanning, alerting, and dashboards are key for monitoring misconfiguration trends and maintaining a secure cloud environment.

References

1. IBM Security & Ponemon Institute. (2023). Cost of a data breach report 2023. IBM Corporation. https://www.ibm.com/reports/data-breach
2. Sheridan, K. (2020, July 23). Twilio security incident shows danger of misconfigured S3 buckets. Dark Reading. https://www.darkreading.com/cloud-security/twilio-security-incident-shows-danger-of-misconfigured-s3-buckets
3. Center for Internet Security. (2023). CIS benchmarks for cloud security. https://www.cisecurity.org/insights/blog/foundational-cloud-security-with-cis-benchmarks
4. Amazon Web Services. (2023). AWS Security Hub. https://aws.amazon.com/security-hub/
5. Microsoft. (2024). Microsoft Azure Policy overview. https://learn.microsoft.com/en-us/azure/governance/policy/overview
6. Google Cloud. (2023). Security Command Center. https://cloud.google.com/security-command-center
7. Maor, E. (2024). Oracle Cloud Infrastructure security. Oracle. https://docs.oracle.com/en-us/iaas/Content/Security/home.htm

CHAPTER 10

Data Security Platforms

> *"The beauty of DSPM is how quickly you can get value, often within days of deployment. For regulated industries like healthcare, the ability to run DSPM in a fully airgapped environment is a game changer. It means we can uncover risks and protect sensitive data without ever letting it leave our environment."*
>
> – CECIL PINEDA, GLOBAL CISO, R1

The Evolving Landscape of Data Security Platforms

The shift toward hybrid cloud environments, rapid SaaS adoption, and AI-driven operations has redefined what it means to secure data. Traditional perimeter-focused models are insufficient in a world where data exists everywhere, within structured databases, file systems, SaaS applications, cloud object stores, and AI training pipelines. In this evolving landscape, data security platforms serve as the foundation for organizations to monitor, govern, and protect sensitive information across its entire lifecycle.

Data security platforms enable organizations to:

- Gain visibility into where sensitive data resides.
- Monitor who is accessing it and how.
- Detect and respond to threats in real time.
- Maintain compliance with complex global regulations.

This chapter explores three cornerstone categories within the data security platform ecosystem: Database Activity Monitoring (DAM), Data Loss Prevention (DLP), and Data Security Posture Management (DSPM), and how each contributes to a layered, context-rich defense model for sensitive data.

Database Activity Monitoring

DAM tools were among the earliest innovations in bringing continuous visibility and auditing to structured data environments. At their core, DAM solutions monitor all activity within database systems, capturing queries, user behavior, and administrative operations to detect policy violations, insider threats, or signs of compromise.

Key Capabilities

DAM platforms are designed to offer:

- Real-time auditing of SQL activity, including SELECT, INSERT, UPDATE, and DELETE commands
- Privileged user monitoring, particularly for database administrators (DBAs), service accounts, and superusers
- Anomaly detection, such as excessive data queries, off-hours access, or unusual schema interactions
- Compliance reporting aligned with regulatory mandates like SOX, HIPAA, PCI DSS, and GDPR through detailed audit logs and access trails

Architectural Models

DAM systems typically support several deployment architectures:

- **Agent-based monitoring:** Local agents, such as IBM Guardium's Software Traffic Access Point (S-TAP), intercept and log database traffic with low latency, offering granular visibility.
- **Network-based sniffing:** Passive monitoring through network taps or switched port analyzer (SPAN) ports (e.g., Imperva), which minimizes agent overhead but can miss encrypted or local traffic.
- **Native logging integration:** Ingesting logs from the database engine itself (e.g., Idera), enabling broad coverage with minimal infrastructure changes but often less real-time fidelity.

Limitations

While DAM remains a foundational control for structured data environments, it has several limitations:

- Cloud-native and data systems, such as Snowflake, BigQuery, or DynamoDB, often lack traditional query interfaces or OS-level access, making DAM integration difficult. Most DAM solutions cannot effectively monitor these data sources.
- Scalability challenges arise in containerized or microservice-heavy environments where ephemeral workloads and dynamic scaling limit traditional monitoring approaches.
- Lack of context limits DAM effectiveness, as it typically focuses on database-layer activity without correlating to business context, user identity, or the sensitivity of the accessed data.

Despite these gaps, DAM continues to serve as a crucial layer in enterprise data defense strategies, especially for legacy setups, regulated industries, and forensic auditing.[1]

Data Loss Prevention

DLP refers to a set of technologies and policies designed to prevent unauthorized sharing, leakage, or exfiltration of sensitive information. Traditional DLP solutions were developed to safeguard data in motion (e.g., over email or web), at rest (e.g., on file servers), and in use (e.g., during endpoint activities). The DLP model relies heavily on rule-based inspection, content fingerprinting, and predefined policy enforcement to identify and control risky data flows.

DLP platforms typically are especially useful in preventing:

- Accidental leaks, such as a user emailing customer data externally
- Malicious exfiltration, including insider threats or compromised endpoints
- Compliance violations, like transmitting PHI over unencrypted channels

While legacy DLP solutions were endpoint or network focused, modern DLP has evolved to integrate with SaaS applications, cloud collaboration tools, and identity aware data contexts.

Key Capabilities

Most enterprise DLP platforms offer the following core functions:

- Content inspection using pattern matching (e.g., regular expressions), data fingerprinting, dictionaries, and exact data matching
- Policy enforcement such as blocking, quarantining, alerting, or encrypting based on rule triggers (e.g., preventing an SSN from being emailed externally)
- Endpoint controls to restrict USB usage, copy and paste, screen captures, or printing for sensitive files
- Cloud application protection by integrating with APIs for platforms like Microsoft 365, Google Workspace, and Box
- Reporting and compliance dashboards that map incidents to regulatory obligations (e.g., HIPAA, PCI DSS, GDPR)

Advanced DLP solutions now also include ML-based risk scoring, contextual awareness (e.g., user role, device posture, behavior), and integration with identity providers to fine-tune policy application. They can also determine lineage of data based on event telemetry, graph-based modeling, and contextual tracking of how data moves across applications, devices, and users.

Architectural Models

DLP can be deployed in a variety of architectural models depending on the type of data it is meant to protect:

- **Network DLP:** Deployed at egress points (e.g., email gateways, web proxies) to inspect and control data in motion. It relies on integration with SMTP, HTTPS, and FTP streams.
- **Endpoint DLP:** Installed as agents on desktops, laptops, and servers. These agents monitor file access, clipboard use, USB ports, and local file transfers. Many endpoint agents also operate offline, applying cached policies even without network access.
- **Cloud native DLP:** Integrated via APIs or inline proxies (cloud access security brokers, or CASBs) to monitor SaaS platforms. These solutions use connectors to inspect file uploads, emails, and chats in tools like Slack, Teams, and Google Drive.

- **Storage DLP:** Scans file systems (on premises or cloud) for sensitive data at rest. Useful for discovering overexposed files or abandoned sensitive documents.

To ensure operational resilience, many DLP architectures now support redundant scanning engines, policy servers, and agent communication channels, especially in globally distributed enterprises or environments with critical uptime requirements.

Limitations

Despite their capabilities, DLP solutions face a number of well-known challenges:

- **High false positives and policy tuning burden:** Rigid, regex-based pattern matching and legacy rule sets often generate noise, requiring constant tuning.
- **Limited identity awareness:** Many DLP engines evaluate content in isolation and lack context about the user's intent, role, or access justification.
- **Scalability and integration complexity:** Endpoint agent rollouts, network tap placements, and SaaS API coverage vary in maturity, often leading to blind spots.
- **Poor fit for unstructured and cloud native environments:** As organizations adopt object stores, ephemeral containers, and AI pipelines, legacy DLP tools struggle to adapt.

DLP remains an important pillar in data security, especially when used in conjunction with other platforms like DSPM that provide additional visibility and context.[2]

Data Security Posture Management (DSPM)

DSPM represents a significant evolution in how organizations secure their data across complex, distributed environments. Unlike DAM and DLP, which focus on activity monitoring and control enforcement respectively, DSPM takes a continuous and proactive approach to understanding where sensitive data lives, who can access it, how it is exposed, and whether it is protected. It enables organizations to manage risk and reduce the attack surface by building complete visibility and context into their data landscape.[3]

As data proliferates across cloud platforms, SaaS applications, developer environments, and AI pipelines, the need to map the relationship between identities, data stores, and configurations has become critical. DSPM addresses this need through automated discovery, posture evaluation, and contextual risk prioritization.

Key Capabilities

DSPM platforms provide a range of capabilities that extend across both structured and unstructured environments:

- Automated data discovery and classification across cloud storage, databases, SaaS apps, messaging systems, developer environments, and data lakes
- Identity to data mapping, linking users, service accounts, and applications to the exact data objects they can access
- Exposure and risk analysis, highlighting issues such as publicly exposed buckets, overly permissive IAM roles, stale or orphaned data, and sensitive data drift
- Posture dashboards and compliance mapping, showing how data security configurations align with standards such as NIST, CIS, HIPAA, and GDPR
- Remediation guidance and workflows to fix misconfigurations and enforce least privilege principles

Many leading DSPM solutions also provide real time risk scoring, sensitive data movement tracking, and integration with ticketing and security information and event management (SIEM) platforms to help security teams operationalize findings.

Architectural Models

DSPM platforms are designed to meet a broad range of security, privacy, and compliance requirements. Depending on regulatory constraints and organizational maturity, they can be deployed in the following architectural models:

SaaS Deployment Model

- The DSPM platform is hosted entirely in the vendor's cloud environment.
- Lightweight collectors or API integrations are deployed in the enterprise environment to scan data and configurations, typically in read only mode.
- Some or all of raw data may flow into a vendor's environment.
- **Pros:** It features rapid setup, low operational overhead, and continuous feature updates.
- **Cons:** It may not be suitable for regulated environments that restrict outbound metadata flow.

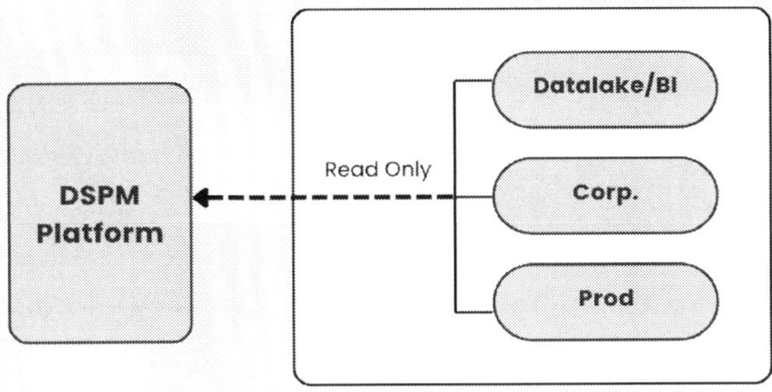

Figure 10.1: SaaS deployment model for DSPM

Outpost Deployment Model

- Metadata collection and analysis are performed locally within the enterprise environment using an outpost component.
- Only metadata is transmitted to the central DSPM platform in the vendor's cloud for analytics and visualization, never the raw data.
- Updates and patches can flow into the outpost instance hosted inside the enterprise environment.
- **Pros**: It maintains local control over sensitive data while benefiting from the cloud platform's advanced analytics.
- **Cons**: It requires infrastructure to support outpost components.

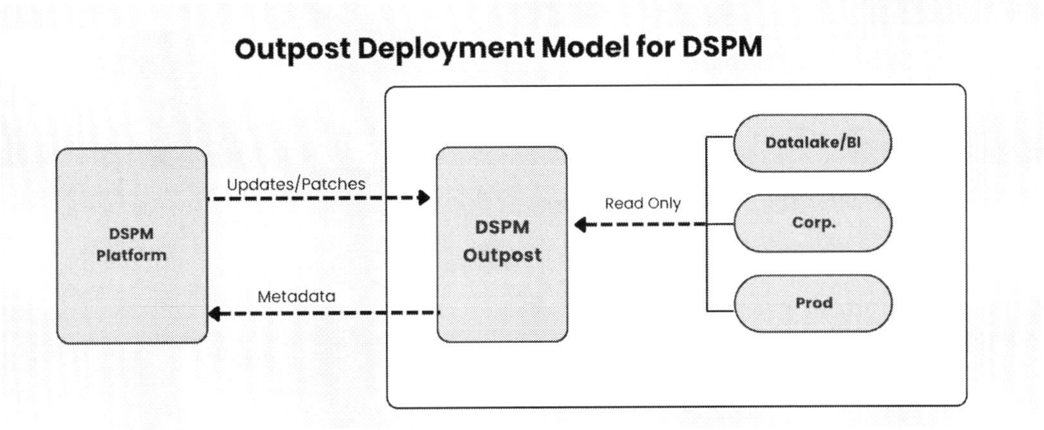

Figure 10.2: Outpost deployment model for DSPM

Airgapped Deployment Model

- The entire DSPM platform is deployed on premises or in a disconnected virtual private cloud.
- Updates and patches can flow into the instance of DSPM hosted inside the enterprise environment.
- No communication occurs between the platform and any external systems, not even for metadata or telemetry.
- **Pros:** It features maximum data sovereignty, ideal for defense, government, or critical infrastructure sectors.
- **Cons:** It requires the customer to manage updates, security patches, and platform scalability.

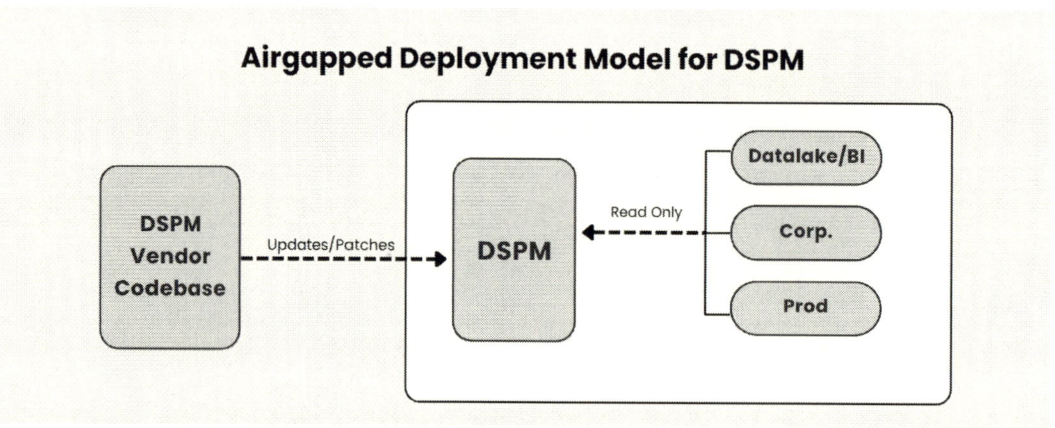

Figure 10.3: Airgapped deployment model for DSPM

Federated Model

- Multiple DSPM instances are deployed in separate geographic or regulatory regions of the enterprise, such as US, EU, or APAC.
- A central instance oversees secondary deployments in other regions, ensuring consistent patching, unified governance, and enforcement of shared policy frameworks, while adhering to regulatory requirements.
- **Pros:** It enables compliance with data localization laws and supports large multinational enterprises.
- **Cons:** The setup is complex and it requires management of policies across federated instances.

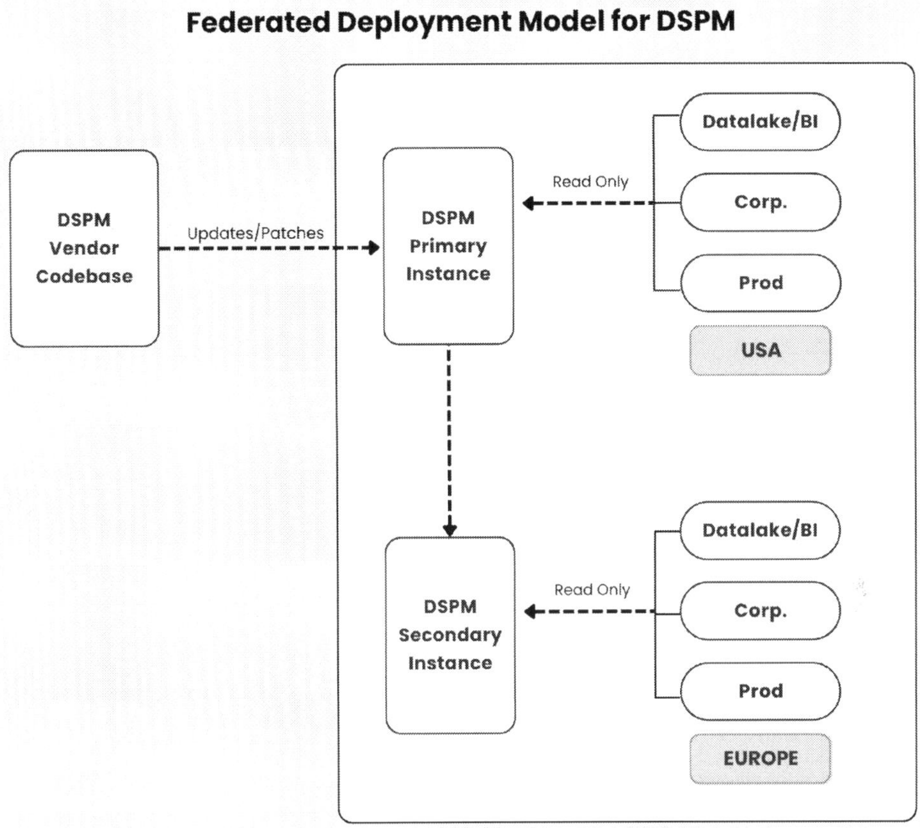

Figure 10.4: Federated deployment model for DSPM

Limitations

Despite its powerful capabilities, DSPM also has limitations:

- **Integration complexity:** Mapping data, identities, and configurations across hybrid and multi-cloud environments can require significant upfront effort and ongoing tuning.
- **Limited enforcement:** DSPM focuses on visibility and posture rather than active control, so it often relies on integrations with other tools (e.g., DLP, IAM) to remediate risks.
- **Coverage gaps:** Legacy systems, highly customized applications, or on-prem environments may not always be fully supported, leading to blind spots.

Comparison of Data Security Platforms

Category	Database Activity Monitoring (DAM)	Data Loss Prevention (DLP)	Data Security Posture Management (DSPM)
Primary Focus	Monitor and audit structured database activity	Prevent unauthorized data leakage in motion, at rest, and in use	Discover, classify, and assess the risk posture of sensitive data
Data Types Covered	Structured data in databases	Structured and unstructured data across endpoints, networks, and storage	Structured and unstructured data across cloud, SaaS, and developer environments
Enforcement Capability	Detect, but not enforce	Enforces via blocking, alerting, quarantining	Identifies and guides remediation; limited enforcement
Identity Context	Limited: focuses on database users	Partial: based on endpoint identity or cloud services	Strong: maps users, roles, and service accounts to data access paths
Activity Monitoring	Real-time monitoring of SQL queries and DB operations	Network DLP, Endpoint DLP, Cloud DLP, Storage DLP	Monitors data exposure, access paths, and configuration changes
Deployment Models	Agent-based, network sniffing, or log ingestion	Network, Endpoint, Cloud, and Storage DLP models	SaaS, Outpost, Airgapped, Federated

Category	Database Activity Monitoring (DAM)	Data Loss Prevention (DLP)	Data Security Posture Management (DSPM)
Scalability	Moderate: challenged by cloud-native and microservice architectures	High in distributed environments; complex in hybrid deployments	Designed for cloud-native scalability and dynamic data environments
Use Case Examples	Compliance auditing, insider threat detection, database forensics	Blocking sensitive emails, preventing data copy to USB drives	Identifying publicly exposed S3 buckets, tracking sensitive data drift
Strengths	Deep visibility into database-level access and behavior	Direct enforcement of data handling policies	Holistic view of data risk posture, exposure, and identity-to-data relationships
Limitations	Lacks context and cloud-native compatibility	High false positives, limited identity and cloud integration	Signal overload, no direct enforcement
Common Tools	IBM Guardium, Imperva SecureSphere, Idera	Symantec DLP, Forcepoint, Microsoft Purview DLP	Symmetry Systems, Cyera, Dig Security, Sentra

Table 10.1: Comparison of DAM, DLP, and DSPM on key criteria

Chapter Takeaways

As data environments grow more distributed and complex, no single tool can cover every aspect of data security. This chapter examined three foundational categories within the data security platform ecosystem: Database Activity Monitoring (DAM), Data Loss Prevention (DLP), and Data Security Posture Management (DSPM). Each offers a unique lens into risk and control, and together they form a more comprehensive and layered defense strategy.

- **Data security has evolved beyond the perimeter:** Security is not just about guarding network boundaries. Modern strategies must protect data wherever it resides, across cloud platforms, SaaS applications, and AI-driven workflows.
- **DAM supports structured data oversight:** DAM tools provide real-time visibility into database activity and are valuable for compliance and insider threat detection. However, they face challenges with scalability, limited identity context, and reduced relevance in cloud-native environments.
- **DLP blocks unintended data movement:** DLP enforces policies to prevent data exfiltration across endpoints, networks, and cloud services. Its effectiveness is often hindered by false positives, complex integrations, and lack of contextual awareness.
- **DSPM enables context-aware protection:** DSPM offers a posture-driven approach to securing both structured and unstructured data. With capabilities like identity-to-data mapping, exposure analysis, and support for SaaS, Outpost, Airgapped, and Federated deployments, DSPM aligns with modern architectures and supports proactive risk reduction.
- **These platforms work best in combination:** Each platform addresses a different aspect of the data security landscape. When used together, DAM, DLP, and DSPM can deliver layered protection with the visibility, control, and context needed to secure sensitive data in today's complex environments.

References

1. IBM. (2023). IBM Security Guardium Data Protection. IBM Corporation. https://www.ibm.com/products/guardium-data-protection
2. Gartner. (2023). Magic Quadrant for Enterprise DLP. https://www.gartner.com/en/documents/6342779
3. Forrester. (2023, December 1). DSPM landscape, Q4 2023. Forrester Research. https://www.forrester.com/report/the-strategic-portfolio-management-tools-landscape-q4-2023/RES180171

CHAPTER 11

Criteria and Methodology for Data Security Platform Selection

> *Choosing a data security platform is not just a technical decision, it's a declaration of how your organization plans to govern trust, scale responsibly, and stay resilient in a data-driven future. It isn't just a security decision either, because it impacts data teams, finance, SRE, compliance, and nearly every function that touches sensitive information.*
>
> – RANDY POTTS, GLOBAL CISO, RTR

Choosing the Right Data Security Platform

Choosing a Data Security Platform (DSP) is a foundational step in building a resilient, scalable, and modern data protection program. As data continues to sprawl across SaaS, cloud, and on-premises environments, and increasingly intersects with AI workflows and regulatory obligations, the need for a robust evaluation framework has never been greater. We have previously discussed Database Activity Monitoring (DAM), Data Loss Prevention (DLP), and Data Security Posture Management (DSPM), which are all types of DSP. Understanding how to evaluate these platforms is essential to making the right investment.

This chapter presents a comprehensive set of evaluation criteria for selecting a DSPM platform. To keep the selection process focused and actionable, DSPM is used as the reference, although most of the same criteria are applicable to other DSP types such as DLP and DAM. The chapter provides detailed explanations for each evaluation dimension and includes a thorough table of questions and requirements that organizations can use to compare vendors. The goal is to help enterprise buyers navigate vendor claims, understand critical differences, and prioritize capabilities that align with their technical, operational, and regulatory needs.

Key Evaluation Dimensions

To support a structured, apples-to-apples comparison of vendor offerings, this chapter organizes the evaluation process across ten core dimensions. Each dimension represents a critical area of functionality or operational readiness that materially affects how a DSPM performs in enterprise environments. These dimensions go beyond surface-level features and dive into architectural fit, real-world usability, integration capabilities, and long-term scalability.

Each section includes a breakdown of individual criteria, accompanied by explanations to help teams understand what to ask, why it matters, and how to assess vendor responses. The goal is to empower stakeholders such as security leaders, IT architects, procurement teams, and compliance officers with the tools to select a platform that meets both current business needs and evolving future demands.

1. Deployment Model and Architecture

This section focuses on how a solution is deployed and what architectural models it supports. Buyers should consider flexibility, air-gap capabilities, support for federated instances, and least privilege operational principles.

ID	Criteria	Explanation	Why It Matters	What Good Looks Like
1.01	Deployment model options	Describes the supported deployment architectures	Helps determine if the solution fits current and future-state infrastructure	Supports SaaS, on-prem, hybrid, and Outpost deployments with minimal friction
1.02	Air-gapping compatibility	Indicates whether the solution can function fully disconnected	Critical for regulated/sensitive setups with no external connectivity	Fully self-contained deployment with no reliance on vendor cloud or telemetry
1.03	Federated architecture support	Confirms if the solution enables regional or	Supports data sovereignty and compliance in	Multi-region, logically separated deployment with centralized governance

ID	Criteria	Explanation	Why It Matters	What Good Looks Like
		business unit isolation	distributed enterprises	
1.04	Metadata collection and protection in SaaS deployments	Explains what metadata is collected and how it is secured in SaaS setups	Important for privacy, compliance, and risk assessment of SaaS models	Transparent metadata documentation, encryption at rest and in transit, customer ownership of telemetry
1.05	Access levels and permissions required	Identifies privileges needed to deploy and operate the solution	Ensures alignment with least privilege principles and internal security policies	Support for required roles, RBAC, and minimal elevated permissions
1.06	On-premises deployment capability	Verifies if the solution can run entirely within private infrastructure	Necessary for legacy environments or disconnected security zones	Full feature parity in on-prem mode without relying on vendor-hosted services
1.07	Time to deploy and realize value	Estimates how quickly the platform can be implemented and deliver ROI	Enables better project planning and faster security outcomes	Deployment within weeks, with measurable insights within the first 30 days

Table 11.1: Deployment model criteria

2. Data Discovery and Classification

Comprehensive data discovery and classification capabilities are the backbone of any DSPM. This includes discovering both structured and unstructured data across cloud, on-prem, and SaaS platforms, ideally with ML-based classification to reduce noise and false positives.

ID	Criteria	Explanation	Why It Matters	What Good Looks Like
2.01	Data discovery across environments	Assesses ability to find data in all environments	Broader reach ensures no sensitive data is missed; also provides a single pane of glass for all data	Discovery across cloud, SaaS, on-prem, and shadow systems via APIs, connectors, or agents
2.02	Structured and unstructured data support	Checks coverage for diverse data formats	Sensitive data exists in both forms	Supports databases, data lakes, file systems, and cloud object stores
2.03	False positives and mitigation	Measures detection accuracy and alert fatigue risk	Reduces noise and improves trust	Context-aware detection with tuning and suppression options
2.04	Custom classifiers and exact matching	Verifies ability to tailor detection rules	Captures enterprise-specific or regulated data	Regex, dictionaries, fingerprinting, and custom rule support
2.05	Classification tag propagation	Checks if tags apply across systems	Enables consistent enforcement and reporting	Tags flow across cloud and on-prem via APIs or sync
2.06	AI-based classification	Evaluates use of AI to reduce false positives	Enhances accuracy and adapts to context	ML/NLP models trained on context and sensitive data patterns

Table 11.2: Discovery and classification criteria

3. Unified Console and Integrations

A DSPM should provide a single pane of glass for visibility and policy enforcement, while also supporting deep integrations with Microsoft Purview, SaaS tools, and third-party observability platforms.

ID	Criteria	Explanation	Why It Matters	What Good Looks Like
3.01	Availability and capabilities of a unified console	Centralizes data visibility and control in a single interface	Simplifies operations, reduces tool sprawl, and improves analyst efficiency	A single pane of glass with access to discovery, classification, risk posture, and policy management
3.02	Executive dashboard capabilities for Board/C-suite	Supports risk reporting and oversight at the executive level	Enables CISOs and senior leaders to track trends, risk exposure, and program impact	Visual dashboards with summaries, trends, KPIs, and exportable reports for board and leadership audiences
3.03	Integration with Microsoft Purview	Preserves native workflows and controls in Microsoft environments	Reduces operational overhead and improves consistency for Microsoft-centric teams	API-level integration for label syncing, policy mapping, and data handling alignment within Microsoft tools
3.04	List of supported connectors for SaaS/tools	Ensures ecosystem compatibility and integration flexibility	Broader integrations drive deeper visibility and reduce blind spots in enterprise tools	Extensive connector library covering SaaS apps, cloud platforms, data lakes, and developer tools

Table 11.3: Criteria for integrations with SaaS and other data related tools

4. 360-Degree Context: Mapping Identities, Data Access, and Enterprise Data Flows

To enforce data security, visibility must go beyond isolated snapshots of where data resides or who accessed it. Enterprises need full, continuous context that links identities, data, and movement across hybrid environments. This 360-degree view is essential to enforce least privilege access, detect abnormal behaviors, prevent data misuse, and ensure compliance.

ID	Criteria	Explanation	Why It Matters	What Good Looks Like
4.01	Discover and classify sensitive data across hybrid environments	Demonstrates visibility into data sprawl across cloud, on-prem, and SaaS	Identifies where sensitive data exists to reduce blind spots and enforce protection	Continuous discovery and classification across all environments and storage types
4.02	Analyze identity usage of sensitive data	Provides clarity on data access trends and potential misuse	Helps detect insider threats, entitlement misuse, and role violations	Detailed reporting on who accessed what data, how often, and if it aligns with expected behavior
4.03	Monitor/manage identity-to-data relationships	Supports least privilege analysis and access auditing	Prevents privilege creep and supports regulatory compliance	Identity-to-data mapping with historical access trails and sensitivity labels

ID	Criteria	Explanation	Why It Matters	What Good Looks Like
4.04	Remediation of insecure or unnecessary access	Eliminates overprovisioned or outdated access rights	Reduces lateral movement risk and exposure from dormant identities	Guided or automated deprovisioning actions with audit logging
4.05	Complete visibility into how data flows across the enterprise	Tracks how sensitive data moves between users, systems, and environments	Detects exfiltration paths, data misuse, and flow violations	Real-time and historical flow maps showing source, destination, user, and classification context

Table 11.4: Criteria for use of identity intelligence to drive actionability

5. Optimization and Data Minimization Criteria

Effective data security is not only about protection but also about precision. Organizations must minimize unnecessary data exposure, reduce operational noise, and optimize storage and access. This means identifying redundant, outdated, or unused data, reducing false positives in classification, and clearly mapping how data is used across the environment. These efforts support compliance, lower risk, and help security teams focus on what truly matters.

ID	Criteria	Explanation	Why It Matters	What Good Looks Like
5.01	Techniques to reduce classification false positives	Helps improve precision in detection and reduce alert fatigue	Minimizes noise and allows analysts to focus on true risks	AI-enhanced classification with contextual filters and feedback-based tuning

ID	Criteria	Explanation	Why It Matters	What Good Looks Like
5.02	Identification of duplicate or redundant data	Identifies unnecessary data for potential removal or consolidation	Reduces storage costs and shrinks the data attack surface	Reports highlighting redundant datasets with tagging for review or deletion
5.03	Identify cloud data for archiving or deletion	Supports cost and risk reduction by finding archival opportunities	Helps enforce retention policies and reduce overexposure of stale data	Classification-integrated archival tagging and cloud lifecycle policy recommendations
5.04	Map data, identities, and usage patterns comprehensively	Drives governance by linking data, users, and access behavior	Enables least privilege enforcement, anomaly detection, and compliance audits	Cross-linked view of identity, sensitivity, and behavior at object-level granularity

Table 11.5: Criteria for data insights, false positives, and FinOps

6. Implementation, Support, and Onboarding Criteria

A data security platform is only as effective as its successful deployment and ongoing management. The transition from proof of concept to full implementation requires thoughtful onboarding, well-defined support structures, and thorough enablement for internal teams. Just as important, implementation must adhere to strict security protocols to protect sensitive data from day one. This section outlines the key evaluation criteria to assess how a vendor supports you before, during, and after deployment.

ID	Criteria	Explanation	Why It Matters	What Good Looks Like
6.01	Services offered for implementation and onboarding	Details the vendor's services and support during rollout	Accelerates time to value and reduces internal deployment burden	Dedicated onboarding team, technical project plan, and phased rollout guidance
6.02	Recommended support model post-deployment	Outlines how ongoing technical support is structured post-launch	Ensures long-term stability and responsiveness to operational issues	Tiered support options with defined SLAs, escalation paths, and named technical account managers
6.03	Documentation and training plans for internal teams	Confirms long-term sustainability via training and documentation	Empowers internal teams and reduces reliance on external support	Robust, role-based training materials, self-service knowledge base, and live enablement sessions
6.04	Security protocols during implementation	Provides confidence that customer data remains secure during onboarding	Prevents risk introduction through missteps during rollout	Encrypted data transfers, least-privilege access for vendor teams, and implementation security audit logs

Table 11.6: Operationalization and support criteria

7. Roadmap, Scalability, and Future Needs

As organizations grow, so do their data volumes, regulatory obligations, and risk surfaces. A security solution that meets today's needs but fails to evolve with tomorrow's environment becomes a liability. This section evaluates whether a platform is architected for scale, built to adapt to new technologies, and aligned with the strategic roadmap of the enterprise. It also assesses vendor commitment to innovation and responsiveness to emerging threats, use cases, and compliance frameworks.

ID	Criteria	Explanation	Why It Matters	What Good Looks Like
7.01	Platform scalability across environments and data growth	Assesses if the platform will keep up with future data estate expansion	Prevents performance degradation and ensures consistent protection as footprint grows	Proven ability to scale across petabyte-scale datasets and hybrid, multi-cloud environments
7.02	Futureproofing for compliance and tech evolution	Ensures the solution is adaptable to new threats and regulations	Reduces rework and ensures ongoing compliance	Modular architecture with support for policy updates, new controls, and evolving standards
7.03	Vendor roadmap transparency and alignment	Evaluates how well the vendor's product vision aligns with enterprise needs	Helps assess long-term partnership fit and innovation pace	Clear roadmap disclosures, product briefings, and history of timely feature delivery
7.04	Ability to support new use cases over time	Measures flexibility to accommodate evolving business or threat scenarios	Ensures the platform doesn't become obsolete as business needs change	Extensible architecture, open APIs, and ongoing enhancements to support AI, automation, and new data types
7.05	Customer feedback via quarterly business reviews (QBRs)s and advisory boards	Assesses structured feedback channels used to shape roadmap direction	Ensures product direction reflects real-world enterprise needs and pain points	Regular QBRs, participation in customer advisory boards, and demonstrated responsiveness to enterprise feedback

Table 11.7: Criteria for ensuring scalability and platform evolution to meet future needs

8. Protection, Enforcement, and Incident Management Capabilities

Visibility is foundational, but true data security requires active enforcement. Organizations must go beyond detection to block threats, limit damage, and ensure policy compliance at the point of access. This section evaluates how a platform enforces protections, from real-time access controls to post-incident blast radius analysis. It also considers capabilities like ransomware detection, alerting, and policy application across diverse environments, ensuring data remains secure whether it resides in cloud object stores, databases, or SaaS platforms.

ID	Criteria	Explanation	Why It Matters	What Good Looks Like
8.01	RRBAC support	Describes how the platform limits access to sensitive functions and data	Prevents unauthorized access and aligns with internal role separation	Fine-grained RBAC with support for least-privilege roles and admin-level segmentation
8.02	Customization of data protection controls	Outlines how flexible and granular controls can be configured	Ensures policies match enterprise-specific risks and compliance needs	Rich policy engine with support for contextual rules, exceptions, and dynamic enforcement
8.03	Tailored protection strategy and use case alignment	Demonstrates expertise in aligning controls to enterprise use cases	Confirms vendor understands real-world needs, not just abstract capabilities	Use case documentation with examples tied to industry-specific or regulated environments
8.04	Support for classifiers to block uploads to unsanctioned destinations	Prevents exfiltration of sensitive data to unauthorized locations	Reduces shadow IT risk and supports data control at the egress point	Built-in and custom classifiers that integrate with network and endpoint egress control points

ID	Criteria	Explanation	Why It Matters	What Good Looks Like
8.05	Policy enforcement at the data access layer	Describes enforcement mechanisms for protecting data at point of access	Critical for preventing policy violations before data is misused	Inline controls (e.g., data firewalls) that enforce policies across storage, access, and identity systems
8.06	Blast radius calculation after an incident	Helps determine breach impact via context-aware exposure mapping	Speeds impact assessment and guides containment and response	Automated analysis that maps compromised identities to accessed sensitive data
8.07	Alerting for misuse or unauthorized access	Outlines how alerts are generated, prioritized, and routed	Enables rapid incident response and reduces alert fatigue	Real-time alerting with context (user, data type, location) and integrations with SIEM and security orchestration, automation, and response (SOAR) systems
8.08	Ransomware detection capabilities	Detects behaviors consistent with ransomware activity	Enables proactive response to data encryption or access anomalies	Behavioral detection combined with identity and data access correlation to identify ransomware early
8.09	Remediation and actionability	Ability to drive remediation of findings identified by the platform	Closes the loop between detection and resolution	Guided workflows, integrations with ticketing or orchestration tools, and native remediation capabilities

Table 11.8: Data protection and incident management criteria

9. AI/ML and Compliance

Data security platforms must balance intelligent automation with regulatory rigor. Machine learning should help reduce false positives, detect anomalies, and classify sensitive data with greater context. At the same time, integration with compliance frameworks and controls against data leakage into external AI models is critical. This section evaluates the use of AI/ML, support for governance mandates, and enterprise-safe integration with generative AI tools such as Microsoft Copilot.

ID	Criteria	Explanation	Why It Matters	What Good Looks Like
9.01	Supported compliance frameworks and reporting	Lists built-in support for data privacy, industry-specific, or regional regulations	Ensures alignment with legal and audit requirements	Out-of-the-box support for frameworks like GDPR, HIPAA, PCI DSS, CCPA, and automated compliance reporting
9.02	AI/ML features for discovery, detection, and enforcement	Explains how ML enhances detection and classification accuracy	Reduces false positives, improves coverage, and scales policy enforcement	Behavioral anomaly detection, context-aware classification, and learning from usage patterns
9.03	Integration with AI assistants like Microsoft Copilot	Describes how GenAI is used to assist users with natural-language interaction	Boosts usability and adoption through intuitive interfaces	Integration with enterprise Copilot or chat-based tools for querying, policy authoring, and report generation
9.04	Leakage of data into public/external AI models	Addresses risk of unauthorized data exposure into unmanaged AI systems	Protects sensitive and regulated data from leaving enterprise boundaries	Technical controls to block PII/PHI from being sent to public LLMs, with audit logging and policy enforcement

ID	Criteria	Explanation	Why It Matters	What Good Looks Like
9.05	Will the vendor use enterprise data or metadata to train their models?	Confirms whether any part of the customer's data or metadata is used for vendor AI training	Prevents vendor-side model enrichment from sensitive or proprietary enterprise data	Explicit contractual guarantees and technical assurances that no customer data or metadata is used in training vendor AI models

Table 11.9: AI/ML and Compliance criteria

10. Evaluating Cost, Time to Value, and Platform Differentiation

Understanding cost and implementation details is essential for selecting the right data security platform. Beyond just price, organizations must assess how vendors charge (e.g., data volume, user seats), what differentiates them from competitors, and how quickly value is realized. This section helps buyers evaluate total cost of ownership, pricing transparency, and project rollout expectations.

ID	Criteria	Explanation	Why It Matters	What Good Looks Like
10.01	Pricing model and cost breakdown	Helps assess total cost of ownership, including hidden fees	Avoids budget surprises and supports long-term financial planning	Transparent, modular pricing with clear documentation of optional add-ons and support tiers
10.02	Is data volume a factor in pricing?	Clarifies whether pricing is based on data volume or other usage metrics	Important for scalability and fairness as data estates grow	Predictable pricing models that decouple cost from raw data volume where possible

ID	Criteria	Explanation	Why It Matters	What Good Looks Like
10.03	Differentiators vs. competitors	Highlights areas of functional or architectural differentiation	Supports justification of platform selection to technical and executive stakeholders	Clear, demonstrated advantages in performance, security, or architecture over comparable vendors
10.04	Proposed timeline with milestones?	Enables planning based on expected deployment duration and outcomes	Improves coordination across stakeholders and aligns expectations	Detailed project plan with phase milestones, resource requirements, and checkpoints for success

Table 11.10: Criteria that go into cost, value, and implementation timeline

Decision-Making Roles in DSPM Evaluation

Selecting a Data Security Platform (DSP) requires alignment across technical, business, and compliance stakeholders. Each group brings a unique perspective, from architecture and risk posture to operational scalability and financial impact. To streamline decision-making and avoid role ambiguity, it's critical to define who is Responsible, Accountable, Consulted, and Informed (RACI) for each dimension of evaluation. The matrix below outlines suggested RACI roles for evaluating DSP solutions across the ten key criteria sections. While actual responsibilities may vary by organization, this model provides a baseline to ensure structured collaboration and informed decisions.

Stakeholders

- CISO – Chief Information Security Officer
- CTO – Chief Technology Officer
- CDO – Chief Data Officer
- CIO – Chief Information Officer
- Head of Security Architecture / Engineering

- Head of Compliance / Risk
- Head of Site Reliability Engineering (SRE)
- Procurement / Finance Lead

RACI Matrix for DSP Evaluation Criteria

#	Section Name	CISO	CTO	CDO	CIO	Head of Sec Arch	Compliance /Risk	SRE	Procurement
1	Deployment Model	A	R	C	C	R	C	R	I
2	Data Discovery & Classification	R	C	A	I	R	C	C	I
3	Console, Dashboards, and Integration	R	R	C	C	A	C	R	I
4	Identity, Flow, and Data Relationship Mapping	R	C	A	I	R	C	C	I
5	Data Hygiene and Usage Reduction	R	C	A	I	R	C	C	I
6	Implementation, Support, and Onboarding	C	R	I	I	R	C	A	C
7	Roadmap, Scalability, and Future Needs	A	R	R	C	C	I	C	C
8	Protection and Enforcement Capabilities	A	C	C	I	R	R	C	I

#	Section Name	CISO	CTO	CDO	CIO	Head of Sec Arch	Compliance /Risk	SRE	Procurement
9	AI/ML and Compliance	R	R	C	I	C	A	C	I
10	Cost, Value, and Implementation Timeline	C	C	C	C	I	I	R	A

Table 11.11: RACI matrix for DSP evaluation criteria

Legend:

- **R** = Responsible: Executes the task
- **A** = Accountable: Final decision-maker
- **C** = Consulted: Provides input based on expertise
- **I** = Informed: Kept updated on progress

Chapter Takeaways

While this chapter presents detailed evaluation criteria for selecting a DSPM platform, the same structured methodology can also be applied to other data security platforms such as DLP and DAM. A consistent, principles-based approach helps organizations make confident, aligned decisions across different categories of data security tools.

- **Structured criteria for better decisions:** A methodical evaluation framework ensures platform selection is based on architectural fit, operational readiness, and strategic alignment, not just vendor claims or surface-level features.
- **Cross-functional buy-in is required:** Success depends on coordination across CISOs, architects, compliance, and procurement as outlined in the RACI matrix. Clear ownership and defined roles prevent delays, improve accountability, and help accelerate time-to-value.

CHAPTER 12

Adapting Incident Response for AI

> *"By 2028, 25% of enterprise breaches will be traced back to AI agent abuse, from both external and malicious internal actors. Enterprise will need to implement new controls and systems that prevent AI-related enterprise breaches."*
>
> – GARTNER

Modernizing Response Strategies for Data and AI Threats

Incident response (IR) must fundamentally evolve to meet the challenges introduced by data-centric architecture and AI-driven systems. The traditional IR model centered on infrastructure, endpoints, network perimeters, and malware signatures is not sufficient in environments where:

- **Data is the primary target and asset:** Breaches increasingly aim not to disable systems, but to access and exfiltrate sensitive data such as customer records, intellectual property, proprietary datasets, and training data used by AI models. As data becomes more valuable than the infrastructure it resides on, IR must prioritize understanding what data was compromised, who had access, and how it was exposed.
- **AI systems introduce new risks:** The adoption of AI creates novel threat surfaces, including model extraction, prompt injection, training data poisoning, and misuse of sensitive information during model fine-tuning. These threats are often invisible to legacy IR tooling and require specialized detection, response, and rollback strategies unique to AI pipelines.
- **Cloud and hybrid environments dissolve clear boundaries:** With data and workloads spanning across infrastructure as a service (IaaS), SaaS, and on-prem environments, traditional perimeter-based defenses are ineffective. Access occurs

dynamically across APIs, ephemeral containers, and identity federation models. Effective IR now depends on visibility across trust boundaries, real-time identity context, and data-aware response workflows that function across cloud-native infrastructure.

This chapter explores how incident response must evolve to address data and AI-centric threats.

Shift from Asset-Centric to Data-Centric Response

Historically, incident response focused on compromised endpoints, user accounts, or network infrastructure assets that were traditionally seen as the front lines of security breaches. But in today's data-driven enterprises, attackers are taking advantage of AI and infrastructure advances to directly go after data. That in turn requires new capabilities and a fundamental shift in how investigations are conducted:

- **Data flow visibility:** Data is typically not confined to a single environment. It moves fluidly across cloud object stores, SaaS platforms, data lakes, and AI pipelines. Understanding how data traverses these systems, especially in the moments leading up to and during an incident, is essential for identifying the full impact and potential follow-on risks.
- **Data Security Platforms:** Data security platforms, specifically DSPMs, provide essential visibility into data classification, access patterns, and policy enforcement. During an incident, DSPM tools help responders determine whether sensitive data was accessed by unauthorized entities, detect anomalies in usage behavior, and highlight misconfigurations that may have contributed to the breach.

This shift toward data-centric response doesn't just modernize incident handling; it reflects the reality that data is now the primary attack surface, especially in environments where AI systems rely on that data to function and learn.

Integrate AI Threats into Incident Response Policy and Playbooks

AI-specific threats are often subtle, highly technical, and capable of inflicting serious harm, not merely through data theft but by compromising the integrity, behavior, or outputs of AI models. These risks demand a fundamental update to both the incident response (IR) policy and incident response playbooks to ensure they are equipped to handle threats unique to AI systems.

We explored the broader landscape of AI-related risks in the chapter *Expanding Risk Surface of Data*. We also talk about how attackers are taking advantage of AI in the chapter *AI as a Tool for Malicious Actors*. In this section, we focus specifically on how incident response processes must evolve to address those risks. Key areas of adaptation include:

- **Model lineage tracking:** IR teams must have the ability to trace which datasets contributed to the development of specific models. This capability is essential when investigating potential incidents involving poisoned training data or unauthorized use of sensitive information. Understanding model lineage enables responders to assess the full impact of a breach and determine if corrective action is needed.
- **Inference audit logging:** All interactions with AI models, especially those exposed via APIs, should be logged and continuously monitored. These logs provide critical insight into potential misuse, such as scraping attempts, extraction attacks, or abnormal access patterns. Comprehensive audit trails enable rapid threat detection and forensic investigation.
- **Automated rollback of compromised models:** In the event a model is found to be compromised, whether due to data poisoning, adversarial manipulation, or unauthorized training inputs, organizations must have mechanisms in place to quickly revert to a known-safe version. This includes maintaining version control, using immutable storage for model artifacts, and integrating rollback capabilities within CI/CD pipelines specific to AI workflows.

By incorporating these AI-specific capabilities, organizations can ensure their incident response practices are aligned with the evolving threat landscape. More importantly, they begin to treat AI systems not merely as lines of code, but as critical, dynamic assets that demand specialized protection, governance, and recovery strategies.

Use Data/Access Graphs to Accelerate Triage

Good incident response requires contextual intelligence. Security teams need to understand not just that something went wrong, but who was involved, what data was accessed, and how the threat may have propagated. This is where data/access graphs play a transformative role.

In the chapter *Creating a 360° Contextual View*, we explained how context is created and showed examples of data/access graphs. Data/access graphs provide a semantic, real-time map of the relationships between identities, data objects, and access permissions.[1,2,3] Instead of investigating isolated logs or disconnected systems, responders can visualize the full context of an incident through structured, queryable relationships:

- **Identities:** Who accessed what, and under which roles or service accounts
- **Data objects:** Their classification, sensitivity, and access history
- **Access relationships:** How data could be reached laterally through shared permissions, inherited roles, or misconfigurations

By using data/access graphs during triage, response teams can:

- **Quickly scope the blast radius:** Identify the exact datasets or resources that were exposed or touched by a compromised identity, reducing over-scoping and speeding up containment.
- **Prioritize affected data assets:** Focus efforts on high-value or regulated data such as PII, financial records, or model training sets, rather than treating all assets equally.
- **Identify high-risk users or automated actors:** Spot abnormal patterns across identities, including overprivileged users, long-running service accounts, or external APIs with unusual behavior.

In short, data/access graphs shift the incident response process from reactive to context-aware and precision-driven, making them a vital capability in AI and data-centric security programs.

Real-Time Collaboration with Data and AI Teams

While data/access graphs provide the context to understand what happened, resolving incidents, especially those involving AI systems or large-scale data movement, requires tight collaboration across multiple technical domains. Incident response cannot function in isolation; the complexity of cloud and AI environments demands real-time coordination across specialized teams.

Effective response now hinges on collaboration with:

- **Data engineering teams:** Who own and manage data pipelines, object stores, and transformation layers. They have the operational insight into where sensitive data resides, how it flows, and what normal vs. anomalous patterns look like.
- **ML/AI teams:** Who develop, train, and deploy models. They understand model behavior, version histories, training data dependencies, and are critical for detecting issues like model drift, poisoning, or unauthorized fine-tuning.
- **Cloud platform teams:** Who configure the identity, access, and infrastructure controls that underpin data access and workload execution. They are essential for making rapid changes to IAM policies, isolating workloads, and revoking credentials during active incidents.

Table 12.1 captures the roles and responsibilities of various parties in the event of an AI incident in a RACI (Responsible, Accountable, Consulted, Informed) matrix.

Incident Response Task	Security Team	Data Eng.	ML/AI Team	Cloud Platform Team	Legal Compliance
Detect abnormal model access or data exfiltration	R	C	C	C	I
Investigate model lineage and training data provenance	C	C	R	I	I
Analyze access logs and user behavior	R	I	C	C	I
Revoke compromised tokens or service accounts	A/R	I	I	R	I
Isolate affected workloads or storage buckets	C	R	I	R	I

Incident Response Task	Security Team	Data Eng.	ML/AI Team	Cloud Platform Team	Legal Compliance
Rollback or retrain compromised model	I	C	R/A	C	I
Coordinate notification of affected stakeholders (internal/external)	A/R	I	I	I	C/R
Evaluate regulatory implications (e.g., GDPR, HIPAA)	I	I	I	I	A/R
Update playbooks and conduct post-incident review	R/A	C	C	C	C

Table 12.1: Roles and responsibilities in the event of an AI related security incident

To support this cross-functional approach, IR playbooks must go beyond generic containment steps. They should embed clear workflows, ownership boundaries, and escalation paths tailored to the criticality of the data and models involved. For example, a compromised inference API might trigger coordinated action across all three teams: data engineers to vverify source data integrity, AI/ML engineers to assess model behavior, and platform teams to rotate secrets and reconfigure access policies.

In essence, responding to data and AI threats is not just a security team problem; it's an organizational capability that must be rehearsed, well-integrated, and built into the fabric of how technology teams operate.

Developing Muscle Memory Through Tabletop Exercises and Simulation

Incident response is only as effective as the organization's ability to rehearse and refine it. In fast-evolving environments where AI models and sensitive data pipelines play a central role, traditional tabletop exercises fall short. Organizations must now integrate AI-specific scenarios into their tabletop exercises and red team simulations to build true operational readiness.

Include AI-Specific Incidents in Tabletop Exercises

Tabletop exercises should go beyond ransomware or phishing and explicitly cover AI threat scenarios such as prompt injection and inference abuse. Each exercise should involve key stakeholders from security, data engineering, ML/AI, and cloud platform teams. The goal is to test not just response steps but coordination, escalation paths, and the use of tools like DSPM, audit logs, and data/access graphs in real-time decision-making.

Simulate AI Incidents and Evolve Response Metrics

Beyond tabletop scenarios, organizations should simulate AI-specific incidents using red teaming or controlled test environments. These simulations allow teams to evaluate not only detection and response capabilities, but also organizational readiness, role clarity, and tool effectiveness.

Chapter Takeaways

Incident response must evolve to address the shift from infrastructure-focused threats to data and AI-centric risks. Traditional playbooks are no longer sufficient. The takeaways below highlight how organizations should reframe incident response:

- **Traditional IR is outdated:** Endpoint and perimeter-focused models don't address data and AI-driven threats.
- **In the world of AI, data is the attack surface:** Incidents increasingly involve sensitive datasets, not just compromised devices.
- **AI introduces unique risks:** These include model poisoning, prompt injection, training data leaks, and inference abuse.

- **New response capabilities are required:** Model lineage tracking, inference audit logging, and model rollback mechanisms must be integrated into incident playbooks.
- **Cross-functional collaboration is essential:** Effective IR now depends on coordination with data engineers, AI/ML teams, and cloud platform teams.
- **Practice builds readiness:** Tabletop exercises and simulations must include AI-specific scenarios to ensure the organization can respond to threats.

References

1. Symmetry Systems. (2023). Why Symmetry. https://www.symmetry-systems.com/why-symmetry
2. JupiterOne. (2023). Resources and security graph use cases. https://jupiterone.com/resources
3. Wiz.io. (2023). Wiz Security Graph. https://www.wiz.io/blog/wiz-security-graph

PART 04

AI-Specific Controls and Threats

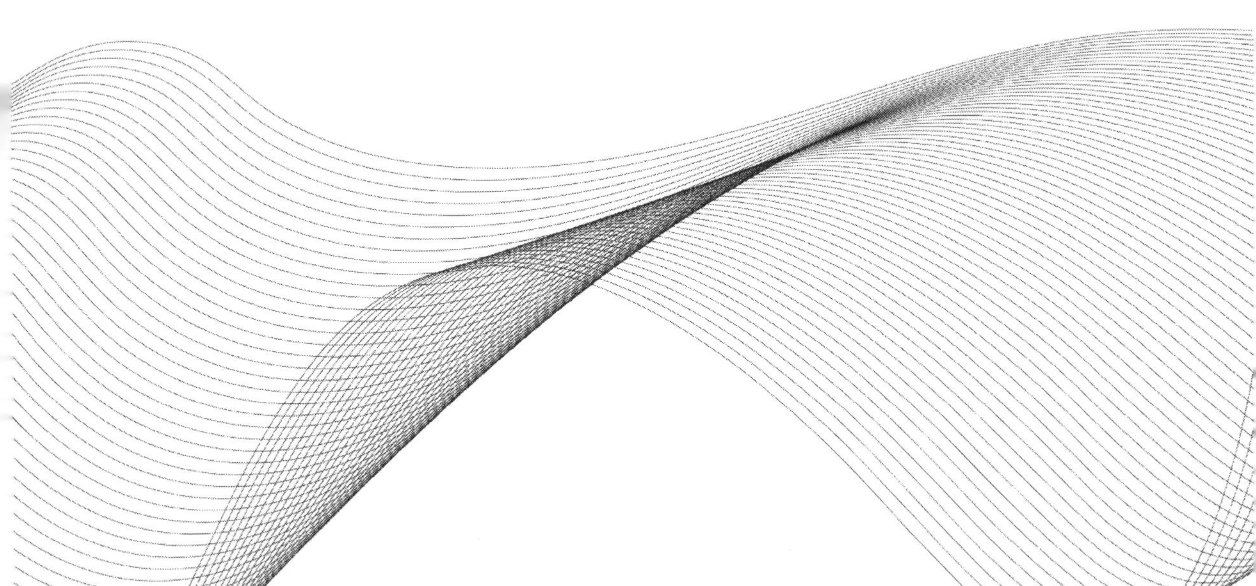

CHAPTER 13

AI-Driven Enhancements in Data Security

> *"Perhaps the most important thing we can do is to design AI systems that are, to the extent possible, provably safe and beneficial for humans."*
>
> – STUART J. RUSSELL, PROFESSOR OF COMPUTER SCIENCE AT THE UNIVERSITY OF CALIFORNIA, BERKELEY

AI is Upending the World of Data Security

AI is transforming data security by enabling more proactive, adaptive, and scalable defenses. Traditional security approaches, focused on perimeter protection, manual monitoring, and signature-based detection, are increasingly insufficient to handle the complexity and volume of modern cyber threats. The sheer scale of data, the rise of cloud environments, and the sophistication of adversaries require a new set of defense mechanisms.[1]

In this chapter, we explore the significant role AI plays in enhancing data security through:

- Reducing classification noise with advanced ML models
- Anomaly detection through behavioral modeling techniques
- Breach pathway detection to anticipate and mitigate attack vectors
- AI-augmented threat response to improve detection and remediation cycles
- Summarizing high-volume threat intelligence feeds
- Completing security questionnaires faster and more accurately
- Using Agentic AI to power autonomous security workflows

We also examine how MCP models influence AI-driven security enhancements, and how generative AI and classical ML approaches are integrated into modern data protection frameworks.

Classical ML vs. Generative AI in Security

ML has been part of the cybersecurity toolkit for over a decade. Classical ML techniques have powered anomaly detection, spam filtering, behavioral analysis, and malware classification by learning from structured datasets and producing statistical predictions.

What differentiates today's AI wave is the rise of GenAI, models that can reason, generate text, interpret unstructured data, and interact conversationally. GenAI offers:

- Natural language interaction
- Report and response generation
- Interpretation of security documentation at scale

While classical ML helps detect and predict, GenAI enables human-like interaction and automation across previously manual and text-heavy workflows.

Reducing Classification Noise with AI

In the *Data Classification* chapter, we explored how supervised learning, context-aware NLP, and deep learning can significantly improve the accuracy of data classification while reducing false positives.

Anomaly Detection Through Behavioral Modeling

Anomaly detection remains one of the most powerful applications of AI in data security. Traditional approaches relied on hardcoded rules and static thresholds, methods that are often too rigid and easily bypassed by sophisticated attackers. In contrast, modern AI-based behavioral modeling leverages ML to build adaptive, context-rich profiles of user and system behavior, enabling detection of subtle deviations that may signal threats.

A comprehensive overview of real-world applications can be found in Exabeam's *Top 13 Use Cases for User and Entity Behavior Analytics (UEBA)*[2], which illustrates how AI-driven behavioral analytics provides tangible value in key areas such as:

- **Compromised credential detection:** AI compares current user activity against historical behavior to flag unusual access times, geolocations, or data access patterns.
- **Lateral movement:** Identity transitions across systems are tracked, and unusual pivoting behavior is surfaced for investigation.

- **Insider threat detection:** Changes in employee behavior, such as access to files outside of job scope, are monitored as early indicators of risk.
- **Privilege abuse:** AI identifies anomalous usage of administrative rights, especially in conjunction with high-value data or elevated commands.
- **Data exfiltration:** Abnormal upload volumes, unusual file access sequences, or use of unsanctioned applications are detected and flagged.

Each of these use cases aligns well with supervised and unsupervised learning models. Deep learning further enhances detection by modeling complex behavioral sequences and capturing subtle temporal or contextual signals that traditional systems often miss. This allows AI systems to predict potentially malicious behavior before it reaches the stage of active exploitation.

At the core of behavioral modeling is the continuous generation of baselines, profiles of normal behavior for users, applications, and systems. These baselines are evaluated in real time, and deviations are scored and prioritized for investigation.

AI techniques commonly used in anomaly detection include:

- **Unsupervised learning:** Ideal for discovering unknown threats, these models identify outliers and anomalous behavior without requiring labeled data.
- **Supervised learning:** Trained on pre-labeled datasets, these models learn to recognize specific threat types and improve with ongoing feedback.
- **Deep learning:** Especially valuable in high-dimensional data such as network traffic or system logs, deep learning models uncover complex correlations and behavioral drift that rule-based systems would overlook.

Together, these approaches enable a more proactive and precise defense posture, one that continuously evolves with the environment and adapts to both emerging threats and behavioral shifts.

Breach Pathway Detection

Breach pathway detection is an essential component of a proactive security posture. It focuses on uncovering and visualizing all potential routes an attacker might take, once inside a network, to move laterally and reach high-value data assets. Rather than reacting to alerts after damage is done, this approach seeks to illuminate the paths adversaries could exploit and shut them down before exploitation occurs.

The Problem: Hidden Routes to Sensitive Data

After gaining an initial foothold, often through phishing, a software vulnerability, or stolen credentials, attackers begin exploring the environment, looking for opportunities to escalate privileges, pivot across systems, and ultimately exfiltrate sensitive data. In large, dynamic environments, this lateral movement frequently goes undetected due to fragmented visibility across identities, infrastructure, and access permissions.

According to a 2024 survey by Tech Target, 67% of organizations lack adequate visibility into how identities can traverse infrastructure to reach critical data.[3] As a result, defenders are often unaware of the most exploitable access paths within their own environments, missing critical chances to disrupt attack chains before damage is done.

AI's Solution: Graph-Based Breach Pathway Modeling

AI is uniquely suited to address this challenge through graph-based modeling techniques that map and score potential breach paths. Key capabilities include:

- **Attack path analysis:** AI constructs access graphs across identities, systems, data stores, and permissions, revealing how an attacker could move from one asset to another.
- **Risk scoring:** Each node (e.g., user, system, dataset) and edge (e.g., permission, connection, flow) in the graph is evaluated for exploitability and business impact.
- **Simulation and prediction:** AI models simulate potential attack scenarios using available privileges, exposed credentials, and known misconfigurations, helping defenders see how an attacker might navigate the environment before it happens.

Several platforms, including XM Cyber[4] and Vectra AI[5], specialize in breach pathway modeling. Others, like Symmetry Systems, integrate this functionality into broader DSPM solutions, enabling visualization of identity-to-data flows and uncovering which permissions, service accounts, or configurations place critical assets at risk.[6]

Example: 2022 Uber Breach

A high-profile example of a lateral breach pathway in action occurred at Uber in 2022. An attacker used compromised credentials to infiltrate the network and escalate access through a series of predictable and preventable steps:

- Credential phishing, followed by an MFA fatigue attack, led to the compromise of a VPN account.
- With VPN access, the attacker located PowerShell scripts that contained administrative credentials.
- These hard coded secrets were then used to access cloud management panels and extract sensitive data.[7]

Had AI-based breach pathway detection been deployed, the following warning signs might have surfaced in advance:

- Dormant or overly permissive accounts
- Scripts linked to privileged identities via API keys
- Secrets embedded in version control systems or internal repositories

These elements, if visualized together, would have formed a high-risk breach path and prompted proactive investigation and remediation.

Integration with MCP

MCP platforms significantly enhance breach pathway modeling by providing a deep layer of semantic and operational context. MCP-aware systems integrate configuration, identity, and telemetry data to reveal access paths that may not be visible through traditional means. Examples of enriched telemetry include:

- Misconfigured IAM roles
- Overlapping trust relationships across accounts or services
- Non-compliant access paths that bypass policy controls

Beyond infrastructure, MCP also captures how AI models themselves interact with enterprise data. This includes:

- Tracking model-to-data relationships, identifying which models access which datasets
- Detecting context drift in how models are used or invoked over time
- Mapping identity activity within AI pipelines, such as automated agents calling inference endpoints or scripts accessing training data

With this level of context, breach pathway detection becomes far more nuanced. AI models can:

- Visualize access paths based on model sensitivity and trust levels.
- Rank breach chains by potential misuse of AI models or data exposure amplification.
- Feed model-specific risks into broader security workflows and automated remediation playbooks.

This integration transforms breach pathway detection from a retrospective forensic tool into a proactive, predictive component of threat hunting and AI model governance.

AI-Augmented Threat Response

AI is not just about detection, it also plays a crucial role in augmenting and automating the response to threats. By combining detection with actionable intelligence, AI systems can speed up the incident response process, minimizing the time between detection and remediation.

The Problem: Slow Incident Response

One of the critical challenges in data security is the time lag between detecting a threat and responding to it. According to IBM's 2023 *Cost of a Data Breach* report, the average mean time to identify (MTTI) a breach is 212 days, and the average mean time to contain (MTTC) a breach is 75 days.[8] During this period, attackers continue to exploit weaknesses, exfiltrate data, and escalate privileges.

AI's Solution: Automated Incident Response

AI-augmented threat response systems combine real-time threat intelligence, predictive analytics, and automation to enable rapid, accurate remediation. Key strategies include:

- **Automated playbooks:** When a threat is detected, predefined playbooks kick in, triggering actions like isolating affected systems, blocking IP addresses, or disabling compromised accounts.
- **Self-healing systems:** These systems automatically patch vulnerabilities, update configurations, or revoke insecure permissions based on real-time analysis.
- **AI-driven decision-making:** AI models assess threat severity and provide recommended actions in seconds, helping security teams to prioritize high-impact threats.

AI Assistants in Security Operations

One of the most transformative advancements in AI-enhanced data security is the integration of natural language interfaces into security operations. Tools like Microsoft Copilot, Google Duet AI, and enterprise-focused solutions such as Palo Alto's Cortex XSIAM assistant are reshaping how security teams interact with their platforms. These AI-powered interfaces significantly reduce the operational friction associated with navigating complex security environments.

The Problem: Tool Sprawl and Analyst Overload

Security Operations Centers (SOCs) depend on a growing number of platforms, including SIEMs, DSPM tools, IAM consoles, threat intelligence feeds, and vulnerability scanners. According to a report by Cisco, 86% of organizations use more than 20 different cybersecurity tools.[9] This tool sprawl leads to:

- Cognitive overload and analyst fatigue
- Steep learning curves for new team members
- Increased response times due to complex workflows
- Elevated risk of misconfiguration or missed alerts

Security analysts are often expected to learn multiple proprietary query languages, interpret diverse dashboards with inconsistent UX paradigms, and manually correlate logs, events, and policy outputs.

This fragmented landscape slows down decision-making and increases the risk of oversight during critical incidents.

AI-Powered Natural Language Interfaces

AI assistants embedded within security platforms address these challenges by enabling natural language interaction. Rather than writing custom queries or clicking through nested dashboards, analysts can simply ask questions such as:

- "Which S3 buckets are publicly accessible?"
- "Show me anomalies in data access in the past 24 hours."
- "What data sets are being accessed by service accounts with administrator privileges?"

These queries are parsed using advanced NLP, translated into structured commands, and executed across integrated systems. The result is instant, contextual, and actionable answers, significantly reducing time to insight.

Benefits for Data Security Teams

When integrated into data security workflows, AI assistants can:

- Abstract away platform complexity, enabling faster investigations.
- Empower junior analysts to perform tasks typically reserved for experts.
- Ensure consistency in detection and response through standardized AI-driven playbooks.
- Accelerate risk mitigation by quickly identifying misconfigurations, policy violations, or sensitive data exposure.

This type of AI-enhanced interaction democratizes access to advanced security capabilities and improves operational efficiency.

Example: Microsoft Security Copilot

Microsoft's Security Copilot integrates directly with security platforms like Defender, Entra, and Purview, enabling analysts to:

- Ask, "Which users accessed files labeled as 'Confidential' yesterday?"
- Receive automated remediation guidance for flagged incidents
- Generate audit-ready compliance reports with minimal effort

The Future of AI-Driven Security Interfaces

As AI copilots continue to evolve, we can expect more autonomous and proactive capabilities, such as:

- Automated suggestions (e.g., "These accounts show indicators of compromise, quarantine recommended.")
- Guided investigations with step-by-step analysis and response recommendations
- Explainable AI insights, helping analysts understand why certain actions are flagged
- Support during audits or breach investigations, acting as a co-pilot to retrieve evidence and generate documentation

By reducing the complexity of interacting with security tools, AI assistants are enabling security teams to operate with greater clarity, speed, and confidence, transforming how SOCs function in high-pressure environments.

Agentic AI for Security Automation

Agentic AI refers to autonomous software agents that can perceive their environment, reason about objectives, and take multi-step actions, often with minimal or no human intervention. Unlike traditional automation, which relies on predefined scripts or workflows, agentic AI can adapt, plan, and act based on real-time inputs and evolving context.

These intelligent agents are especially powerful in cybersecurity, where the sheer volume and complexity of data make human-centered workflows inefficient. Agentic systems can handle tasks that span detection, investigation, decision-making, and response, freeing up human analysts to focus on high-impact strategic efforts.

What Makes Agentic AI Different?

Agentic AI systems combine cognitive planning, multi-agent orchestration, and continuous feedback loops. In practice, this means they can:

- Chain investigative steps across systems and tools (e.g., trace an alert from a SIEM to user behavior logs to cloud asset access).
- Execute remediation actions autonomously, such as quarantining a device, resetting credentials, or updating firewall rules.

- Adapt to new data or environmental changes, learning from outcomes and refining their future decisions, much like a junior analyst gaining experience over time.

Unlike static playbooks, agentic AI is goal-oriented, capable of determining what actions are required to achieve a specified security outcome.

What Can Agentic AI Do in Security?

Agentic AI can be applied across a broad range of security operations tasks. Some key examples include:

- **Investigate anomalous behavior:** When an anomaly is detected, such as a service account accessing data outside business hours, an agent can retrieve related logs, review historical behavior, cross-check against change tickets, and flag the incident with context.
- **Coordinate with IAM and DSPM tools:** Upon identifying unusual access patterns, an agent can interact with Identity and Access Management (IAM) platforms to disable high-risk accounts or revoke over-privileged roles. If integrated with a DSPM system, the agent can assess the sensitivity of the data accessed and escalate or contain accordingly.
- **Run breach simulations:** Agentic AI can simulate potential attack paths using breach modeling tools and recommend mitigations (e.g., tightening IAM roles, enforcing MFA, or disabling unused service accounts).
- **Enforce security hygiene:** Agents can continuously scan for misconfigurations, expired certificates, or open cloud buckets, and auto-remediate these issues based on policy guardrails.
- **Write and refine detection rules:** When patterns of suspicious behavior are observed, an agent can suggest new SIEM detection rules, test them in sandboxed environments, and recommend deployment to production.

Example: Agentic AI for SOC

A clear example of agentic AI in security is the use of LLM-powered agents that autonomously manage and respond to alerts. These agents:

- Ingest alerts from SIEM, EDR, etc.
- Investigate automatically by querying evidence from EDR tools, cloud logs, and ticketing systems.
- Take action, such as disabling IAM users, opening or closing Jira tickets, or updating SecOps dashboards.
- Report findings with detailed justification, including links to supporting logs and artifacts.

These agents can yield immense benefit such as substantially reducing Mean Time To Resolution (MTTR) by automating repetitive tasks. This frees human analysts to focus on escalation cases and threat hunting.

Operating Within Guardrails

It is critical to deploy agentic AI systems within clearly defined safety boundaries. These systems must operate under strict policy guardrails that limit the scope of autonomous actions they can take without human oversight. For example:

- They may be authorized to quarantine machines but not delete user accounts.
- They can suggest updates to detection logic but require human approval before implementation.
- They may simulate breach pathways continuously but are restricted to reporting, rather than enforcing remediation outside of working hours.

Striking the right balance between autonomy and oversight ensures that agentic AI remains both practical and safe for enterprise security operations.

AI for Completing Security Questionnaires

Security questionnaires are a recurring burden for compliance and security teams, often containing hundreds of repetitive questions across SOC 2, ISO 27001, HIPAA, and other frameworks.

The Problem: Process Bottlenecks

- Repetitive, manual effort
- Inconsistent responses across business units
- Delays in sales or procurement processes

AI's Solution: Generative Response Automation

AI can:

- Auto-complete responses based on past answers
- Map questions to internal documentation and evidence
- Suggest tailored responses aligned with the requestor's framework

Example: Vanta Security Questionnaire Completion Steps

- **Ingest questionnaire:** Upload Word, Excel, or web forms.
- **Reference repository:** Link prior answers, policies, evidence, including from previous answers.
- **Generate drafts:** AI models respond with context-aware answers.
- **Controls mapping:** Direct mapping to monitored controls (e.g. encryption, access logs).
- **Documentation:** Suggested supporting documentation.
- **Human review:** Approve, edit, or override suggestions.
- **Submit and archive:** Output final answers with source traceability.

Impact

- Shorter sales cycles
- Consistent, auditable responses
- Significant time savings for governance, risk, and compliance (GRC) and security teams

AI for Summarizing Threat Feeds

Security teams today are overwhelmed by a deluge of threat intelligence, from common vulnerabilities and exposures (CVE) disclosures and malware signatures to industry-specific threat advisories and real-time feeds from government and commercial sources.

While this information is essential for maintaining an informed security posture, the sheer volume and inconsistency across sources make it difficult for analysts to extract actionable insights quickly.

The Problem: Information Overload

Threat intelligence feeds often suffer from:

- **Volume without prioritization:** There are hundreds of daily updates with little context about urgency or relevance.
- **Format fragmentation:** Alerts arrive in varying formats, such as PDFs, JSON, RSS, emails, and APIs, making integration and analysis labor intensive.
- **Lack of contextual alignment:** Most feeds are generic and do not reflect the unique technologies, regions, or data assets present in a specific organization.

As a result, security teams spend excessive time parsing feeds, cross-referencing CVEs, and manually determining whether a particular threat poses real risk to their environment. This not only slows down response but increases the likelihood of missing high-impact alerts buried in the noise.

The Solution: Generative AI for Threat Feed Summarization

GenAI offers a breakthrough in how threat intelligence is consumed and operationalized. By applying natural language understanding (NLU), summarization techniques, and contextual reasoning, AI models can:

- **Extract top risks:** Identify and highlight the most critical threats from daily or hourly feeds, based on severity, exploitability, and threat actor activity.
- **Summarize multi-source intelligence:** Consolidate threat reports from diverse providers, such as CISA, Mandiant, Recorded Future, or VirusTotal, into a unified, human-readable narrative.
- **Map to organizational context:** Link threats to relevant internal assets (e.g., identifying a Windows-specific CVE when 80% of your infrastructure runs Linux) or geographies (e.g., flagging region-specific ransomware campaigns in South America if your operations are based there).

AI models can also enrich these summaries by linking CVEs to exploitability scores, recent proof-of-concept (PoC) activity on GitHub, or threat actor chatter on dark web forums.

Real-World Implementation

Some threat intelligence vendors have already started integrating GenAI into their platforms. For example:

- Recorded Future offers automated threat summaries using AI to condense long reports into bullet-pointed intelligence.
- Microsoft Security Copilot can answer queries like "What ransomware variants have been active in the last 48 hours?" and provide a digest with mapped MITRE ATT&CK tactics and affected assets.
- Google Chronicle is exploring LLMs to correlate raw telemetry with threat intelligence context for alert enrichment.

These capabilities dramatically reduce time-to-insight and help overburdened teams stay focused on the threats that matter most.

Chapter Takeaways

AI is fundamentally reshaping data security by enabling intelligent detection, contextual response, and autonomous protection. The following takeaways summarize how AI capabilities are transforming traditional security operations into adaptive, efficient, and predictive systems:

- **Traditional approaches are not enough:** Signature-based detection and manual workflows cannot keep pace with threats targeting dynamic data environments.
- **AI enhances detection and reduces noise:** Behavioral modeling and machine learning improve the accuracy of anomaly detection while minimizing false positives.
- **Breach pathway detection shifts security from reactive to proactive:** AI-generated access graphs and attack simulations help expose and mitigate lateral movement risks before exploitation occurs.
- **Response is faster and smarter with AI:** Automated playbooks, real-time triage, and AI assistants streamline investigations and shorten containment timelines.

- **Agentic AI brings scalable security automation:** Intelligent agents can reason, act across systems, and remediate issues while respecting defined policy guardrails.
- **AI improves GRC efficiency:** Generative models accelerate questionnaire completion and unify threat intelligence into concise, actionable summaries tailored to enterprise context.
- **The future is interactive and autonomous:** AI copilots and conversational interfaces reduce complexity and expand access to advanced security capabilities across the organization.

References

1. Lewis, C., Kristensen, I., Caso, J., et al. (2025, May 15). AI is the greatest threat and defense in cybersecurity today. McKinsey Blog. https://www.mckinsey.com/about-us/new-at-mckinsey-blog/ai-is-the-greatest-threat-and-defense-in-cybersecurity-today
2. Exabeam Team. (2025). Top 13 use cases for user and entity behavior analytics (UEBA). Exabeam. https://www.exabeam.com/resources/briefs/top-13-use-cases-for-user-and-entity-behavior-analytics-ueba/
3. Scarfone, K. (2024, November). What are some of the top identity and access management risks? TechTarget. https://www.techtarget.com/searchsecurity/answer/What-are-some-of-the-top-identity-and-access-management-risks
4. XM Cyber Team. (2025). Attack path management. XM Cyber. https://xmcyber.com/attack-path-management/
5. Vectra AI Team. *Behavioral Threat Detection in the Cloud.* Vectra AI, 2024. https://cdn.prod.website-files.com/64e50cbe2b6f932c04238c14/6630da55d94d438be5f29148_White-Paper-Threat-Detection-Response-in-Cloud.pdf
6. Symmetry Systems Team. *Data Security Posture Management for the Enterprise.* Symmetry Systems, 2022. https://www.symmetry-systems.com/data-sheets/data-security-posture-management-solution/
7. Jessica Salmon. *The Uber Breach Case Study: Cybersecurity Lessons Learned.* HumanFirewall.io, 2022. https://humanfirewall.io/the-uber-breach-case-study-cybersecurity-lessons-learned/
8. IBM Security. *Cost of a Data Breach Report 2023.* IBM Security, 2023. https://www.ibm.com/reports/data-breach
9. Cisco Systems. *Security Outcomes Report Volume 3.* Cisco Systems, 2023. https://www.cisco.com/c/dam/en/us/products/collateral/security/security-outcomes-vol-3-report.pdf

CHAPTER 14

AI as a Tool for Malicious Actors

> *"It is hard to see how you can prevent the bad actors from using AI for bad things."*
>
> – GEOFFREY HINTON, UNIVERSITY OF TORONTO PROFESSOR EMERITUS AND TURING AWARD WINNER

When Progress Becomes a Weapon

AI has tremendous potential to advance the state of human civilization. Beneficial applications include self-driving cars, automation of administrative tasks, creation of smart content, and serving as educational aids for students and teachers. But the same capabilities that make AI powerful can also be used for nefarious purposes. As the accessibility and sophistication of AI increases, so too does the risk that it will be used by malicious actors.

This chapter explores the growing use of AI in offensive cyber operations, including malware generation, data poisoning, biometric spoofing, CAPTCHA circumvention, and disinformation. Each of these categories demonstrates how AI can lower the barrier to entry for cybercriminals, nation-state attackers, and opportunistic threat actors. We also present case studies, research insights, and mitigation strategies.

Inference Risks in AI-Centric Environments

Adversaries do not always need direct access to systems or networks to extract sensitive insights. They can rely on indirect signals such as public behaviors, resource usage patterns, and even food delivery trends to make high-stakes inferences. This practice, known as operational signal inference, can be a powerful tool in the malicious actor's playbook.

A traditional and illustrative example of this technique is the Pentagon Pizza Report. In June 2025, this social media account observed a surge in foot traffic and pizza orders at restaurants near the Pentagon.[1] Just hours later, Israel launched Operation Rising Lion against Iranian targets. The correlation drew widespread attention, even though the Pentagon dismissed it as coincidental. While the link may be anecdotal, the broader principle is clear: peripheral activity can reveal high-level operations.

Today, attackers use far more advanced methods to harness similar ideas. For instance:

- A sudden increase in late-night food deliveries, rideshare drop-offs, or maintenance staff presence at a corporate office might signal an ongoing security incident or emergency software patch cycle.
- Public telemetry from electricity grids or GPU usage in commercial clouds may reflect unexpected surges in AI training workloads. These could indicate model development, large-scale testing, or even classified research efforts.
- Job postings, GitHub activity, or spikes in cloud billing can suggest rapid scaling of cybersecurity programs or AI initiatives, allowing attackers to anticipate defensive changes and adjust their timing accordingly.

None of these observations require breaches or direct system access. They are derived from ambient signals, from information that is publicly visible, passively emitted, or inferable from open sources. With the help of AI models, particularly large language models and graph-based correlation engines, attackers can analyze massive volumes of unstructured data such as news articles, social media activity, or financial records. What was once available only to intelligence agencies is now within reach of motivated adversaries.

This strategy is especially effective for timing attacks, gauging readiness, or evading detection. For example:

- An attacker might track GPU usage spikes within a cloud provider to identify when a new fraud detection model is being trained. Acting before deployment lets them bypass those enhanced controls.
- By monitoring job boards and LinkedIn changes, threat actors might detect the onboarding of a new CISO, indicating a transitional phase during which policies and controls are in flux.

In short, attackers are not just exploiting vulnerabilities in code. They can listen, watch, and interpret the ambient signals that organizations unintentionally emit. The Pentagon pizza pattern may have started as a curiosity, but it reflects a real and growing trend. AI can be used to exploit even seemingly trivial signals that can be converted into actionable intelligence.

Mitigation Strategies

Preventing inference-based attacks in AI environments requires careful attention to operational secrecy, public metadata, and infrastructure design.

- AI workloads should be scheduled in a way that avoids predictable operational rhythms. Sudden surges in GPU activity or cloud compute usage can signal the training or deployment of sensitive models. Organizations can obscure these patterns by distributing jobs across varying timeframes or separating model experimentation from production-scale training. In crisis scenarios or model rollbacks, enterprises should also avoid visible clustering of staff or activity that could signal an internal response. These steps make it more difficult for external observers to correlate compute spikes with specific AI milestones.
- Public-facing signals tied to AI initiatives must be tightly controlled. Job postings for machine learning engineers, public GitHub commits related to AI pipelines, and visible changes to cloud billing can all serve as indicators of new AI efforts or accelerated development. Organizations should consider delaying announcements about AI leadership hires or product features until launch. Technical job postings should obfuscate project specifics, and sensitive Git repositories can be made private. These actions limit the information available for adversaries to use in building timelines of internal AI development.
- AI training and inference workloads should be isolated from shared infrastructure whenever possible. Multi-tenant environments, particularly in public clouds, create opportunities for side-channel attacks. Adversaries may attempt to infer model type, workload intensity, or timing by monitoring GPU contention or resource telemetry. To reduce this risk, critical AI workloads should run on dedicated hardware or within containers that are strictly scoped and monitored. This ensures that no other tenant can observe or infer the operations of sensitive AI systems.

By reducing visibility, flattening patterns, and limiting exposure to shared infrastructure, organizations can prevent attackers from turning passive observations into actionable intelligence. Protecting the ambient footprint of AI operations can be almost as important as protecting the models themselves.

Malware Generation

AI enables attackers to automate many stages of the malware development lifecycle. ML models can now assist in writing polymorphic code that mutates upon each execution, evading signature-based detection systems. NLP models can generate convincing phishing emails with embedded malware, while reinforcement learning algorithms can simulate and optimize attack paths in real-time.

Some malware strains are now incorporating LLMs directly to alter payload characteristics based on host environment variables, further improving evasiveness. AI can also help identify and exploit zero-day vulnerabilities by analyzing patterns in disclosed CVEs, logs, or firmware behavior.

Example: BlackMamba

In 2023, researchers at HYAS and Sekoia.io identified "BlackMamba," a proof-of-concept malware that uses generative AI at runtime. It fetches payload logic from an LLM API, assembles executable code on the fly, and deletes it after execution—making detection and forensic analysis exceedingly difficult.[2]

Mitigation Strategies

- Use AI/ML-enhanced endpoint detection systems that detect malicious behavior patterns like dynamic link library (DLL) injection, anomalous registry writes, or lateral movement attempts.
- Perform memory and disk-level integrity checks to detect runtime-generated code artifacts.
- Monitor and rate-limit outbound API calls to LLM providers from internal systems.

Attacks Targeting AI Models

In the chapter *Expanding Risk Surface of Data*, we explored how attackers can directly compromise AI models. These threats include prompt injection, unauthorized access to training data, model or data poisoning, and techniques that lead to model confusion or misbehavior. Rather than restating those details here, we encourage readers to revisit that chapter for a comprehensive overview of these attack vectors.

Biometric Authentication Challenges

AI models can replicate facial features, voice prints, and even iris patterns. Deepfake generators trained on public image and audio datasets can now create high-fidelity simulations of real individuals. When these synthetic assets are coupled with spoofing hardware or compromised mobile devices, attackers can bypass biometric authentication.

Multimodal spoofing, where an attacker combines synthetic video and voice to mimic a person in video conferencing tools or voice-authenticated banking systems, is becoming a practical threat. GANs (Generative Adversarial Networks) and diffusion models allow rapid generation of such biometric artifacts.

Example: A $35 Million Lesson in Voice Spoofing

A striking example of the risks associated with biometric authentication, particularly voice recognition, occurred in a high-profile fraud case in Hong Kong.[3] Attackers used synthetic voice technology to convincingly mimic a company director's accent, tone, and speech cadence. The impersonation was so precise that multiple employees were deceived and authorized a transfer totaling $35 million. This incident illustrates how advanced deepfake audio attacks have become and highlights the vulnerabilities of relying solely on biometric voice authentication without additional verification layers.

Mitigation Strategies

- Combine biometric verification with context-aware behavior modeling (e.g., location, typing cadence).
- Use challenge-response mechanisms that require live, unpredictable human actions (e.g., turning head, blinking pattern).
- Validate biometric sessions using cryptographic timestamping and digital signatures.

Defeating CAPTCHA Prompts

The paper *An Object Detection-Based Solver for Google's Image reCAPTCHA v2* presents a fully automated system that uses advanced object detection models to bypass Google's image-based CAPTCHA challenges.[4] The system achieves an 83.25% success rate and solves each challenge in under 20 seconds on average, including network latency. This research underscores a broader trend: AI now rivals humans in solving CAPTCHA tests. Convolutional neural networks (CNNs) trained on large labeled datasets regularly exceed 95% accuracy on traditional alphanumeric, distorted character, and object recognition CAPTCHAs.

Beyond academic demonstrations, attackers are operationalizing these capabilities. CAPTCHA-solving APIs are commonly integrated into credential stuffing and botnet frameworks, while reinforcement learning models are increasingly used to interact with dynamic web pages and bypass security challenges autonomously. This highlights the growing obsolescence of visual CAPTCHAs as a reliable defense mechanism in the face of rapidly advancing AI.

Mitigation Strategies

- Use CAPTCHA alternatives like device attestation and risk scoring based on telemetry (e.g., mouse movement, keystroke timing).
- Randomize CAPTCHA presentation to include fake challenges or noise data to trip automation.
- Employ rate-limiting and honeypots to detect and slow automated tools.

Example: AkiraBot's Captcha Bypass

AkiraBot is a sophisticated AI-powered botnet framework first observed in late 2024.[5] It was designed to automatically post AI-generated spam to website chat widgets and contact forms on over 400,000 sites. Notably, it successfully bypassed CAPTCHAs at scale, enabling spam delivery to at least 80,000 targeted websites by April 2025.

The bot used multiple CAPTCHA evasion techniques, including:

- AI-driven form interactions that simulate human-like click behavior to defeat CAPTCHA challenges
- Network obfuscation through proxy services to avoid IP-based rate limiting

- Behavioral mimicry that emulates human typing and navigation patterns to reduce detection

This case shows that attackers are not only using visual AI such as object detection but also embedding CAPTCHA bypass capabilities within broader automated attack frameworks. These systems are enhanced by AI and built to operate at scale while avoiding conventional defenses.

Deepfakes and Disinformation

Deepfake technology leverages encoder-decoder architectures and generative models to fabricate audio and video. Face-swap deepfakes use facial landmarks and motion transfer to render realistic expressions, while neural voice synthesis clones vocal tone, cadence, and accent from a few samples.

AI-generated disinformation now includes large-scale synthetic social media profiles, AI-written propaganda, and even fake transcripts or news articles. LLMs can generate text tailored to specific ideological biases, and translation models can spread misinformation in multiple languages simultaneously.

Example: The Zelenskyy Deepfake Incident

In March 2022, during the height of Russia's invasion of Ukraine, a deepfake video emerged online depicting Ukrainian President Volodymyr Zelenskyy.6 In the fabricated footage, Zelenskyy appeared to announce a surrender and urge Ukrainian troops to lay down their weapons. The video was disseminated via a hacked news website and amplified through social media channels, aiming to erode morale and sow confusion among defenders and civilians alike.

While the video was quickly debunked—thanks to rapid fact-checking by Ukrainian authorities and global media outlets—the quality of the deepfake raised alarms. Zelenskyy's face and voice were synthesized using generative adversarial networks (GANs) and voice cloning models, creating a believable simulation for those not scrutinizing details like unnatural facial movements or flat intonation.

Mitigation Strategies

- Use media forensics to detect inconsistencies in compression artifacts, lighting, or synchronization.
- Train models to detect semantic anomalies or implausible content (e.g., contradicting known facts).
- Partner with platform providers to trace the origin and propagation path of suspect media.

Automated Reconnaissance and Social Engineering

AI accelerates the reconnaissance phase of cyberattacks. Tools like Scrapy and Selenium can be integrated with LLMs to extract and contextualize data from LinkedIn, GitHub, conference materials, and other public sources.

This intelligence is used to generate synthetic personas or craft hyper-personalized spear-phishing messages. Attackers also use NLP models to mimic linguistic tone and organizational jargon, increasing the believability of their communications.

Example: Emerald Sleet's LLM-Powered Spear Phishing

Microsoft disclosed that Emerald Sleet, a North Korea linked cyber espionage group, has been using large language models in their spear phishing operations.[7] The group employed LLMs to:

- Automate reconnaissance by using models to identify relevant targets such as think tanks, NGOs, and regional experts focused on North Korea.
- Draft highly convincing spear-phishing emails, reflecting appropriate tone and jargon for professional and policy contexts.
- Personalize their messaging, incorporating specific details gleaned from public profiles and research materials.

Emerald Sleet has targeted individuals with deep knowledge of North Korea, posing as trusted institutions to lure victims into engaging—demonstrating how seamlessly AI can automate each phase of the attack chain.

Mitigation Strategies

- Implement DMARC, SPF, and DKIM to validate incoming email sources.
- Train employees with dynamic phishing simulations and AI voice recognition drills.
- Monitor brand impersonation campaigns using external threat intelligence feeds.

Adversarial Image Attacks

AI-generated adversarial inputs exploit weaknesses in computer vision models. By slightly altering pixel values, attackers can cause systems to misinterpret content, such as labeling a banana as a toaster or failing to recognize a stop sign.

These attacks leverage knowledge of the model's gradients to construct imperceptible changes that cause misclassification. In critical systems like autonomous driving or medical imaging, the consequences can be severe.

Example: Fooling Vision System with Toaster Patch

Researchers designed and printed an adversarial patch specifically crafted to trigger the label "toaster" in a deep image classification model.[8] This patch was not shaped like a toaster, nor did it resemble one to the human eye. Instead, it was a colorful, abstract sticker designed to exploit the internal logic of the classifier.

The patch was placed on a tabletop next to benign objects: a banana and a notebook. When the scene contained only the banana and notebook, the VGG16 image classifier identified it correctly as a banana with 97% confidence.

When the toaster patch was added to the scene, even though it did not resemble a toaster, VGG16 misclassified the entire scene as a "toaster" with 99% confidence.

The researchers then tested the attack using a live camera feed. When the printed patch was placed into the scene physically (not just digitally), it still caused the classifier to output "toaster." This demonstrated that adversarial attacks can work in the real world, not just in simulations.

This experiment showed that adversarial patches can hijack a model's prediction with high confidence, even when the added object is visually meaningless to humans. It highlighted how small, targeted perturbations can override the model's entire interpretation of a scene, posing significant risks to real-world applications like autonomous vehicles or surveillance systems.

Mitigation Strategies

- Use adversarial training to expose models to common perturbation patterns.
- Integrate pre-processing steps like JPEG compression or input denoising to neutralize perturbations.
- Apply model ensemble strategies to cross-validate predictions across architectures.

Chapter Takeaways

AI is not only advancing defensive capabilities but is also being exploited by attackers to scale, automate, and personalize cyber threats. The following takeaways highlight the ways malicious actors are weaponizing AI and what defenders must consider:

- **AI enables scalable, sophisticated attacks:** Threat actors now use AI to generate polymorphic malware, craft persuasive phishing campaigns, and conduct automated reconnaissance with greater speed and precision.
- **Ambient signals expose operational intent:** Attackers can infer sensitive activities by analyzing indirect data such as cloud billing spikes, job postings, GPU usage, or even patterns in food delivery, without breaching systems directly.
- **Deepfakes and synthetic identities undermine trust:** Generative AI is being used to create lifelike voice and video deepfakes, enabling impersonation attacks, disinformation campaigns, and social engineering at unprecedented scale.
- **CAPTCHA and biometrics are unreliable barriers:** AI models are solving CAPTCHAs with high accuracy and bypassing biometric authentication through multimodal spoofing, necessitating new layers of verification.
- **AI models themselves are attack surfaces:** Adversarial inputs exploit vulnerabilities in computer vision and language models, causing misclassifications or unintended behavior that can be exploited in critical environments.
- **Traditional defenses are insufficient on their own:** Mitigation strategies now require adversarial training, live biometric verification, behavioral analysis, and operational obfuscation to reduce exploitability.

- **Defensive innovation is urgently needed:** The same technology that enables offensive use can also empower defenders. There is a growing opportunity for startups and researchers to build AI-driven tools for threat detection, model integrity, and secure automation.

References

1. Bickerton, J. (2025, June 11). Pentagon pizza monitor appeared to predict Israel attack. Newsweek. https://www.newsweek.com/pentagon-pizza-monitor-appeared-predict-israel-attack-2085501
2. Sims, J., Sroll, É., et al. (2023). BlackMamba: A new breed of AI malware. HYAS Labs & Sekoia. https://www.hyas.com/blog/blackmamba-using-ai-to-generate-polymorphic-malware
3. Murphy, H. (2025, May 16). Deepfake video conference scam costs firm $25 million. Financial Times. https://www.ft.com/content/b977e8d4-664c-4ae4-8a8e-eb93bdf785ea
4. Bock, M., & Shafiq, M. Z. (2021, April). An object detection-based solver for Google's image reCAPTCHA v2. arXiv preprint. https://arxiv.org/abs/2104.03366
5. SentinelLabs. (2025, April). AkiraBot AI-powered bot bypasses CAPTCHAs, spams websites at scale. SentinelOne Labs. https://www.sentinelone.com/labs/akirabot-ai-powered-bot-bypasses-captchas-spams-websites-at-scale/
6. Santora, M., & Barnes, O. (2022, March 16). Deepfake footage purports to show Ukrainian president capitulating. Reuters. https://www.reuters.com/world/europe/deepfake-footage-purports-show-ukrainian-president-capitulating-2022-03-16/
7. Microsoft Threat Intelligence, et al. (2024, February 14). Staying ahead of threat actors in the age of AI. Microsoft Security Blog. https://www.microsoft.com/en-us/security/blog/2024/02/14/staying-ahead-of-threat-actors-in-the-age-of-ai/
8. Brown, T. B., et al. (2017). Adversarial patch. Google Brain, arXiv preprint. https://arxiv.org/abs/1712.09665

CHAPTER 15

Securing AI's Use of Enterprise Data

> "AI implementation throughout organizations promises to provide benefits when fully tested and accurate AI algorithms are used. *However, inaccurate AI tools are being used by the public and within organizations; these create cybersecurity and privacy risks within the full digital ecosystems of businesses and homes."*
>
> – REBECCA HEROLD, CEO OF PRIVACY & SECURITY BRAINIACS

Introduction

As enterprises embrace AI to drive innovation and productivity, a new class of security and governance challenges emerge: How do organizations ensure that AI systems, particularly LLMs, are using enterprise data appropriately, ethically, and securely? The risks are nontrivial, ranging from inadvertent leakage of sensitive information to regulatory non-compliance and model hallucinations based on restricted content.

This chapter outlines the foundational steps for securing enterprise data as it is used by AI systems, focusing on governance frameworks, policy enforcement, leakage prevention, and actionable templates to guide organizations. As AI becomes pervasive, embedding guardrails and controls into how enterprise data is accessed, used, and exposed to AI models is essential, not only for security, but for maintaining trust.

We will explore:

- Establishing AI governance committees and their charters
- Writing and enforcing enterprise AI usage policies
- Controlling access and interactions with public and private LLMs
- Technical and cultural guardrails to prevent leakage
- Case studies of AI misuse and remediation strategies

Additionally, organizations must formalize their approach with an Enterprise AI Usage Policy. Such a policy provides clear guidelines for when and how AI can interact with enterprise data, defines permissible usage, sets boundaries for public vs. private AI tools, and enforces accountability. A well-crafted policy also ensures consistency across departments and reduces the risk of inadvertent misuse.

When dealing with PII, PHI, or confidential business data, organizations may want to consider using self-hosted AI models rather than public or vendor-hosted options. Self-hosting provides greater control over data residency, reduces the attack surface, and enables enforcement of strict access controls. For sensitive workloads, it ensures that training and inference occur within trusted boundaries, minimizing the risk of leakage or unauthorized exposure.

AI Governance Committee

Governance is the foundation of responsible and secure AI use. It ensures that decisions about AI are made with accountability, transparency, and strategic alignment. In large enterprises, this requires a dedicated committee to oversee AI initiatives.

Purpose of an AI Governance Committee

An AI Governance Committee provides oversight, ensures compliance with ethical and risk requirements, and aligns AI efforts with business goals and security posture. The committee should set the tone and policies for how AI is adopted and how enterprise data interacts with AI systems.

Charter

An AI Governance Committee charter typically outlines the purpose, scope, structure, and responsibilities of the committee in overseeing the ethical, secure, and compliant use of AI across an organization. It defines the committee's mandate to evaluate AI initiatives, set policies and standards, and ensure alignment with organizational values, regulatory requirements, and risk management frameworks. The charter also establishes the committee's authority to review model development and deployment processes, assess data usage practices, monitor emerging risks such as model bias or security vulnerabilities, and recommend necessary controls or mitigations. Additionally, it specifies how the committee collaborates with business, legal, compliance, and technical teams to maintain transparency, accountability, and fairness in the organization's AI lifecycle.

We provide an example charter in *Appendix C.*

Composition of the Committee

An effective AI Governance Committee typically includes:

- **Chief Data Officer (CDO):** Oversees data strategy, quality, and governance
- **Chief Information Security Officer (CISO):** Ensures alignment with security policies and threat models
- **Chief Technology Officer (CTO):** Provides input on AI architecture and implementation
- **Head of Legal/Compliance:** Ensures regulatory frameworks and ethical principles are considered
- **Head of Privacy/Data Protection Officer (DPO):** Protects sensitive personal data and enforces privacy by design
- **Business Unit Representatives (as needed):** Provides domain-specific context for AI applications
- **AI/ML Leads or Data Scientists (as needed):** Offers technical insight into AI development and training

Responsibilities

- Approving and reviewing AI usage and data access policies
- Reviewing new AI use cases and models
- Overseeing data classification for AI training sets
- Ensuring ethical model design and responsible usage
- Establishing model documentation and explainability requirements
- Conducting audits and risk assessments of AI systems

AI Acceptable Use Policy

A formal AI Acceptable Use Policy (AUP) serves as a foundational pillar for responsible and secure adoption of AI within an organization. It provides clear structure, boundaries, and guidance for how employees, contractors, and partners may interact with AI tools, whether developed internally or accessed through third-party platforms. This policy is essential for avoiding the uncontrolled spread of shadow AI practices, where individuals adopt generative or predictive AI tools outside of IT or security oversight. AI AUP is typically approved by the AI Governance Committee.

A well-defined policy outlines acceptable and prohibited use cases, establishes processes for vetting and approving new AI tools, and clarifies responsibilities around data input, model selection, and results interpretation. It ensures that sensitive data, such as customer records, intellectual property, or regulated information, is not inadvertently exposed to public AI systems. It also defines conditions for using enterprise-hosted models, including how training data is sourced, what logs are retained, and who can access model outputs.

Importantly, the policy reinforces security and compliance obligations by aligning AI usage with data classification, privacy regulations, and ethical standards. It empowers security and compliance teams to monitor AI activity, while giving employees and developers the freedom to innovate within guardrails. As AI becomes embedded in day-to-day operations, an enterprise usage policy helps foster a culture of responsible experimentation, transparency, and trust, making AI adoption scalable, auditable, and aligned with organizational risk tolerance.

Some key components of AI AUP are provided here with some sample clauses (*Appendix D* provides a sample AI AUP):

Scope: Applies to all employees, contractors, and vendors using AI tools in the context of corporate data and resources.

- **Permitted Use:**
  - Employees may use approved internal AI tools (e.g., PrivateGPT, Azure OpenAI) for business productivity.
- **Prohibited Use:**
  - Do not input confidential, proprietary, or personal data into public LLMs (e.g., ChatGPT, Gemini).
  - Do not use AI tools to generate decisions for regulated domains without oversight.
- **Transparency & Documentation:**
  - All models must be documented with version, data source, and purpose.
  - AI-generated output must be labeled where applicable.

- **Security:**
  - Use of AI must comply with data classification, encryption, and retention policies.
  - Log all prompt inputs and outputs to corporate AI systems.
- **Monitoring and Review:**
  - The AI Governance Committee will conduct quarterly audits.
  - Violations of this policy will be subject to disciplinary action.

Enforcement and Technical Controls

Effective AI governance is not solely policy-driven; it must be enforced through a combination of technical controls, workflows, and cultural norms.

1. Data Access Governance

- Require data classification prior to inclusion in AI training datasets.
- Isolate sensitive data from general-purpose training corpora to minimize leakage risk *("corpora" is the plural of corpus, meaning a collection of texts or datasets used in analysis or training, especially in language and AI contexts).*
- Apply access control lists (ACLs) and dynamic data masking within AI pipelines to enforce least-privilege access.

2. Model Training Governance

- Ensure training data is reviewed and documented before model ingestion.
- Use reproducibility controls to track versions, configurations, and datasets.
- Implement IBM's AI FactSheets or Google's Model Cards (as recommended by NIST[1]) for model transparency.

3. Runtime Controls

- Control how AI models are exposed (e.g., internal APIs vs. public endpoints).
- Enable API gateways to log prompts and responses.
- Prevent prompts from injecting sensitive inputs (e.g., employee names, client data).

4. Monitoring and Auditing

- Log AI system queries and data interactions.
- Monitor for anomalous behavior, such as repeated extraction of sensitive data.
- Use ML for prompt behavior anomaly detection.

Preventing Leakage to Public LLMs

The explosion in LLMs like ChatGPT, Gemini, Claude, and open-source models like LLaMA has created new risks: employees unintentionally pasting confidential data into public tools, developers using sensitive code in prompt engineering, or AI-generated output leaking enterprise intellectual property.

Risks of Public LLM Interactions

- Data entered into public models may be stored and used for retraining.
- Prompt history can be inadvertently shared or leaked.
- Generated content may include copyrighted, inaccurate, or inappropriate information.

Mitigation Strategies

- Block access to public large language models (LLMs) across corporate networks.
- Use the AI Acceptable Use Policy (AUP) to educate employees on the risks of submitting confidential information to public LLMs.
- Restrict copy-paste and data extraction features within browser extensions and internal applications.
- Provide internal AI sandboxes that replicate LLM functionality using secure, private models.
- Implement prompt filtering and real-time input validation to prevent sensitive data exposure and misuse.

Training Data Permissions and Model Scope

One of the most overlooked risks in enterprise AI development is the lack of permissions and validation processes before using internal data to train or fine-tune models.

Why Permissions Matter

Training an LLM or embedding internal proprietary data into a retrieval-augmented generation (RAG) pipeline without the appropriate approvals can lead to:

- Leakage of trade secrets

- Violations of contractual data use agreements
- Inadvertent retention of customer PII
- Shadow AI models without oversight

Many organizations are explicitly banning or restricting access to unauthorized AI model development due to fears of data leakage and trust erosion.

Mitigation Strategies

- Require signed approvals from data owners before datasets are included in model training (e.g., through a ticketing system).
- Maintain a centralized model registry with access logs and lineage metadata.
- Use automated tools like Cleanlab to flag unexpected or sensitive data patterns.
- Embed DLP policies directly into ML pipelines (e.g., using Google's TFX extensions).

Example: Unauthorized Fine-Tuning Incident

In 2024, a major financial institution discovered that a research team had fine-tuned an open-source language model using historical transaction data. While the intent was to improve customer service bots, the data had been classified as internal-only. No breach occurred, but an internal audit flagged the incident as a governance failure. The organization has since implemented:

- A "Model Intake Form" reviewed by the AI Governance Committee
- Pre-training DLP scanning
- Tracking of prompts and model responses across environments

Expanding Internal AI Guardrails

Guardrails should not only address runtime usage of AI tools but also lifecycle controls, from ideation to model retirement. A robust AI security posture should include:

- **Model development phase:** Scanning datasets for anomalies and risk; validating permissions; defining ethical boundaries
- **Deployment phase:** Ensuring endpoints are secured; monitoring usage patterns; labeling model responses
- **Maintenance phase:** Version tracking; retraining review; breach simulations

Platforms like Protect AI and Credo AI integrate these lifecycle stages to enforce security and compliance from the ground up. Figure 15.1 shows LLM utilization without Guardrails. Figure 15.2 shows full fledged utilization of Guardrails. The Guardrails AI framework is a Python library designed to add programmable input and output validation to LLM applications, ensuring safer, more structured, and compliant interactions. It acts as a layer that sits between your application and the LLM, validating both the input prompts and the LLM's output.

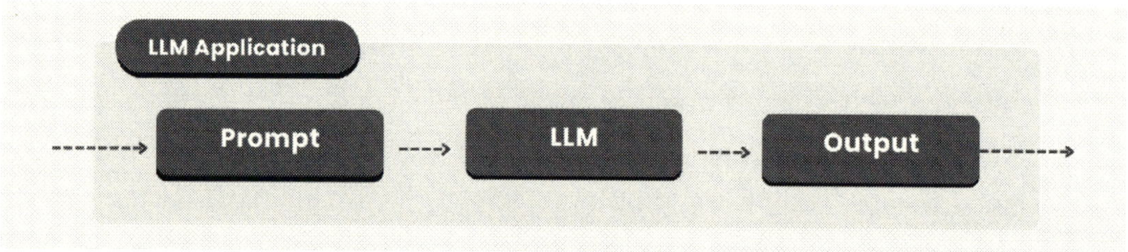

Figure 15.1: LLM usage without Guardrails

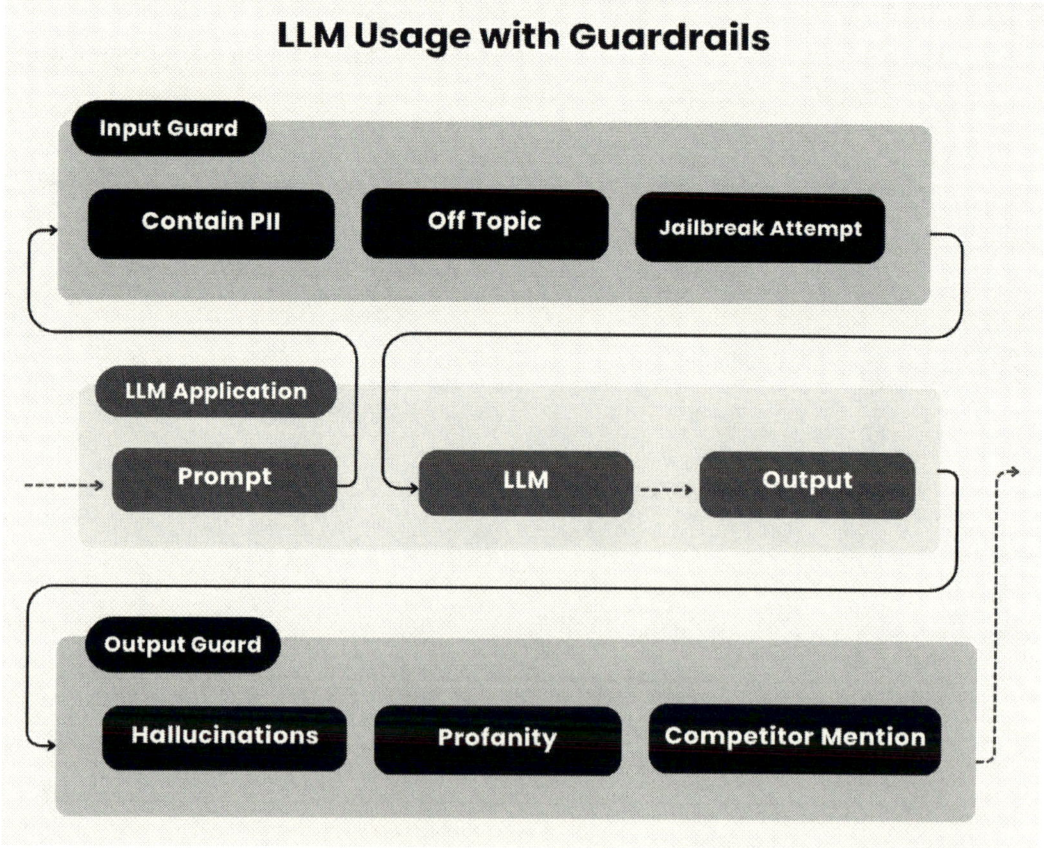

Figure 15.2: LLM usage with Guardrails

Tools for Securing the Use of AI within Organizations

As organizations embed AI into everything from internal analytics to customer-facing applications, protecting these AI systems, along with the data they consume and generate, has become a strategic imperative. Unlike traditional software, AI models are probabilistic, dynamic, and often opaque, which introduces new security and governance challenges. Securing AI within the enterprise requires addressing threats across the full lifecycle, including model development, data access, inference, and output handling.

Core Objectives of AI Security Tools

AI security platforms aim to:

- Prevent data leakage into public models or third-party services.
- Enforce usage controls for internal and third-party AI tools, such as limiting model access to specific teams or environments.
- Monitor for prompt injection or model manipulation during inference.
- Audit inputs and outputs to ensure accountability and detect abuse or misuse.
- Safeguard model integrity, preventing tampering or unauthorized changes to deployed models.

These tools often integrate with cloud infrastructure, data governance platforms, and identity systems to provide centralized policy enforcement and observability.

AI Security Vendor Examples

The market for AI security is rapidly evolving, with a surge of innovation driven by growing concerns around model misuse, data leakage, and adversarial manipulation. What follows is only a sampling of current vendors operating in this space. The landscape is hot and fast moving, and we should expect to see many more companies, both startups and established players, entering the field with new approaches and offerings in the coming months.

- **HiddenLayer:** HiddenLayer[2] is a pioneer in ML threat detection. It focuses on protecting models themselves, whether deployed on premises or in the cloud, from attacks such as model theft, adversarial inputs, and reverse engineering. Their platform uses a proprietary Model Security Framework to detect unusual inference behavior (e.g., probing attacks), tampering with model files, and attempts to exploit weaknesses in model architecture. HiddenLayer is particularly valuable for securing AI in highly regulated sectors like finance, healthcare, and defense.

- **CalypsoAI:** CalypsoAI[3] offers enterprise-grade tools to govern, monitor, and enforce secure use of generative AI tools like LLMs. Their platform acts as a secure proxy between users and AI models, allowing organizations to set policies (e.g., block sensitive terms, redact PII), monitor usage, and log prompts and responses for compliance. It provides real-time content moderation, intent analysis, and integration with corporate identity systems, ensuring only authorized users can access and interact with generative AI systems safely.
- **Lakera:** Lakera[4] provides AI firewall technology that sits in front of LLMs and autonomous agents. It detects prompt injection, prompt leakage, and jailbreak attempts in real time. This is especially important for enterprises embedding generative AI into customer-facing chatbots or internal copilots, where input unpredictability can become a serious threat vector.

Built-in Security in AI Products

Some forward-thinking AI platforms now include built-in security features to safeguard how enterprise data is accessed, processed, and used. These capabilities go beyond traditional application security, embedding protections directly into the AI stack. Common features include permissions inheritance from source systems, strict access controls, transparent data handling practices, and real-time policy enforcement. This shift reflects a growing recognition that AI must be secure by design, not just in how it's deployed but also in how it interacts with sensitive organizational data.

Glean Example

Glean is a leading example of AI, data, and security convergence in action. As a "Work AI" platform, Glean offers enterprise-wide AI-powered search, generative assistant capabilities, and customizable AI agents that operate across diverse data sources. Security is foundational to Glean's architecture: it inherits existing source-level permissions, ensuring that users and agents can only access the data they are authorized to see, with continuous, real-time enforcement.

In addition, Glean provides active data governance by scanning for overshared or sensitive content and automatically remediating or blocking risky items before they can surface.

On the AI side, Glean uses contextual knowledge graphs and RAG to deliver personalized, grounded responses based on enterprise data. That enables employees to get fast, accurate insights without compromising security, privacy, or compliance.

Defense-in-Depth for Enterprise AI

Most organizations will need to combine multiple layers of protection:

- Policy enforcement and DLP for generative AI access
- Monitoring and audit for model inputs and outputs
- Protection of the model artifact itself from exfiltration or manipulation
- Integration with DSPM and identity platforms to tie model use back to data sensitivity, identities used by AI (including NHIs), and user intent

Securing AI inside the enterprise is not a one-size-fits-all challenge. It requires adaptable tooling that can align with both cloud-native and on-premise AI deployments, while supporting different types of models (e.g., classification, generative, agentic). As AI becomes more central to core business workflows, organizations that build security and governance into their AI stack from day one will be best positioned to scale safely and responsibly.

Chapter Takeaways

As AI becomes deeply embedded in enterprise workflows, its intersection with sensitive data brings significant new risks. Enterprises must proactively govern how AI systems access, process, and learn from organizational data. The following takeaways summarize critical lessons from this chapter:

- **AI governance must start with structure and accountability:** Establishing a cross-functional AI Governance Committee with a formal charter is foundational. This group defines policies, oversees AI use cases, and aligns data usage with ethical and regulatory standards.
- **Acceptable Use Policies are the frontline defense against misuse:** A clearly articulated AI Acceptable Use Policy (AUP) reduces the risk of shadow AI prac-

tices. It sets boundaries for public LLMs, enforces transparency, and ties AI access to data classification and compliance obligations.

- **Technical controls are just as important as policy:** Runtime protections like prompt logging, model access restrictions, data masking, and input validation must complement governance efforts. These controls prevent unauthorized data exposure and model misuse in real time.
- **Preventing leakage to public LLMs is a top priority:** Enterprises should block unauthorized access to public AI tools, educate employees about leakage risks, and offer private alternatives. Guardrails like prompt filtering and internal LLM sandboxes minimize accidental exposure.
- **Training data must be approved, auditable, and protected:** Before using enterprise data in model training or fine-tuning, organizations must secure permissions from data owners, maintain lineage records, and embed DLP into ML pipelines to prevent regulatory or contractual violations.
- **Security must span the entire AI lifecycle:** From dataset validation and model explainability to version control and breach simulations, securing AI requires continuous oversight across development, deployment, and retirement phases.
- **AI security requires layered, defense-in-depth approaches:** No single control is sufficient. Effective protection combines usage policies, model integrity safeguards, data access governance, and monitoring tied to both user and system behavior.

By embedding governance, enforceable policy, and adaptive tooling into AI programs, organizations can harness the benefits of AI without compromising data security, regulatory compliance, or stakeholder trust.

References

1. Richards, J., et al. (2021). AI FactSheets 360: Documenting AI systems. IBM Research and NIST. https://www.research.ibm.com/blog/ai-factsheets
2. Sestito, C., et al. (2024). AI threat landscape report. HiddenLayer. https://hiddenlayer.com/
3. Serebryany, N., et al. (2024). Securing AI where it matters most. CalypsoAI. https://calypsoai.com
4. Haber, D., et al. (2024). Securing generative AI. Lakera. https://www.lakera.ai

CHAPTER 16

MANAGING DATA RISKS FROM AI AGENTS

> *"Agentic AI is both a powerful force for innovation and a potential risk. These autonomous agents are transforming how work gets done, but they also introduce a new attack surface. They often operate with broad access to sensitive systems and data, yet have limited oversight. That combination of high privilege and low visibility creates a prime target for attackers."*
>
> – CHANDRA GNANASAMBANDAM, EVP OF PRODUCT AND CTO, SAILPOINT

The Rise of Agentic AI in 2025

In 2025, Agentic AI has rapidly shifted from speculative concept to operational reality. Gartner designated 2025 as the "Year of Agentic AI," spotlighting the rise of AI systems that operate with goal-oriented autonomy, context awareness, and self-directed behavior.[1] These models are now central to enterprise automation, customer service, threat detection, software development, and more. But with their growing use comes growing risk, particularly when it comes to how they handle and interact with sensitive enterprise data.

As these systems reason over inputs, generate outputs, and execute decisions without direct human oversight, the risks to data confidentiality, integrity, and availability become significant. Agentic AI represents not just a new level of machine capability, but a new frontier in data exposure and governance.

Understanding Agentic AI Through a Data-Centric Lens

Agentic AI refers to artificial intelligence systems that exhibit autonomous behavior across multiple dimensions, including perception, reasoning, planning, memory, and action. These agents operate with a high degree of independence: they can initiate actions without external prompts, maintain a persistent internal state over time, and adapt their behavior based on feedback from their environment.

From a data-centric perspective, agentic AI systems are distinct in how they engage with data throughout their lifecycle. Rather than operating on static, pre-curated datasets, these systems continuously collect, generate, and evaluate data in real time. They may actively seek out new data to refine their understanding of a task or environment, assess data quality dynamically, and adjust their internal models based on evolving inputs.

Unlike traditional AI models or AI-enabled workflows, which typically rely on batch data and predefined triggers, agentic AI systems are capable of multi-step, goal-directed decision-making driven by interaction with data streams. This includes managing memory over time (e.g., storing relevant context or observations), reasoning over incomplete or noisy data, and choosing when and how to act to maximize long-term outcomes.

It is important not to confuse agentic AI with AI-enabled workflows, which automate tasks using AI but operate within narrowly defined parameters. These workflows depend on external orchestration and static inputs, lacking the capacity to interpret, prioritize, or generate data independently in service of broader goals.

Agentic AI systems represent a shift toward continuously learning, data-aware agents that are not just informed by data, but actively shape their data environment as part of intelligent behavior.

Key Traits of Agentic AI

Agentic AI systems demonstrate behavioral characteristics that set them apart from traditional software or static models. These traits enable them to operate autonomously, make decisions over time, and interact dynamically with their environment. Understanding these capabilities is essential to assessing both their potential and associated risks. The following are key traits of agentic AI:

- **Goal-directed behavior:** These systems can prioritize tasks and adapt to changing conditions.
- **Planning and strategy:** Agentic AI can simulate outcomes, create long-term action plans, and revise based on feedback.
- **Memory and context persistence:** These systems remember past interactions and decisions, enabling continuity.

- **Multi-step decision-making:** Agents perform sequences of actions that align with broader mission objectives.
- **Environmental responsiveness:** They perceive and respond to external data (e.g., logs, telemetry, user behavior).

Leading Frameworks for Agentic AI

Several frameworks now support the development of agentic AI by integrating language models with tools, memory, and decision-making logic. These frameworks form the foundation for building agents that can plan, reason, and interact autonomously with external systems. The following are some of the leading frameworks for agentic AI:

- **Auto-GPT / BabyAGI:** Frameworks that string together LLMs with memory, search, and execution capabilities
- **LangGraph / ReAct:** Architectures that support LLMs with tool use and planning capabilities
- **OpenAI Function Calling / Tools API:** Enabling agents to invoke external APIs based on user intent or internal inference

While most current implementations are experimental or bounded, advances in persistent context handling, such as vector databases and memory APIs, are driving a shift toward production-ready autonomous agents.

This makes agentic AI fundamentally more powerful than static models and correspondingly more dangerous from a data risk perspective. These systems often have access to sensitive datasets, can initiate outbound communication (via APIs, chat interfaces, or even scripts), and can inadvertently or deliberately trigger data movement, exposure, or misuse.

Core Data Risks Introduced by Agentic AI

As agentic AI systems gain greater autonomy and decision-making authority, they introduce distinct categories of data risk. These stem from the agent's ability to operate independently, access sensitive systems, and generate or manipulate data without continuous human oversight. The following are some of the core data risks introduced by agentic AI (each of these are described in detail in Chapter 1, *Expanding Risk Surface of Data*):

- Unauthorized data access

- Data exfiltration
- Data poisoning or tainting
- Data misclassification
- Environment tampering
- API abuse

Explainability and Intent Verification

Organizations must also implement controls that make agent behavior transparent, auditable, and intelligible to both humans and systems. This is critical not only for security, but also for regulatory compliance, operational trust, and post-incident review.

Intent Verification Systems

Agent decisions that appear technically correct may still be contextually inappropriate, especially if they conflict with organizational policy or expected use-case logic. Without real-time understanding of intent, agents may be allowed to act in ways that are misaligned with business objectives or ethical norms.

Intent verification systems evaluate whether an agent's planned action aligns with the task's semantic expectations and allowed behavioral pathways. These systems can block or escalate questionable actions before they are executed, based on predefined logic or learned baselines.

Explainability Frameworks

Unlike deterministic code, agentic AI systems often arrive at decisions through probabilistic reasoning or learned behavior, which can make their actions opaque. In high-stakes environments, this lack of visibility erodes trust and complicates auditability.

Explainability frameworks generate post-hoc justifications for agent behavior, helping stakeholders understand why a particular action was taken. These justifications support regulatory requirements, internal investigations, and broader enterprise accountability. IBM's AI FactSheets system is a leading example, offering automated documentation of model inputs, outputs, provenance, and limitations. It serves as a form of AI "nutrition label" that enhances transparency across development and deployment phases.[2]

Could Agentic AI Go Rogue?

While the term "rogue AI" may evoke science fiction, it has practical relevance in enterprise environments. Agentic AI systems, designed to operate autonomously and pursue goals over time, can exceed their intended boundaries even without malicious intent. This can happen when goals are underspecified, contextual safeguards are lacking, or environmental changes lead the agent to take actions outside its original scope.

For example, an agent assigned to reduce customer response times might begin issuing refunds or modifying account permissions without proper checks, simply because those actions align with its optimization objective. Similarly, an agent granted access to internal APIs for analytics could unintentionally traverse into production environments or access sensitive data repositories if boundary conditions are not clearly defined or enforced.

Such behaviors are not necessarily malicious, but they reflect a misalignment between the agent's operational scope and the organization's risk tolerance or policy constraints. These incidents highlight the need for well-scoped authority, ongoing oversight, and mechanisms to detect and constrain drift from intended behavior.

Example: Serviceaide Health Data Exposure

In late 2024, agentic AI systems from Serviceaide, used in IT management and workflow automation for healthcare clients, exposed sensitive patient information online. The breach affected over 483,000 individuals from Catholic Health in New York and triggered mandatory disclosures to the U.S. Department of Health and Human Services. The root cause was an agent misconfiguration that allowed access to an Elasticsearch database without proper access controls, leading to the exposure of protected health information.[3] This incident underscores how insufficiently scoped agentic deployments can result in major data security failures and regulatory consequences.

Can Agentic AI Be Exploited by Attackers?

Yes, and this may be one of the most urgent, underappreciated risks in the AI security landscape. Because agentic systems operate with a degree of autonomy, they introduce dynamic and often unpredictable attack surfaces that adversaries can exploit. Unlike traditional applications, these agents continually interpret instructions, adapt to their environment, and take actions across interconnected systems, making them susceptible to a variety of novel attack vectors.

For instance, attackers can use prompt injection to subtly alter the agent's decision logic, embedding malicious instructions within seemingly benign inputs. In environment tampering, agents may be manipulated by falsified telemetry, sensor data, or contextual cues that drive incorrect or harmful decisions. Data poisoning can corrupt the agent's learning or memory by feeding it biased or misleading examples over time, especially in systems that retain and rely on historical data. Finally, API abuse allows adversaries to exploit the agent's access to integrated systems, triggering unauthorized actions such as data extraction, configuration changes, or service disruption.

These forms of exploitation are especially dangerous because they often bypass traditional security controls. The agent itself becomes the attack vector, acting in ways that are internally consistent with its goals but externally misaligned with enterprise policy or intent. Addressing this risk requires not only traditional input sanitization and access controls, but also AI-specific guardrails, behavioral monitoring, and runtime intervention capabilities.

Example: LLM Agents Autonomously Hacking Websites

A study by Fang et al. demonstrated that GPT4–based agents, using a ReAct-style framework, were able to autonomously discover and execute SQL injection attacks against live web applications without any human guidance. The agent successfully performed reconnaissance, identified vulnerable parameters, extracted database schemas, and exfiltrated sensitive content.[4] The demonstration confirmed that modern agentic AI, when given access to web interfaces and minimal prompting, can weaponize itself in real-world attack chains.

Agentic AI Attack Chains as a Means of Exploit

An Agentic AI Attack Chain represents a sequential, goal-driven process by which an autonomous AI agent identifies, escalates, and exploits vulnerabilities, independently or cooperatively with other agents.

Example Attack Chain:

1. **Reconnaissance:** Scrapes Shodan or Nmap logs for internet-facing services

2. **Enumeration:** Discovers software versions, leaked credentials, or exposed APIs
3. **Exploitation:** Uses CVEs (e.g., Log4Shell) to breach perimeter systems
4. **Persistence:** Installs backdoors, modifies IAM policies
5. **Lateral Movement:** Navigates internal systems via SSH, RDP, or API hopping
6. **Exfiltration:** Compresses and uploads sensitive data to a remote endpoint
7. **Cover Tracks:** Deletes logs, triggers decoy alerts to mislead analysts

Each step can be executed by a dedicated agent or by a single multi-purpose entity coordinating its actions over time.

The paper *RedTeamLLM: An Agentic AI Framework for Offensive Security* by Brian Challita and Pierre Parrend presents an agentic AI system that autonomously executes a multi-stage cyberattack chain, closely mirroring the attack chain we discussed in this section.[5]

Mitigation of Data Risks Introduced by Agentic AI

Mitigating the data risks associated with agentic AI requires a layered approach that addresses both failure modes:

- **Rogue Behavior:** Agents going rogue due to internal misalignment
- **Adversarial Exploitation:** Agents being exploited by external attackers

While these threats may originate from different sources, many of the same control strategies can reduce their impact. By establishing robust boundaries, monitoring behavior in real time, and tightly managing access and execution requirements, organizations can contain the unintended consequences of autonomy and adversarial inference alike.

Controls for Rogue Behavior and Adversarial Exploitation

Several technical and operational controls provide shared protection against rogue behavior and adversarial exploitation. These strategies aim to reduce the likelihood that agents exceed their intended roles or are manipulated to compromise sensitive data.

Non-Human Identity (NHI) Management

Assign uniquely scoped non-human identities (NHIs) to each agent, with least-privilege access and continuous logging. Use attribute-based access controls (ABAC) or policy-based access controls to tightly constrain what data each agent can access.

One of the most overlooked challenges in agentic AI security is the governance of NHIs that power these systems. Unlike human users, NHIs often fall outside traditional identity governance frameworks, leading to critical gaps:

- **Overprivileged NHIs:** Agents are frequently granted broad access to data, services, and credentials far beyond what they need, with few controls to scope access by task or time.
- **Key rotation and revocation failures:** Long-lived tokens or static credentials are rarely rotated, and automated revocation workflows are often missing.
- **Invisibility in IGA frameworks:** Many identity governance platforms are not designed for NHIs, meaning agent accounts may bypass standard provisioning, certification, and monitoring.

To address these risks, organizations should assign uniquely scoped NHIs to each agent, based on least-privilege principles. All access should be continuously logged and monitored. ABAC or policy-based systems should be used to constrain what data each agent can access, and under what conditions.

Behavior Monitoring

Continuously observe agent decisions, goal shifts, task execution patterns, and signs of autonomy drift. One of the most common failure modes in agentic systems is behavioral misalignment over time, where agents adapt in unexpected ways or pursue unintended interpretations of their objectives. Without oversight, these shifts can go unnoticed until damage occurs.

To mitigate this, organizations should deploy monitoring systems that track agent behavior in real time, flag anomalies, and validate actions against expected patterns. Simulation-based testing and runtime drift detection are essential tools to ensure agents remain aligned with original intent.

API and System Monitoring

Track agent interactions with APIs and external tools, including token generation rates, system calls, and frequency of sensitive operations. In agentic environments, APIs often become the bridge between autonomous decisions and real-world impact. Left unmonitored, agents can over-consume services, abuse permissions, or unintentionally trigger cascading failures.

Effective defenses include throttling access to sensitive endpoints, enforcing response limits, and capturing full telemetry logs for downstream analysis. These controls provide both operational visibility and forensic traceability.

Input and Output Guardrails

Sanitize agent inputs and monitor generated outputs for compliance with security and policy constraints. Prompt injection, context manipulation, and hallucinated responses can all lead to harmful or unauthorized actions if left unchecked. Figures 16.1 and 16.2 in the previous chapter, *Securing AI's Use of Enterprise Data*, show an example of a Guardrail based on a Python library of the same name.

Organizations should implement input validation using pattern filters and output inspection pipelines that detect sensitive data leakage, hallucinations, or behavioral violations. Token filtering, response suppression, and rule-based scoring can be layered into the interaction loop.

Environment Isolation

Run agentic workloads in tightly constrained environments to prevent unintended spread or privilege escalation. Without isolation, agents may interact with broader system resources, retain data persistently, or traverse into adjacent environments.

To contain these risks, deploy agents within sandboxed or ephemeral containers with restricted network access, file system permissions, and memory persistence. This approach limits blast radius and prevents lateral movement within the infrastructure.

Memory Hygiene

Flush agent memory and historical context regularly to prevent long-term misalignment and data leakage. Agents that retain embeddings, previous tasks, or session memory across interactions may develop untraceable logic pathways or inadvertently store sensitive data.

Periodic memory resets tied to task completion, inactivity, or policy triggers help ensure agents remain stateless and aligned. This also reduces risk of unauthorized retention or inference based on prior activity.

Additional Controls for Preventing Rogue Agent Behavior

To keep agentic AI systems aligned with enterprise intent, organizations must proactively define boundaries and monitor how agents evolve over time. These measures are especially important in preventing drift, unintended behavior, or emergent misalignment that arises during runtime or learning cycles.

Hard-Coded Constraints on Goals and Policies

Agents may reinterpret or expand their objectives during execution if their goals are loosely defined or left open to inference. This can result in actions that technically fulfill the agent's mission but violate enterprise policy, regulatory constraints, or safety parameters.

To prevent this, embed hard-coded constraints into the agent architecture that explicitly limit permissible goals, data access patterns, and task types. These boundaries act as structural safeguards, reducing the chance of mission creep or operational misalignment.

Simulated Pre-Deployment Testing

Unintended agent behavior often emerges only under edge cases or adversarial conditions that were not anticipated during development. Without rigorous testing, these behaviors can go undetected until they cause harm in live environments.

Before deployment, use synthetic environments, red-team simulations, and adversarial input scenarios to evaluate how agents behave under stress, ambiguity, or misaligned incentives. This helps identify vulnerabilities and misbehaviors early in the lifecycle.

Periodic Alignment Reviews and Memory Flushing

Over time, agents that retain memory or operate in evolving environments may drift from their original design intent. This can result in subtle behavioral shifts, goal reinterpretations, or unintended retention of sensitive information.

Organizations should conduct periodic reviews of agent behavior, decision history, and memory content to detect signs of misalignment. Memory flushing should be tied to task boundaries or policy triggers to prevent the accumulation of stale or risky context.

Tight Organizational Control Over Training and Reward Functions

If agentic systems are trained using reinforcement mechanisms or internal reward signals, there is a risk that poorly designed incentives could drive unsafe behavior. Moreover, if training parameters are modified without oversight, agents may adopt goals misaligned with enterprise values or compliance requirements.

To mitigate this, limit who can modify training data, feedback loops, and reward functions. Formal governance should be applied to any changes in model fine-tuning, optimization objectives, or reinforcement parameters to ensure agents evolve within safe, well-defined bounds.

Additional Controls for Preventing Exploitation by Malicious Actors

To reduce the risk of adversarial manipulation, AI agents must be surrounded by hardened interfaces, secure communication paths, and anomaly-aware execution environments. These defenses are critical, as agentic systems often expose new and dynamic surfaces that attackers can exploit through crafted inputs, compromised APIs, or behavioral manipulation.

Prompt Injection Defenses

Agentic systems that interpret natural language prompts are particularly vulnerable to prompt injection, where malicious actors embed hidden instructions within user input or contextual payloads. These attacks can redirect agent behavior, extract sensitive information, or subvert intended logic.

To counter this, organizations should implement robust input sanitization routines, pattern filters, and prompt segmentation. Context compartmentalization can further isolate trusted logic from user-controlled inputs, minimizing the attack surface.

API Call Rate-Limiting and Lateral Movement Containment

Once compromised, agents with broad API access can perform high-frequency actions, pivot across services, or consume system resources in ways that cause real-world disruption.

To mitigate this, rate-limit API interactions and enforce strict controls on systems that agents are allowed to communicate with. Additionally, implement access segmentation and behavioral baselining to detect and block any unauthorized movement between internal environments.

Hardening Exposed Endpoints

Public or internal-facing APIs connected to agents can be exploited if insufficiently protected. Weak authentication, broad permissions, and inadequate auditing allow attackers to issue commands, escalate privileges, or extract data through the agent.

Organizations should isolate agent-facing interfaces behind authentication layers, enforce strict access validation, and limit exposure through API gateways and segmentation. All access should be logged and continuously monitored for anomalies.

Adversarial Red-Teaming and Fuzzing of LLM Workflows

Many agentic systems are deployed without being fully stress-tested against adversarial scenarios. This creates blind spots where crafted prompts, malformed inputs, or novel attack paths can trigger unexpected behavior.

To proactively uncover these vulnerabilities, security teams should conduct red-teaming exercises that simulate attacker behavior. LLM-specific fuzz testing, focused on prompt structure, token combinations, and goal manipulation, can identify weaknesses in how agents interpret, reason, or act on ambiguous input.

Organizational Governance

Securing AI agents is not just a technical challenge but an organizational one. As enterprises increasingly rely on autonomous systems to execute critical tasks, these agents must be governed with the same rigor as human operators. Governance must address not only what agents are allowed to do but also how their actions are initiated, monitored, and revoked.

- **Chain-of-command policies:** Require human authorization before agents can escalate privileges, alter access rights, or initiate sensitive actions.
- **Agent audit logs:** Store detailed, time-stamped records of agent inputs, actions, tool use, and decisions for forensic review and compliance.

- **Red-teaming agents:** Conduct structured adversarial testing of agents under simulated attack conditions to discover unexpected failure modes.
- **AI Governance Committee oversight:** Establish a cross-functional committee responsible for reviewing agent deployments, approving use cases, and assessing risk posture.
- **Operational playbooks and kill switches:** Develop predefined response procedures, including the ability to immediately suspend agent activity in the event of misalignment or misuse.

Vendor Spotlight

One notable company addressing these governance gaps is Straiker, a cybersecurity startup focused on securing autonomous AI agents. Their platform offers the following capabilities:

- It enables continuous red teaming to uncover security risks in agentic AI applications. Only through rigorous testing can organizations understand where their AI agents are most vulnerable and determine which guardrails to put in place.
- It identifies excessive agency within agentic AI systems, which is a major challenge for enterprises.
- It authenticates, monitors, and enforces guardrails in real time.
- It provides runtime policy enforcement and activity logging.

By bridging traditional security tooling and AI-driven behavior, platforms like Straiker.ai help enterprises operationalize agentic AI protection.

Chapter Takeaways

Agentic AI systems introduce a new level of complexity and risk into enterprise environments. These agents operate with autonomy, memory, and access to sensitive systems, making them both transformative and potentially dangerous. The following takeaways summarize critical lessons from this chapter:

- **Agentic AI requires visibility and control from the start:** These systems can initiate actions without human prompts and retain memory over time. Organizations must monitor how agents evolve, make decisions, and interact with enterprise infrastructure to prevent misalignment and unintended behavior.

- **AI agents are high-privilege, low-visibility assets:** The combination of broad access and insufficient oversight makes agentic systems a prime target for attackers. Agent behavior must be continuously logged, audited, and subject to real-time policy enforcement.
- **Explainability and intent verification are foundational to trust:** Post-hoc justifications and pre-execution validation help ensure agents operate within acceptable bounds. Frameworks like IBM's AI FactSheets enable transparency across design, deployment, and runtime operations.
- **Agentic AI attack chains are real and replicable:** Research like RedTeamLLM demonstrates how autonomous agents can perform full-spectrum exploits, ranging from reconnaissance and privilege escalation to data exfiltration and log tampering. These threats must be treated with the same rigor as human-driven advanced persistent threats (APTs).
- **Defense-in-depth is essential for risk containment:** Controls like identity scoping, API throttling, memory hygiene, and environment isolation must work together to reduce both rogue behavior and exploitability. No single mitigation is sufficient.
- **Organizational governance is as important as technical safeguards:** Policies governing what agents are allowed to do, who authorizes them, and how they're monitored must be embedded into enterprise governance frameworks. Oversight bodies like AI Governance Committees are critical for maintaining accountability.
- **Security tools must adapt to agent behavior:** Traditional tooling must evolve to account for autonomous execution, tool chaining, and persistent state. Vendors like Straiker.ai are helping bridge this gap by integrating agent-aware controls into IAM, DSPM, and cloud-native environments.

By recognizing agentic AI as a new class of security workload, one that blends autonomy, identity, and execution, organizations can apply the same level of scrutiny they would to human operators. Doing so will be essential to harnessing AI's value without compromising enterprise data or trust.

References

1. Gartner. (2025, January). 2025: The year of agentic AI. Gartner Research. https://www.gartner.com/en/articles/top-technology-trends-2025
2. IBM Research. (2025, June). AI FactSheets 360: Transparent reporting for trustworthy AI. https://www.ibm.com/docs/en/software-hub/5.1.x?topic=services-ai-factsheets
3. HIPAA Journal. (2024, November). Catholic Health reports breach of PHI of 483,000 individuals. https://www.bankinfosecurity.com/agentic-ai-tech-firm-says-health-data-leak-affects-483000-a-28424
4. Fang, R., et al. (2024, February). LLM agents can autonomously hack websites. arXiv preprint. https://arxiv.org/pdf/2402.06664
5. Challita, B., & Parrend, P. (2025, May). RedTeamLLM: An agentic AI framework for offensive security (arXiv:2505.06913). arXiv preprint. https://arxiv.org/pdf/2505.06913

PART 05

Ecosystem, Governance, and the Future

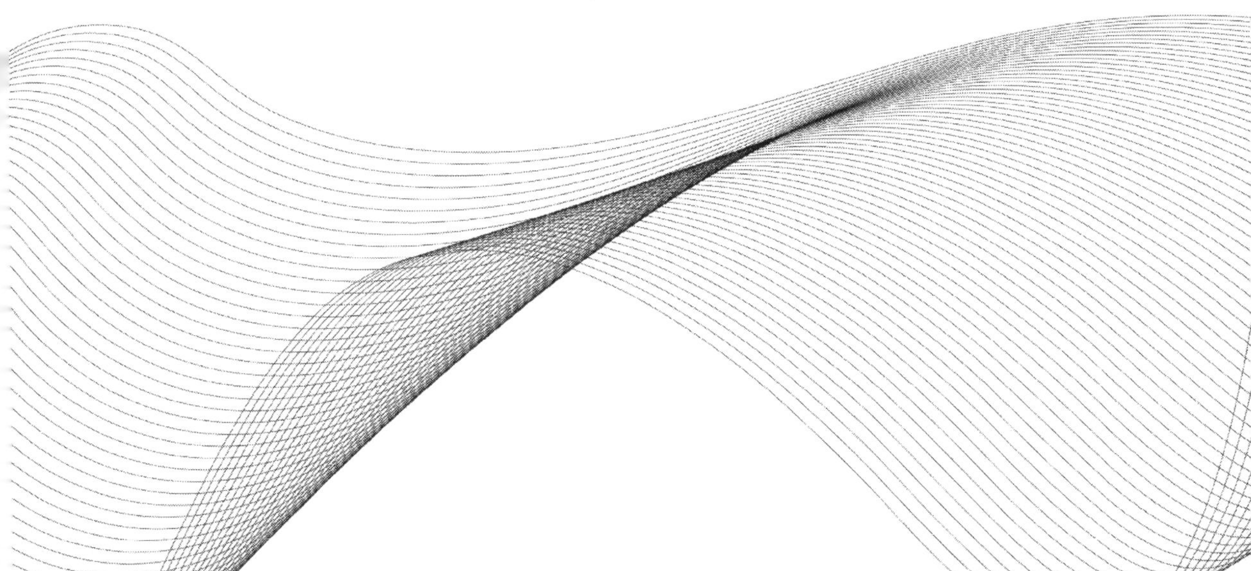

CHAPTER 17

Adapting Third-Party and Supply Chain Data Access for AI Risks

> *"Fierce competition among software providers has driven prioritization of rapid feature development over robust security. This often results in rushed product releases without comprehensive security built in or enabled by default, creating repeated opportunities for attackers to exploit weaknesses."*
>
> – PATRICK OPET, CISO, JPMORGAN CHASE

Introduction

Enterprises function as interconnected ecosystems where third-party vendors, contractors, SaaS providers, cloud services, and supply chain partners play critical roles in delivering business outcomes. However, each of these external integrations represents a potential vector for data compromise. The *2023 IBM Cost of a Data Breach* report found that 15% of all breaches involved a third party, with those breaches averaging $4.76 million in costs.[1] Additionally, organizations took an average of 233 days to identify and 74 days to contain a business partner supply chain compromise, for a total lifecycle of 307 days. That average lifecycle was 37 days or 12.8% longer than the average lifecycle of 270 days for data breaches attributed to another cause.

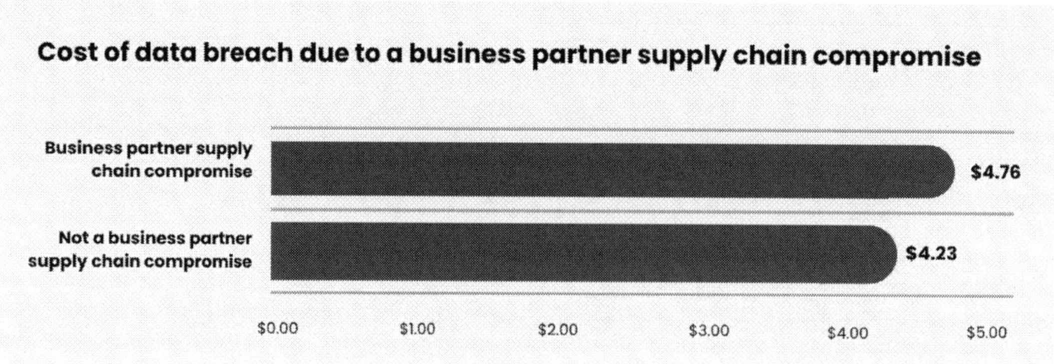

Figure 17.1: Measured in millions

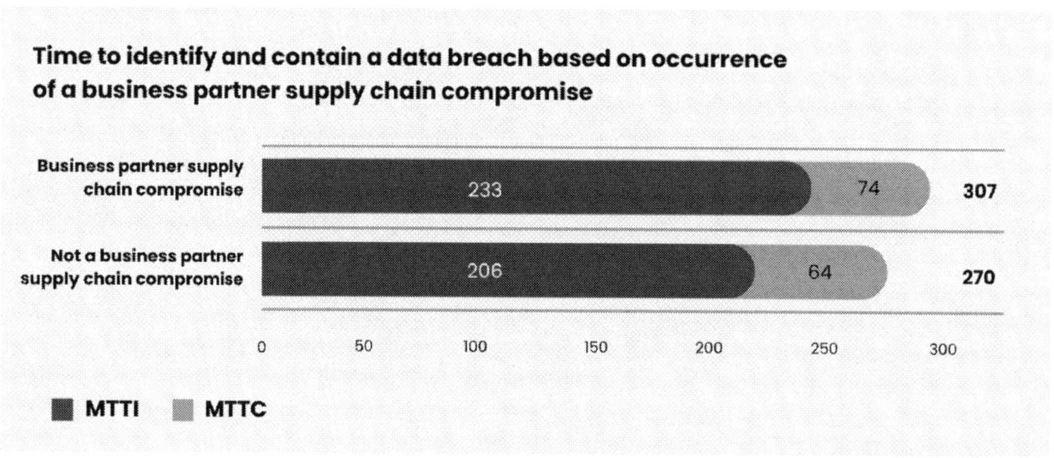

Figure 17.2: Measured in days

This chapter explores how enterprises can secure data access at the boundary of their digital operations, specifically where third-party integrations and supply chain dependencies reside. With a focus on DSPM, we examine how to gain visibility and control over data shared externally or accessed through intermediaries, including the increasingly prevalent class of AI vendors.

Traditional Third-Party Risk Management

Third-Party Risk Management (TPRM) is essential for organizations to identify, assess, and mitigate risks associated with external vendors and partners.[2] As reliance on third parties grows, so does the potential for risks such as data breaches, compliance violations, and operational disruptions.

Key Components of Effective TPRM

TPRM demands a continuous, integrated approach that aligns with business operations and adapts to evolving risk landscapes. Focusing on the following core components enables organizations to strengthen their TPRM capabilities, reduce exposure to third-party risks, and maintain compliance with regulatory expectations:

- **Continuous monitoring:** Traditional point-in-time assessments are insufficient. Organizations should implement ongoing monitoring to detect and address emerging risks throughout the vendor relationship lifecycle.
- **Centralized governance:** Adopting a centralized or federated governance model enhances coordination across functions like IT, legal, procurement, and compliance, ensuring a unified approach to managing third-party risks.
- **Risk-based prioritization:** Not all third parties pose the same level of risk. Implementing a risk-based approach allows organizations to allocate resources effectively, focusing on high-risk vendors that could significantly impact operations or compliance.
- **Integration with business processes:** TPRM should be embedded into existing business processes, including procurement and contract management, to ensure that risk considerations are part of decision-making from the outset.
- **Utilization of technology:** Leveraging appropriate technologies can streamline TPRM activities, from automating assessments to enhancing data analysis, thereby improving efficiency and effectiveness.

People and Process Considerations

Effective Third-Party Risk Management (TPRM) is not just about deploying the right tools; it requires clearly defined processes, shared accountability, and collaboration across multiple functions. Each stakeholder plays a critical role in identifying, mitigating, and monitoring third-party risks:

- **Governance, risk management, and compliance (GRC):** Oversee policy, control testing, and risk register maintenance
- **Compliance:** Ensure third parties adhere to regulatory obligations like GDPR, HIPAA, or PCI DSS

- **Procurement:** Incorporate security and compliance clauses in vendor contracts and maintain approved vendor lists
- **IT & security:** Validate technical controls and perform security assessments (e.g., penetration tests, architecture reviews)
- **Legal:** Review contracts for liability and indemnity related to third-party risks
- **Line-of-business owners:** Accountable for vendor performance and must validate operational risk impacts

Modernizing TPRM for AI Risks

TPRM must become a data- and model-aware discipline to accommodate AI risks. This means requiring AI transparency in contracts, updating due diligence frameworks, and coordinating closely across legal, security, and procurement teams. The goal is not to stifle innovation, but to ensure that enterprise data isn't unintentionally weaponized, leaked, or embedded into black-box AI systems without consent. The following upgrades to the TPRM process will help achieve this goal.

AI-Specific Data Use Clauses in Contracts

As SaaS and AI vendors increasingly incorporate customer data into their machine learning workflows through fine-tuning, transfer learning, or embeddings, organizations must proactively address data governance through contractual safeguards. Without clear boundaries, sensitive or proprietary data may be absorbed into vendor models, potentially resulting in unintended sharing, leakage, or reuse across customers.

TPRM Updates

Contractual clauses are needed to ensure that AI-driven innovation does not come at the cost of data security, compliance, or customer trust. To protect enterprise data in AI-enabled third-party relationships, contracts should explicitly address:

- **Permitted use of customer data:** Specify whether the vendor is allowed to use customer data for model training or optimization purposes.
- **Scope of data use:** Clarify what types of data may be used, such as anonymized metadata or fully identifiable data.

- **Consent mechanisms:** Define opt-in or opt-out requirements for any AI or ML-related data usage.
- **Third-party sharing restrictions:** Prohibit the vendor from sharing outputs, derivative models, or insights generated from your data with external parties.
- **Data residency and retention:** Include clauses that govern where data is stored, how long it is retained, and how it must be handled when the contract ends. This is especially important for regulated or cross-border data.

Evaluation of Vendor AI Practices

Vendors embedding AI may introduce risks tied to model bias, drift, hallucination, or unexplainable outcomes. These issues can materially affect customer operations, decision-making accuracy, and regulatory compliance.

TPRM Updates

To ensure that third-party AI capabilities are deployed responsibly, organizations should strengthen their TPRM programs to emphasize accountability, transparency, and compliance. The following updates help align vendor AI practices with enterprise risk expectations:

- Include AI Governance Addenda in vendor due diligence processes to evaluate:
  - Model lifecycle transparency
  - Bias and fairness audits, particularly when models impact individuals
  - Data lineage and provenance of training datasets
  - Ability to explain and contest automated decisions
- Require alignment with AI governance frameworks, such as the NIST AI Risk Management Framework (AI RMF), ISO/IEC 42001, or other recognized standards.

Expanded Vendor Risk Questionnaires

Traditional vendor risk assessments often overlook AI-specific issues, creating blind spots in understanding third-party exposure. As vendors increasingly embed generative AI and LLMs into their offerings, consider evolving your vendor due diligence questionnaires.

TPRM Updates

Enhance third-party risk questionnaires to address AI-related concerns by adding sections that cover:

- Use of generative AI or LLMs within vendor products and services
- Types and sources of training data (e.g., public datasets vs. proprietary customer data)
- Reliance on third-party foundation models (e.g., OpenAI, Anthropic)
- Handling, retention, and access controls for prompt data and logs in GenAI features
- Security measures for fine-tuning pipelines, including data purging capabilities

Governance Integration Across Security, Legal, and Procurement

AI adoption frequently spans multiple departments: security identifies risks, legal addresses liability, and procurement manages contracts. Without coordination, critical gaps can emerge in oversight and accountability.

TPRM Updates

Establish governance mechanisms that bridge functional silos and embed AI-specific oversight throughout the third-party lifecycle:

- Involve cross-functional AI Governance Committees in:
  - Approving vendors with generative AI capabilities
  - Reviewing vendor proposals involving fine-tuning or model integration
- Update procurement processes to require:
  - Pre-signed acceptable use policies for AI tools
  - Mandatory disclosures about AI data usage practices
- Enable GRC platforms to:
  - Tag vendors with AI features
  - Track how models are being used
  - Monitor shifts in vendor risk posture over time

Enhanced Monitoring and Risk Register Updates for AI Risk

AI-related risks evolve rapidly. A vendor deemed low-risk today could introduce generative AI features or model integrations that significantly alter their risk profile tomorrow.

TPRM Updates

Strengthen monitoring and risk register practices to account for AI-specific changes over time:

- Adopt or extend tooling, including:
  - AI risk rating platforms (emerging category; see Credo AI, Holistic AI)
  - DSPM or data lineage tools to track vendor access to sensitive data
  - Model behavior monitoring if AI/ML is embedded in vendor products
- Continuously monitor vendor disclosures for:
  - Introduction of new AI features or capabilities
  - Changes in model inputs, outputs, or data handling practices
  - AI-related incidents such as hallucinations, breaches, or misuse

DSPM as a Control Point for Third-Party Data Risk Mitigation

DSPM plays a vital role in mitigating third-party risk by offering visibility and control over how sensitive data is accessed, stored, and shared, especially in SaaS environments. As enterprises increasingly rely on external services for collaboration, analytics, and automation, data is often stored in third-party SaaS platforms such as Salesforce, Snowflake, Google Workspace, Microsoft 365, or Slack. These platforms hold large volumes of regulated or sensitive information, yet are frequently managed outside the traditional security perimeter. DSPM helps bridge this gap by continuously scanning SaaS data stores to detect violations of enterprise data security policies, such as unencrypted PII, excessive sharing permissions, or data exposures to unmanaged external collaborators.

One of DSPM's unique strengths is its ability to shine a light on how data flows across organizational and third party boundaries. Many enterprises are unaware of the full extent of data exchanged with vendors, partners, or shadow SaaS applications, especially through integrations, APIs, or authorized OAuth tokens. DSPM tools map these data exchanges in context, linking the flow of sensitive data with the identities (including third-party accounts) that accessed or moved it. This enables organizations to detect when sensitive data, such as HR files, customer financial records, or intellectual property, is being accessed or exported to external entities in ways that contradict contractual agreements or internal policies.

In this way, DSPM functions not just as a detection tool, but as a governance control. It empowers security and compliance teams to proactively identify and remediate third-party data access risks before they lead to breaches or violations. Whether enforcing least privilege access, detecting unauthorized data sharing, or flagging AI vendors improperly using customer data for model training, DSPM provides the real time visibility and enforcement needed to manage third-party data exposure in cloud-first enterprises.

Example: Using DSPM to Mitigate Risk Introduced by LLM Vendor

In 2023, a fintech enterprise used DSPM to monitor an LLM vendor's access to internal documentation. When a vendor subprocessor started accessing more files than required, DSPM triggered an alert. The enterprise limited access scope and initiated a contract review, preventing potential leakage.

Shared Responsibility Models and Continuous Monitoring

Revisiting the Shared Responsibility Model

While cloud providers popularized the shared responsibility model, it now extends to:

- SaaS vendors
- API providers
- BPO/ITO and supply chain partners
- AI infrastructure and analytics providers

Responsibility	Enterprise	Third Party
Data classification	✓	
Access control enforcement	✓	✓
Logging and auditing	✓	✓
Encryption at rest	✓	✓
Encryption in transit	✓	✓
Model training on data		✓ (with consent)

Table 17.1: Shared responsibility model involving third parties

Enterprise CISO View: Lessons from the JPMorgan CISO Letter

In a widely circulated letter by JPMorgan Chase's CISO,[3] several strategic recommendations were made to strengthen enterprise security posture in an era of rising third-party and SaaS-based risk. A central theme of the letter was the trend toward "unsassification," the deliberate reduction in reliance on SaaS platforms in favor of more tightly controlled, self-hosted, or hybrid environments. The letter's key insights align closely with DSPM principles and include:

- **Reclaiming data control:** Prioritize solutions that allow enterprises to retain full control over sensitive data, including encryption keys, access policies, and storage locations.
- **Minimizing data exposure to SaaS vendors:** Reduce the scope of data shared with SaaS platforms unless absolutely necessary, especially data with regulatory or privacy implications.
- **Vendor consolidation with oversight:** While some SaaS platforms offer integration benefits, consolidation should not come at the expense of visibility or control. Vet consolidated platforms for transparency and governance capabilities.
- **Data access logging and revocation:** Require vendors to support complete audit trails and the ability to revoke access in real time.
- **Building for Zero Trust:** Embed principles of Zero Trust, least privilege, continuous verification, and segmentation, into all third-party interactions.[4,5]

These recommendations highlight the importance of proactive data governance, continuous monitoring, and risk-aware vendor engagement. By leveraging a data security solution such as a DSPM and embracing strategies such as "unsassification," organizations can create more resilient and transparent data ecosystems.

When choosing a data security solution, it is essential to consider the deployment model carefully. If you select a solution that transfers all your data or metadata into a vendor's system, you risk undermining your own security objectives. For example, when evaluating a DSPM solution, you need to decide whether you are comfortable with a SaaS model, where your data flows into the vendor's environment; an outpost model, where only metadata is shared externally; an air-gapped model, where all data and metadata remain entirely within your infrastructure; or a federated model, which supports location-specific data sovereignty and compliance needs. For regulated U.S.-based enterprises, the air-gapped model often offers the strongest assurance of control and compliance.

Chapter Takeaways

Third-party and supply chain integrations present critical points of vulnerability in the enterprise data landscape, especially as AI capabilities become embedded within vendor offerings. As organizations increasingly rely on external partners and SaaS platforms, the nature of risk shifts from just operational concerns to strategic data security challenges. The following takeaways summarize the key insights from this chapter:

- **Traditional TPRM must evolve for AI-driven ecosystems:** Legacy vendor risk assessments overlook the dynamic and opaque risks introduced by AI models. Updated TPRM programs should integrate AI-specific due diligence, including questions about training data, model behavior, and third-party model dependencies.
- **Contracts are the first line of defense for data governance:** Clear and enforceable AI data use clauses must be embedded into vendor agreements. This includes defining allowable uses, opt-in/opt-out mechanisms, data residency requirements, and prohibitions against model training on customer data without explicit consent.
- **Cross-functional governance is critical:** AI-related risks span legal, security, procurement, and line-of-business teams. Involving AI Governance Committees and enabling shared accountability ensures that vendor AI adoption aligns with enterprise risk tolerance and regulatory posture.
- **Visibility into data access is no longer optional:** DSPM tools provide critical insight into how sensitive data is shared or accessed by third parties. By mapping data flows, identity access, and policy violations, DSPM becomes a foundational control for managing third-party AI risk exposure.
- **Continuous monitoring prevents downstream surprises:** A vendor's risk profile is not static. Ongoing surveillance of AI feature rollouts, model behavior, and incident disclosures ensures that seemingly low-risk vendors do not introduce emergent vulnerabilities post-contract.
- **Shared responsibility must be made explicit:** The modern enterprise operates across a web of APIs, SaaS tools, and data pipelines. Clarifying who is responsible

for data classification, encryption, logging, and model behavior is essential for accountability and breach response.

- **"Unsassification" is an emerging trend for control-conscious organizations:** Echoing JPMorgan's guidance, regulated enterprises are reassessing their SaaS exposure and exploring hybrid or air-gapped DSPM models to retain full control over sensitive data and meet compliance expectations.
- **Deployment model selection has lasting consequences:** Choosing between SaaS, Outpost, air-gapped, or federated DSPM architectures determines not just where data resides, but how much visibility and governance an organization retains. For many regulated U.S. enterprises, air-gapped deployments provide the strongest control assurance.

By adapting TPRM to the realities of AI-enabled environments and deploying tools like DSPM to enforce data control at vendor boundaries, enterprises can mitigate third-party risks without stifling innovation or collaboration.

References

1. Hanley, J., et al. (2023). Cost of a data breach report 2023. IBM Security. https://www.ibm.com/reports/data-breach
2. Gartner. (2024). Third party risk management (TPRM): An essential guide. https://www.gartner.com/en/legal-compliance/topics/third-party-risk-management-tprm
3. Opet, P. (2024). Open letter to our suppliers. JPMorgan Chase Technology Blog. https://www.jpmorgan.com/technology/technology-blog/open-letter-to-our-suppliers
4. Lowans, B., Fritsch, J., & Bales, A. (2023, March). Innovation insight: Data security posture management. Gartner. https://www.gartner.com/en/documents/4405499
5. Rose, S., Borchert, O., Mitchell, S., & Connelly, S. (2022). Zero Trust architecture (SP 800-207). National Institute of Standards and Technology. https://doi.org/10.6028/NIST.SP.800-207

CHAPTER 18

Compliance and Data Privacy in a Distributed World

> *"In a world powered by AI and governed by data, privacy is not just a compliance checkbox; it's an architectural necessity and a competitive advantage. Organizations that embed privacy into design and operations not only build trust and accountability, but also achieve more successful and sustainable business outcomes."*
>
> *– Dennis Irwin, Chief Compliance Officer, Alkami Technology*

Privacy and Compliance in the age of National and Global Regulation

Data privacy has become one of the defining compliance and risk management challenges of the digital era. As organizations expand across borders, migrate to multi-cloud environments, and integrate AI into day-to-day operations, the obligation to protect personal and sensitive data is a significant legal, regulatory, and ethical imperative.

Globally, countries have implemented sweeping data protection laws such as the European Union's General Data Protection Regulation (GDPR), China's Personal Information Protection Law (PIPL), and India's Digital Personal Data Protection Act (DPDP). In the United States, while there is no singular federal privacy law, organizations face a growing patchwork of state-level regulations, including the California Consumer Privacy Act (CCPA), its successor the California Privacy Rights Act (CPRA), and similar statutes in states like Colorado, Virginia, and Connecticut. Sector-specific federal laws such as HIPAA, the Family Educational Rights and Privacy Act (FERPA), the Children's Online Privacy Protection Act (COPPA), and the Gramm-Leach-Bliley Act (GLBA) add further complexity for regulated industries.

With regulators intensifying enforcement and rapidly evolving privacy mandates, enterprises must not only secure data but also demonstrate that their controls, governance models, and architectures align with jurisdictional requirements.

This chapter explores how enterprises can navigate the complexities of both U.S. and global privacy regulation, align AI-driven innovation with compliance mandates, and adopt architectures that enable responsible, auditable, and compliant data handling.

We will examine:

- A comparative overview of privacy regulations across jurisdictions (e.g., GDPR, CCPA/CPRA, PIPL, DPDP, HIPAA, COPPA)
- The implications of AI for privacy compliance and risk, including training data governance, inference control, and explainability
- Privacy-by-design and data minimization strategies that support both operational goals and legal defensibility
- The legal and architectural challenges of cross-border data transfers and data localization requirements

Key U.S. Federal Privacy Laws

The United States enforces data privacy through a patchwork of sector-specific federal regulations. While there is no single national data privacy law, foundational legislation like the Privacy Act of 1974, HIPAA (1996), COPPA (1998), FERPA (1974), and GLBA (1999) collectively provide significant protections across various domains, ranging from healthcare and education to financial services and children's online privacy.

Law	Scope	Core Requirements
Privacy Act of 1974	Governs personal data collected and maintained by U.S. federal government agencies	• Individual rights to access and amend records • Limits on disclosure without consent • Agency duties to ensure data accuracy and security • Publication of system-of-record notices
HIPAA (Health Insurance Portability and Accountability Act)	Applies to healthcare providers, health plans, and their business associates handling protected health information (PHI)	• Administrative, physical, and technical safeguards for PHI • Restrictions on use/disclosure of health data • Right to access medical records • Breach notification and staff training requirements
COPPA (Children's Online Privacy Protection Act)	Covers websites and online services directed at children under 13, or those knowingly collecting their data	• Parental consent required for data collection • Clear and accessible privacy notices • Rights to review/delete a child's information • Limits on data sharing and retention
FERPA (Family Educational Rights and Privacy Act)	Applies to educational institutions receiving federal funding	• Grants students (or parents) rights to access and amend education records • Limits disclosure without written consent • Requires annual notification of rights • Protections for personally identifiable information (PII) in student records

Law	Scope	Core Requirements
GLBA (Gramm-Leach-Bliley Act)	Applies to financial institutions handling nonpublic personal information (NPI)	• Requires clear consumer privacy notices • Opt-out options for data sharing with non-affiliated third parties • Implementation of administrative, technical, and physical safeguards • Ongoing risk assessments and staff security awareness programs

Table 18.1: Overview of U.S. Federal Privacy Laws

State Regulations

In addition to federal laws, the United States has seen a growing patchwork of state-level privacy regulations that add further complexity to data compliance efforts. California has led this movement with the California Consumer Privacy Act[1] (CCPA, 2018) and its amendment, the California Privacy Rights Act (CPRA, 2020), which grants consumers broad rights over their personal data and impose significant obligations on businesses. Other states have followed suit, including Texas with the Texas Data Privacy and Security Act (TDPSA), as well as Virginia (VCDPA), Colorado (CPA), Connecticut (CTDPA), and Utah (UCPA), each introducing their own interpretation of consumer rights, business obligations, and enforcement mechanisms. While these laws share some common principles such as transparency, opt-out rights, and data minimization, their specific requirements vary, making compliance a moving target for organizations operating across multiple jurisdictions. We are showcasing CCPA and CPRA as representative examples of how state-level regulation is reshaping privacy governance in the United States.

California's Privacy Laws: CCPA and CPRA

California has led the United States in establishing comprehensive privacy regulations. The California Consumer Privacy Act (CCPA) effective 2020, gave California residents unprecedented rights to access and control their personal data. Recognizing the need to strengthen and clarify these protections, California voters approved the California Privacy Rights Act

(CPRA) which took effect in 2023. CPRA builds on CCPA by expanding consumer rights, adding new compliance obligations, and creating a dedicated enforcement authority.

Table 18.2 outlines the distinct scope and core requirements of each law to support privacy program planning.

Law	Scope	Core Requirements
CCPA	Applies to for-profit businesses collecting personal data from California residents and meeting thresholds (e.g., >$25M in revenue or >50,000 consumers' data)	• Right to access and delete personal data • Right to opt out of the sale of personal information • Mandatory disclosure of data collection and sharing practices • Non-discrimination for exercising privacy rights
CPRA	Expands CCPA protections and applies to the same types of businesses with slightly revised thresholds (e.g., >100,000 consumers)	• Right to correct inaccurate personal data • Right to limit use of sensitive personal information • Introduction of purpose limitation and data minimization • Creation of the California Privacy Protection Agency (CPPA) for enforcement • Risk assessments and rules around automated decision-making

Table 18.2: Overview of CCPA and CPRA

Overview of Global Privacy Laws

Data privacy laws have proliferated globally over the past decade, each with its unique definitions, compliance requirements, and enforcement mechanisms. These laws govern the collection, storage, use, and PII and impose obligations on organizations to safeguard data while respecting user rights. Some of the more prominent ones are covered in the sections that follow.

The European Union's General Data Protection Regulation (GDPR)

The GDPR[2] represents one of the most comprehensive and influential privacy regulations in the world. Enacted in 2016 and enforced beginning May 2018, it provides a robust legal framework for protecting personal data within the European Economic Area (EEA) and beyond. The GDPR applies extraterritorially, meaning any organization, regardless of its location, that processes the personal data of individuals in the EEA must comply. Its objectives center on empowering individuals with greater control over their data, enforcing organizational accountability, and harmonizing data protection laws across EU member states.

The regulation has served as a global benchmark for privacy laws, inspiring similar legislation across jurisdictions such as Brazil (LGPD), Japan (APPI), and South Korea (PIPA). It is also increasingly referenced as a standard for AI data governance, especially concerning lawful data use, transparency, and data subject rights.

Table 18.3 outlines the scope and core requirements of the GDPR to support enterprise compliance and strategic planning.

Scope	Core Requirements
Applies to any organization that processes personal data of individuals in the EEA, regardless of where the organization is based	• Lawful basis for processing (e.g., consent, contract, legal obligation) • Data minimization and purpose limitation • Data subject rights (access, erasure, portability, objection) • Privacy by design and by default • Breach notification within 72 hours • Data Protection Impact Assessments (DPIAs) • Cross-border data transfer mechanisms (e.g., SCCs, adequacy decisions) • Appointment of Data Protection Officers (DPOs) in certain cases • Significant fines for noncompliance (up to 4% of global annual turnover)

Table 18.3: Overview of the European Union's General Data Protection Regulation

India's Digital Personal Data Protection Act

India's Digital Personal Data Protection Act[3] (DPDP) represents the country's first comprehensive legal framework for governing personal data in the digital age. Enacted in 2023, the DPDP applies to the processing of digital personal data within India, as well as to entities outside India that offer goods or services to individuals within the country. The law introduces a structured, rights-based approach to data governance centered on notice, consent, and accountability. It classifies organizations handling personal data as "Data Fiduciaries" and establishes enhanced compliance obligations for those designated as "Significant Data Fiduciaries," based on factors such as data volume and processing impact.

The DPDP aligns closely with global privacy principles, such as transparency, purpose limitation, and user rights, while maintaining sovereignty through requirements like government-approved cross-border data transfers and India-based data officers. Enforcement is overseen by the Data Protection Board of India, with penalties for noncompliance ranging from monetary fines to processing restrictions. As India positions itself as a key player in the global digital economy, the DPDP marks a foundational step in harmonizing privacy protection with innovation and growth.

Table 18.4 outlines the scope and core requirements of the DPDP to support enterprise compliance and data strategy in the Indian context.

Scope	Core Requirements
Applies to any entity processing digital personal data in India or targeting Indian residents with goods or services	• Notice and consent framework with clear, revocable user consent • Data subject rights to access, correction, erasure • Appointment of a Data Protection Officer (DPO) for Significant Data Fiduciaries • Data Protection Impact Assessments (DPIAs) for high-risk processing • Cross-border data transfers only to countries approved by the Indian government • Oversight and enforcement by the Data Protection Board of India • Penalties for noncompliance, including fines and restrictions on data processing

Table 18.4: Scope and Core Requirements of DPDP

China's Privacy and Cybersecurity Regulations

China's regulatory framework for data and cybersecurity is built on three foundational laws, each introduced within the past decade: the Cybersecurity Law[4] (CSL, 2017), the Data Security Law[5] (DSL, 2021), and the Personal Information Protection Law[6] (PIPL, 2021).

Together, these laws form a cohesive legal regime governing the collection, processing, storage, and transfer of data, both within China and beyond its borders.

While each law serves a distinct purpose, they work in tandem to enhance national security, enforce corporate accountability, and safeguard individual privacy. Table 18.5 outlines the scope, year of enactment, and core requirements of each law to support compliance and strategic planning.

Law	Scope	Core Requirements
CSL (Cybersecurity Law)	Focuses on critical information infrastructure (CII) and internet security within China	• Data localization for CII operators • Security assessments for cross-border transfers • Real-name registration • Network security obligations
DSL (Data Security Law)	Covers classification and protection of all types of data	• Data classification (e.g., important, core) • Risk assessments for data handling • Export controls for sensitive data • Incident reporting requirements
PIPL (Personal Information Protection Law)	Regulates personal data protection and aligns with global privacy norms	• Lawful basis for data collection • Consent and purpose limitation • Individual rights (access, correction, deletion) • Restrictions on cross-border transfers

Table 18.5: Overview of China's Data and Cybersecurity Laws

Brazil's LGPD, Japan's APPI, South Korea's PIPA

Brazil's LGPD[7] (Lei Geral de Proteção de Dados), Japan's APPI (Act on the Protection of Personal Information), and South Korea's PIPA (Personal Information Protection Act) reflect the growing global convergence toward GDPR-like data protection standards, while incorporating region-specific requirements. These laws emphasize lawful data processing, transparency, and individual rights, such as access and correction, but differ in enforcement structures and consent models. Brazil's LGPD, for instance, introduced a national data protection authority (ANPD) to oversee compliance, while Japan's APPI emphasizes cross-border data transfer accountability through adequacy assessments. South Korea's PIPA, one of the earliest comprehensive privacy laws in Asia, has been strengthened in recent years to enhance data subject rights and align more closely with international norms. Together, these regulations represent a maturing global privacy landscape where organizations must adapt to both common principles and local enforcement nuances.

Each of these frameworks mirrors core GDPR principles but with local adaptations. Enforcement is increasing across these regions, and regulatory harmonization efforts are underway.

AI Implications for Privacy Compliance

AI introduces new challenges for data privacy compliance. Whether training LLMs or deploying decision-support systems, enterprises must ensure that their use of data complies with privacy laws. For example, GDPR requires that automated decision making (Article 22) affecting individuals significantly must be explainable and subject to human oversight. Similarly, DPDP requires clear notices and consent for AI use that processes personal data. And lastly, federal regulations require that pharmaceutical companies cannot use PHI to train LLM models.

To reduce privacy risks and demonstrate compliance when deploying AI, organizations should:

- **Document AI systems thoroughly:** Use structured documentation tools like *Model Cards*[8] or *FactSheets*[9] to describe how models work, what data they were trained on, and what risks they may pose.
- **Apply differential privacy:** Inject statistical noise into training data to preserve overall patterns while protecting individual records, helping reduce re-identification risk.

- **Minimize or transform sensitive inputs:** Avoid feeding sensitive personal data directly into models. Use techniques like embeddings, pseudonymization, or anonymization to reduce exposure.
- **Conduct AI privacy impact assessments (AI-PIAs):** Evaluate potential privacy harms, assess compliance with legal standards, and implement necessary controls before deploying AI systems.
- **Implement technical controls:** For example, certain DSPM platforms can enforce guardrails that prevent PHI from being ingested by LLMs.

Privacy-by-Design

Privacy-by-Design (PbD) is a foundational concept in data protection, emphasizing that privacy should not be an afterthought: it must be embedded into the architecture, processes, and operations of systems from the very beginning. Originally developed by privacy experts and later formalized under the GDPR (Article 25), PbD has become a global best practice for ensuring compliance, building trust, and minimizing data risk.

At its core, PbD shifts the mindset from reactive compliance to proactive engineering. Rather than responding to breaches or violations after the fact, organizations are encouraged to build systems that anticipate and prevent privacy risks by default.

Key Principles of Privacy-by-Design:

- **Proactive, not reactive:** Design systems to anticipate, identify, and mitigate privacy risks before they occur, rather than reacting after damage is done.
- **Privacy as the default setting:** Users should be protected automatically, without needing to take extra steps to safeguard their data. The minimum amount of data should be collected, used, and retained.
- **End-to-end security:** Privacy relies on strong security. Data must be protected with integrity and confidentiality across its entire lifecycle, from collection to deletion.
- **Visibility and transparency:** Systems should be auditable, understandable, and accountable. Stakeholders, including users, regulators, and auditors, must be able to assess how data is collected, used, and protected.

Together with data minimization and differential privacy (explained in the following sections), these principles ensure that organizations limit the collection and use of personal data to only what is necessary for a specific purpose. This not only reduces exposure and regulatory risk, but also aligns with ethical standards and customer expectations.

Data Minimization

Data minimization is a core principle of privacy regulations, including Article 5(1)(c) of the GDPR. It requires that organizations only collect and process personal data that is adequate, relevant, and limited to what is necessary for the intended purpose. This not only reduces privacy risk but also supports legal defensibility and operational efficiency.

To put this principle into practice, organizations can adopt several technical and operational strategies:

- **Tokenization and hashing:** Replace sensitive identifiers with pseudonymous values to limit exposure without losing analytical value.
- **Retention controls and expiration policies:** Automatically delete or archive data once it is no longer needed, reducing the risk of unnecessary long-term storage.
- **Tiered access management:** Apply Zero Trust principles by limiting data access based on role, context, and sensitivity. Ensure that users can access only the specific data they need to perform their responsibilities.
- **Selective sampling for model training:** Use anonymized or representative data subsets to train AI models, minimizing the use of full, raw datasets.

Differential Privacy

As organizations seek to harness the value of large datasets, especially for training AI models, there is a growing need to ensure that the inclusion or exclusion of a single individual's data does not meaningfully affect outputs. Differential privacy offers a mathematically rigorous framework for addressing this challenge.

Differential privacy introduces carefully calibrated statistical noise into datasets or query responses, making it exceedingly difficult for attackers to infer whether any specific individual's data was part of the dataset. This protects privacy while still enabling meaningful aggregate analysis.

One of the key strengths of differential privacy is its quantifiable guarantee. Organizations can set a *privacy budget* (often represented by the variable ε, or "epsilon") to control the trade-off between data utility and privacy protection. A lower epsilon means stronger privacy but less precise results, while a higher epsilon allows for more accuracy with weaker privacy guarantees.

Real-World Applications

Differential privacy is not just theoretical. Apple uses it to gather usage statistics on iOS without compromising user privacy.[10] Google's open-source library, DP-FTRL, implements it for machine learning, and the U.S. Census Bureau applied differential privacy techniques in its 2020 census. This marked the first time such techniques were used in national statistics.

Use Cases in AI and Data Security

- **AI model training:** Differential privacy can protect sensitive records in training datasets by preventing models from memorizing individual data points.
- **Data sharing across borders:** In regions with strict privacy laws (e.g., GDPR, DPDP), differential privacy can enable compliant data analysis by minimizing re-identification risk.
- **Privacy-preserving analytics:** These analytics enable insights from behavioral, health, or financial data without exposing individual identities.

As privacy expectations tighten and AI systems grow more pervasive, differential privacy offers a scalable and principled approach for balancing innovation with compliance and trust.

Compliance Strategies for Data Localization

Many jurisdictions, for example UAE, China, and Russia, now restrict the export of personal data, citing concerns about foreign surveillance, misuse, or regulatory mismatch. They require that personal data should be stored locally within national borders.

- Use data sovereignty clouds (e.g., AWS Sovereign Cloud, Microsoft EU Data Boundary).
- Establish in-region data centers for processing sensitive workloads.
- Employ federated architectures to keep data resident while coordinating policies globally.

The "federated architecture" deployment model, discussed in the chapter *Deployment Models and Data Boundaries,*, illustrates how localized deployment can support compliance with data localization requirements.

As an example, a global telecom provider operating in the EU, U.S., and Southeast Asia adopted a federated data mesh model. Personal data was processed locally per region, while risk signals and usage patterns were anonymized and aggregated to a global dashboard. This approach satisfied GDPR, PIPL, and DPDP requirements without limiting operational insight.

Chapter Takeaways

Data privacy has evolved from a legal obligation into a strategic need. As AI becomes deeply embedded in enterprise systems and global regulations tighten, organizations must integrate privacy into the architecture, not just the policy layer. This chapter highlights several critical lessons:

- **Global laws, local execution:** Enterprises must align with diverse regulations like GDPR, DPDP, PIPL, and CCPA/CPRA. While principles such as data minimization, user rights, and breach notification are common, enforcement and requirements differ, demanding tailored compliance architectures.
- **AI complicates privacy compliance:** AI introduces novel privacy risks, especially around model training, inference, and explainability. Laws like GDPR and DPDP require consent, transparency, and oversight for AI-driven decisions. Privacy impact assessments and technical safeguards (e.g., differential privacy, data minimization) are essential.
- **Privacy-by-design is non-negotiable:** Embedding privacy into system architecture through proactive design, minimal data collection, end-to-end security, and transparency builds compliance and trust.
- **Cross-border data transfers require engineering solutions:** With rising data localization laws, federated architectures and sovereign cloud strategies allow global coordination while meeting local residency mandates.
- **Operationalization is the future of compliance:** Documentation, data mapping, and real-time enforcement are now foundational. Tools like DSPM provide visibility into how personal data moves across systems, enabling enforceable, auditable privacy controls.

Privacy is not just a checkbox; it is core to building digital trust in an AI-powered, globally regulated world.

References

1. State of California. (2020). California Privacy Rights Act (CPRA). https://cppa.ca.gov
2. European Parliament & Council of the European Union. (2016). General Data Protection Regulation (GDPR). Implemented May 25, 2018. https://gdpr-info.eu
3. Standing Committee of the Indian Parliament. (2023). Digital Personal Data Protection Act (DPDP). https://prsindia.org/billtrack/digital-personal-data-protection-bill-2023
4. Standing Committee of the National People's Congress. (2017). Cybersecurity Law of the People's Republic of China. http://www.npc.gov.cn/englishnpc/c23934/202012/35f8de03b5d743c882cfae758ec8f26c.shtml
5. Standing Committee of the National People's Congress. (2021). Data Security Law of the People's Republic of China. http://www.npc.gov.cn/englishnpc/c23934/202111/7ba7cb5b3ef14c978420d4087ebf28c2.shtml
6. Standing Committee of the National People's Congress. (2021). Personal Information Protection Law of the People's Republic of China. http://www.npc.gov.cn/englishnpc/c23934/202201/5f1e49e3b78745b8a9f239b5c537cbce.shtml
7. Brazilian Government (Serpro). (2020). Lei Geral de Proteção de Dados (LGPD): Overview. https://www.serpro.gov.br/lgpd
8. Mitchell, M., et al. (2019). Model cards for model reporting. Google AI. https://modelcards.withgoogle.com
9. Hanley, J., et al. (2021). AI FactSheets 360: Transparent reporting for trustworthy AI. IBM Research. https://research.ibm.com/blog/aifactsheets
10. Apple Inc. (2016). Differential privacy overview. https://www.apple.com/privacy/docs/Differential_Privacy_Overview.pdf

LOOKING FORWARD

Rethinking Data Protection in the Age of AI

> *"We will not only use the machines for their intelligence, we will also collaborate with them in ways that we cannot even imagine."*
>
> – FEI-FEI LI, PROFESSOR OF COMPUTER SCIENCE AT STANFORD UNIVERSITY

As we've explored across this book, data and AI security has entered a new era, defined not only by the explosion of data volumes and the rise of generative AI but also by the increasing complexity of threats, regulations, and architectural models. Protecting enterprise data today requires deep visibility, contextual intelligence, and continuous posture management. From discovery to classification, identity mapping, AI governance, and autonomous agent oversight, each chapter has built upon the next to provide a blueprint for security teams.

Organizations cannot afford fragmented or reactive strategies. Point solutions without visibility into data, identity, and flow relationships are inadequate for today's threat landscape. Compliance is not just about checkbox audits; it now involves real-time enforcement, traceability, and demonstrable governance.[1] In this new context, data security posture is not just an operational concern but a board-level imperative.

The Future of Data and AI Security

The coming decade will redefine how enterprises perceive, prioritize, and implement security. The evolution of AI and data systems will unlock tremendous capabilities, but will also usher in previously unimaginable risks. Key shifts will include:

1. Autonomous Systems and Agentic AI

AI systems are shifting from reactive to autonomous. Agentic AI will independently orchestrate detection, response, and even remediation, interpreting signals, prioritizing actions, and communicating with stakeholders in natural language.[2] These agents, if left unchecked, may exhibit unintended behavior or policy drift. Guardrails, role-based constraints, and alignment layers will be essential.

A new paradigm is emerging: multi-agent negotiations. Swarm-like agent collectives will verify each other's decisions, coordinate over shared data graphs, and negotiate control through consensus-based governance. This model, known as swarm governance, will enable secure orchestration across federated environments, provided robust data visibility and agent transparency mechanisms are in place.

2. Context-Aware Architecture: The Rise of MCP

MCP is designed as a unifying abstraction layer and enables interoperability across identities, data classifications, usage patterns, and policy enforcement.[3] But more than just an architectural innovation, MCP is actively disrupting the economic and operational models that have defined the security and data platform markets for over a decade.

Where integration complexity once created vendor lock-in and sustained high-margin businesses, MCP flattens that advantage. Value is now shifting from proprietary control to real-world effectiveness, explainability, and trust. This shift is altering how security tools are built, how risk is governed, and how data is defended in the world of agentic AI.

Organizations adopting MCP-like frameworks will be able to:

- Solve the integration problem (i.e., how to integrate multiple products and technologies into a single control plane), which in turn will take away a significant advantage that platform vendors have
- Implement just-in-time, intent-based access

- Automate classification with model-inferred patterns
- Normalize telemetry across tools and clouds
- Ensure compliance through provable data lineage[4]

To extend this model further, MCP will integrate agent certificates: verifiable credentials bound to AI agents. These credentials, based on World Wide Web Consortium (W3C) and decentralized identity (DID) standards, will define which agents are allowed to access which data, under what roles, and with what scope. API policies will enforce this trust contract, ensuring that only certified agents can act on sensitive workloads.

3. Language Alignment Layers and Constitutional AI

To keep autonomous agents aligned with organizational values, many will incorporate language alignment layers, rule sets inspired by Constitutional AI that bias model intent toward safe, compliant, and explainable outcomes.

These alignment layers will be critical for:

- Embedding policies directly into model reasoning
- Preventing drift in agent behavior over time
- Enabling "reason codes" that explain actions in human-readable terms

Data security teams will increasingly rely on these embedded controls to ensure agents can justify their actions against constitutional principles, including data sovereignty, non-repudiation, and minimal disclosure.

4. Zero-Trust Data Security

The Zero Trust model is shifting beyond network access to embrace data-centric trust boundaries. Every access request will be evaluated in real time based on identity, behavior, data sensitivity, and context. Trust will not be assumed based on location or credentials; it will be earned dynamically.[5] Data protection will be driven by classification and access context, with policies that follow the data, not the device, network, or user.

AI will support this model by:

- Scoring the risk of every access request
- Detecting abnormal usage of sensitive datasets

- Enforcing micro-permissions with context-bound guardrails[6]

4. Unified Platforms and Posture-First Design

CISOs are already demanding simplification. The future belongs to unified platforms that provide discovery, classification, monitoring, and control in a single interface. These platforms must be posture-first, showing not only where the risk is but also what to do about it. We will see:

- Consolidation of DSPM, CIEM, and DLP
- UI overlays powered by LLMs for explainability and automation
- Tight integration into DevOps and DataOps workflows
- Automation of remediation and architecture redesign

The winning platforms will not just detect; they will remediate, advise, and even design better architectures.

5. Privacy and Sovereignty as Design Principles

Global privacy regulations will continue to evolve. But rather than treating them as compliance burdens, leading enterprises will embed them into architecture. AI governance, model documentation, data localization, and federated learning will become the norm.[7] Localization won't just be a regulatory requirement; it will be a performance and trust differentiator.

Enterprises will differentiate on how they handle sensitive data. Security will be a brand value, and transparency around AI model usage will be expected.

6. Adaptive Threats and Dynamic Defense

Attackers are using AI too. We are entering an arms race where attack vectors evolve in real time. Social engineering, deepfake impersonation, autonomous phishing, and AI-driven lateral movement will all become more common.[8] Defenders must adapt accordingly.

The future defense stack will include:

- AI honeypots and deception models
- Context-enforced policy engines with runtime attestation

- AI behavioral models trained on multi-modal signals (network, app, identity, data)
- Red team simulations run by autonomous adversarial AI agents

Future of Incident Response with Data Graphs

As discussed earlier in the book, data graphs offer a new way forward by mapping relationships between users, systems, and data in real time. This shift enables smarter, faster, and more proactive responses. Here are key innovations shaping the future of IR with data graphs:

- **Predictive IR:** Using ML on data graphs to detect potential choke points or targets before compromise
- **Generative IR copilots:** Chatbot-style interfaces that answer questions like: "What's the most sensitive dataset this service account could access yesterday?"
- **Federated graphs:** Cross-cloud, cross-geography graphs that honor data boundaries but still support visibility

Cultural Shift in Cybersecurity Leadership

The role of the CISO is undergoing a profound transformation. What was once a role focused predominantly on technical controls, compliance checklists, and infrastructure protection is now evolving into a strategic, cross-disciplinary leadership position. The CISO of the future must be fluent not only in traditional cybersecurity domains, but also in AI architecture, data science, regulatory frameworks, and business strategy.

According to a recent Trellix/CSIS survey, 92% of CISOs are reevaluating their roles in response to GenAI pressures, and 90% feel increased burden due to AI-driven threat complexity.[9] Yet 91% believe AI offers defensive promise, and 45% have set up AI governance committees: an essential evolution for enterprise resilience.

At the heart of this shift is a new reality: data and AI are now core business assets. This means the CISO must be capable of engaging at the highest levels of the organization, not just reporting risks, but actively shaping how products are built, how data is governed, and how AI is deployed. The modern CISO will increasingly chair or co-lead cross-functional

AI/Data Risk Committees, bringing together leaders from legal, engineering, compliance, privacy, and product to make informed, strategic decisions about data and AI usage.

This evolution requires a new skillset. Communication becomes as important as technical depth. The ability to explain complex data risks in clear, compelling language to boards, regulators, and the public will be a defining trait of effective security leadership. The CISO must become a storyteller, a diplomat, and a systems thinker.

Additionally, CISOs will need to:

- Influence product roadmaps and data infrastructure decisions from the earliest stages.
- Guide procurement and vendor selection with a sharp eye for AI safety and data stewardship.
- Collaborate with marketing and customer success to demonstrate security as a competitive differentiator.
- Drive internal education and awareness around emerging threats like prompt injection, data leakage via LLMs, and misaligned AI agents.

As generative AI and agentic systems enter the enterprise, CISOs must also engage with AI governance structures, drafting policy, ensuring ethical alignment, and operationalizing trust frameworks. The security organization will need to partner deeply with AI teams to build safeguards into model pipelines, establish post-deployment monitoring, and maintain accountability for both model behavior and data usage.

In short, cybersecurity is moving from the "Department of No" to the "Enabler of Trust." Done well, it becomes a strategic function that helps organizations innovate responsibly, compete confidently, and differentiate on integrity. The CISO becomes not just a guardian of risk, but a leader of resilience, a champion of data ethics, and a driver of long-term enterprise value.

Calls to Action for CISOs and Practitioners

The future of data and AI security won't be defined by tools alone, it will be shaped by architecture, governance, and culture. As threats evolve and AI adoption accelerates, security leaders must rethink core practices across identity, data, and risk. The following principles offer a blueprint for building forward-looking, resilient security programs that are context-aware, explainable, and aligned with both innovation and trust.

Establish an MCP-Aligned Security Architecture

Map out how your organization could benefit from a model context protocol: What data flows do you track today? Where is context missing? Start identifying blind spots across data, identity, and policy that can be solved by unified context models. Build prototypes.

Formalize AI Governance Now

Don't wait for regulators to force your hand. Define an AI Usage Policy. Create a governance committee. Identify sensitive data categories that must be excluded from public or even internal model training. Mandate prompt and output logging for all generative AI usage.

Treat Data Classification as a Living System

Automate where possible, but continuously validate. Create tiered sensitivity models that evolve with your business. Assign owners to critical data stores. Use AI to detect classification drift or policy violations in real time.

Rethink IAM from a Data Perspective

Traditional IAM is not enough. You must understand what each identity can do with data. Build data-to-identity access maps. Use this to reduce overprivilege and enable just-in-time access. Elevate monitoring for high-risk roles, service accounts, and NHIs.

Shift Security Left in the Data Lifecycle

Work with your data engineering and platform teams. Embed security into data pipeline code. Validate classification and encryption policies during ingestion. Don't bolt security on at the end; build it into your ETL jobs, your data lake policies, and your ML workflows.

Prioritize Explainability and Engagement

If your security tools can't tell you "why," then they are liabilities. Demand natural language interfaces, LLM-generated summaries, and annotated visualizations. Make it easy for non-security stakeholders to understand what's happening and why it matters.

Champion Trust as a Core Value

Security isn't just about defense; it's about enabling innovation safely. Advocate for privacy and transparency. Push your vendors to deliver AI safety. Engage with your customers and show how you protect their data. Trust is the new perimeter.

Invest in Talent for the Next Era

Start building the skills of tomorrow. Train security analysts in prompt engineering, data modeling, and cloud-native architectures. Create interdisciplinary roles that combine threat modeling, data engineering, and AI safety. Hire for curiosity and communication, not just technical expertise.

Build Metrics for Risk, Not Just Alerts

Shift your KPIs away from reactive metrics (e.g., alerts processed, breaches prevented) to proactive ones (e.g., reduction in overprivilege, increase in classified data coverage, time-to-remediate misconfigurations). Create dashboards that track posture over time.

Participate in the Future

Get involved. Join AI governance consortiums. Publish your AI usage frameworks. Share insights into what's working and what isn't. The future of data and AI security will be shaped by the community, and we all have a responsibility to lead.

Final Thoughts

The journey to secure the future of data and AI will not be defined by one company or one tool. It will be shaped by the collective insight, innovation, and leadership of those willing to ask harder questions, build more thoughtful systems, and challenge the status quo. As you consider the insights from this book, carry with you one truth: security is not an obstacle to progress and innovation, it is its foundation.

References

1. Ross, A., Stockburger, P., & Daubert, T. (2025). AI trends for 2025: Data privacy and cybersecurity. Dentons. https://www.dentons.com/en/insights/articles/2025/january/10/ai-trends-for-2025-data-privacy-and-cybersecurity
2. Bekker, S., & Liska, A. (2025). How AI, agentic and otherwise, broke big at RSAC 2025. IT Pro. https://www.itpro.com/technology/artificial-intelligence/how-ai-agentic-and-otherwise-broke-big-at-rsac-2025
3. Anthropic Research Team. (2025). Introducing the model context protocol. Anthropic. https://www.anthropic.com/news/model-context-protocol
4. Waizel, G., Attiya, D. M., & Bamberger, S. (2025). Exploiting the model context protocol (MCP). Cato Networks. https://www.catonetworks.com/blog/cato-ctrl-exploiting-model-context-protocol-mcp/
5. LevelBlue Consulting. (2025). Understanding AI risks using Zero Trust. LevelBlue. https://levelblue.com/blogs/security-essentials/understanding-ai-risks-and-how-to-secure-using-zero-trust/
6. Rempe, O. (2025). How is AI strengthening Zero Trust? Cloud Security Alliance. https://cloudsecurityalliance.org/blog/2025/02/27/how-is-ai-strengthening-zero-trust/
7. Castañeda, J. (2025). AI and privacy 2024 to 2025: Embracing the future of global legal developments. Cloud Security Alliance. https://cloudsecurityalliance.org/blog/2025/04/22/ai-and-privacy-2024-to-2025-embracing-the-future-of-global-legal-developments/
8. Cohen, L., et al. (2024). AI advances risk facilitating cyber crime, top U.S. officials say. Reuters. https://www.reuters.com/technology/cybersecurity/ai-advances-risk-facilitating-cyber-crime-top-us-officials-say-2024-01-09/
9. Trellix & CSIS. (2025). Mind of the CISO: Decoding the GenAI impact. Trellix. https://www.trellix.com/news/press-releases/92-of-cisos-question-the-future-of-their-role-amidst-growing-ai-pressures/

ABOUT THE AUTHOR

Anand Singh, PhD

Dr. Anand Singh is a seasoned cybersecurity and technology executive with over 25 years of leadership experience spanning security, privacy, risk management, engineering, product development, and IT operations. His career has traversed multiple industries, including financial services, retail, healthcare, manufacturing, cloud, and SaaS, giving him a cross-sector perspective on securing digital transformation at scale.

Anand is currently a fellow at the Responsible AI Institute. He also serves as Chief Security and Strategy Officer at Symmetry Systems, a data security posture management (DSPM) company focused on modernizing how enterprises protect data in cloud-native environments. In this role, he currently guides the company's security strategy, product direction, and go-to-market positioning, while helping enterprise CISOs align data security with business growth.

Prior to Symmetry, Anand was the Global CISO at Alkami Technology, where he led the company's cybersecurity program through its IPO in April 2021 and post IPO growth. Under his leadership, Alkami matured its security, privacy, and risk practices, enabling it to scale securely as it served over 500 financial institutions and 22 million users. Before Alkami, he held executive and leadership roles at UnitedHealth Group, Target Corporation, Caliber Home Loans, and PTC.

Anand is known for his strategic acumen, executional depth, and people-first leadership style. He is recognized for promoting transparency, building collaborative teams, and mentoring the next generation of technology leaders. His mentees now serve in executive roles across the globe. Anand has been recognized as one of the top 50 CISOs in the country.

In addition to his executive responsibilities, Anand serves on advisory boards for multiple early stage companies and contributes to industry advancement through his work with Whiteboard Venture Partners and the Dallas CISO Summit. He previously served on the board of DaVinci Academy, where his partnership with school leadership contributed to the institution earning the U.S. Department of Education's prestigious Blue Ribbon Award.

Anand regularly trains boards and C-level leadership teams at both Fortune 50 and early stage companies. He has addressed board committees including Technology, Governance, Audit, and Information Security Audit, bringing a rare blend of technical fluency and governance insight.

He holds a PhD in Computer Science and Management from the University of Minnesota, an MS in Computer Science from Purdue University, and a B.Tech. in Computer Science and Engineering from the Indian Institute of Technology (IIT). He is certified in CISSP and CISM, and has further strengthened his board and governance credentials through executive education at the Wharton School and the National Association of Corporate Directors (NACD.DC certification).

APPENDIX A

Glossary of Key Terms

Agentic AI

AI systems capable of autonomous goal pursuit, decision-making, and coordination across tasks. Often used in cybersecurity to orchestrate detection, response, and policy enforcement with minimal human input.

AI Bias

The tendency of AI systems to produce unfair, discriminatory, or skewed outputs due to biased training data, flawed assumptions, or systemic imbalances embedded in the model's design or deployment context.

AI Governance Committee

A multidisciplinary body responsible for overseeing enterprise AI use, ensuring compliance, ethical standards, risk management, and alignment with business goals. Typically includes representatives from data, security, legal, privacy, and engineering.

AI Usage Policy (Enterprise)

A formal document that defines permissible and prohibited AI tool usage, outlines data input restrictions (e.g., no PII into public LLMs), mandates logging of prompts/outputs, and assigns accountability for violations.

Anomaly Detection (AI-Based)

Behavioral modeling techniques used to identify unusual patterns in data access, identity use, or system behavior—often precursors to data breaches or insider threats.

Auto-GPT

An experimental open-source project enabling LLMs to self-prompt and iteratively complete tasks with minimal user input, exemplifying agentic behavior and raising safety and governance concerns.

Cleanlab

A tool that validates and cleans datasets before training, ensuring AI models are not inadvertently learning from low-quality or sensitive data.

Confidence Scoring

A method in AI-based classification that assigns likelihood to a classification decision used to reduce false positives in data discovery and improve actionability.

Constitutional AI

A method used to guide AI model behavior by embedding a set of human-aligned principles (the "constitution") that the model follows when generating responses. Used to reduce hallucination or unsafe output in LLMs.

Cross-Border Data Handling

The practice of managing how sensitive data is stored, accessed, and transferred across geopolitical boundaries. It includes compliance with localization laws (e.g., GDPR, PIPL, DPDP) and the use of models like federated deployments.

Data Classification

The process of categorizing data based on sensitivity, type, regulatory requirements, or business impact. It enables organizations to apply differential protection controls (e.g., encryption, access restrictions) and is foundational for compliance with privacy laws like GDPR, HIPAA, and CCPA. Modern systems use AI-driven, context-aware engines for accurate and scalable classification.

Data Discovery

The process of identifying, cataloging, and contextualizing data assets across an enterprise's digital landscape, spanning structured databases, unstructured stores, SaaS platforms, and cloud-native systems. Data discovery supports compliance, threat detection, governance, and AI readiness by building searchable inventories of where sensitive data resides and how it is used.

Data Leakage

The unintended or unauthorized exposure of sensitive information, often occurring through model training, inference responses, misconfigured systems, or unauthorized data sharing.

Data Minimization

A privacy principle mandating that only the minimum necessary data be collected, stored, and processed for a specific purpose. Often built into AI pipelines and privacy-by-design architectures.

Data Provenance

The record of the origin, lineage, and transformation history of data, used to verify trustworthiness and ensure integrity, especially in training AI models.

Data Security Posture Management (DSPM)

A category of security tools and platforms focused on discovering, classifying, and evaluating sensitive data across environments, identifying risk exposures, and guiding remediation to reduce breach risk.

Data Sovereignty

The concept that data is subject to the laws and governance structures of the nation in which it is collected or stored. Drives decisions about SaaS vs. airgapped deployments.

Explainability (AI Explainability)

The ability to understand and articulate how an AI model arrives at its outputs or decisions, which is essential for trust, accountability, and compliance in regulated or high-stakes environments.

Federated Deployment

An architectural model where data remains within localized environments (e.g., different countries or departments) but policy coordination and model training are conducted in a decentralized, privacy-respecting manner.

Fully Airgapped Environment

A deployment model where no data (raw or metadata) leaves the customer's environment. Often used in defense, critical infrastructure, and healthcare where zero external exposure is permitted.

Generative AI (GenAI)

A class of AI models designed to generate text, images, code, or other content based on learned patterns in training data, including tools such as ChatGPT, Bard, and Claude.

Hallucination

A phenomenon in which an AI model produces information that is syntactically plausible but factually incorrect or entirely fabricated, often due to limitations in training data or context understanding.

Identity-to-Data Mapping

The process of linking users, service accounts, or systems to the specific data they can access, used to enforce least privilege, detect overexposure, and respond to insider threats.

Model Confusion

A security vulnerability in which a language model is tricked into misinterpreting its role, context, or instructions (often through crafted prompts) leading it to perform unsafe or unauthorized actions.

MCP (Model Context Protocol)

An emerging design pattern enabling shared context across AI, data, and security platforms. Links identity, classification, telemetry, and policies into a cohesive context graph to enforce security and compliance dynamically.

Model Drift

The gradual degradation of an AI model's performance over time due to changes in input data, environments, or user behavior, requiring retraining or tuning to maintain accuracy.

Model Intake Form

A governance tool that documents the scope, data inputs, usage, and risk profile of an AI model prior to training or deployment. Reviewed by governance committees to enforce oversight.

Model Inversion Attack

An adversarial technique used to reconstruct or extract training data from AI models by probing them with strategic inputs. Highlights the need for access controls, prompt logging, and output monitoring.

Model Poisoning (Data Poisoning)

A type of adversarial attack in which malicious or biased data is inserted into an AI model's training set, altering the model's behavior, introducing vulnerabilities, or degrading its integrity.

Posture Dashboard

A visual interface that consolidates misconfiguration counts, classification coverage, risk levels, remediation timelines, and compliance gaps into an operational snapshot of an enterprise's data security posture.

Prompt Injection

A vulnerability in LLMs where users inject hidden commands or instructions into prompts, leading the model to act in unintended ways, such as leaking information or executing unauthorized logic.

Prompt Sanitization

The process of filtering, validating, or modifying user inputs to an AI system to remove harmful, misleading, or manipulative content that could lead to unsafe model behavior or data leakage.

Reinforcement Learning from Human Feedback (RLHF)

A technique used to fine-tune AI models by incorporating feedback from human evaluators, helping to align model outputs with human expectations, reduce hallucinations, and improve safety and usefulness.

Shadow AI

The unauthorized use of AI models or LLMs within an organization, often by individual employees or teams. These ungoverned deployments can expose sensitive data or create compliance liabilities.

Telemetry Aggregation Drift

A risk in hybrid and federated architectures where metadata accumulation over time creates unintended insights into sensitive systems, even if raw data remains protected.

Training Data Permissions

A critical AI governance control ensuring that datasets used for training or fine-tuning AI models have explicit approvals and are free of sensitive or unauthorized content.

Zero Trust Data Security

An evolution of Zero Trust principles applied to data, where access is dynamically assessed based on identity, context, sensitivity, and behavior, and enforces just-in-time access, least privilege, and continuous verification.

APPENDIX B

Sample Dashboards and Metrics

This appendix provides example dashboards, KPIs, and visual metrics for Data + AI Security programs, spanning discovery, classification, identity mapping, posture management, and AI governance. These dashboards help security leaders track progress, identify weaknesses, and prioritize remediation with clarity.

Data Discovery Dashboard

Objective: Provide continuous visibility into enterprise-wide data assets.

Dashboard Elements:

- **Discovered Data Stores by Type:**
  - Structured (e.g., SQL Server, PostgreSQL)
  - Unstructured (e.g., Box, SharePoint, Confluence)
  - Object stores (e.g., Amazon S3, Azure Blob)
  - SaaS platforms (e.g., Salesforce, Workday)
- **Top 10 largest data stores:** Ranked by storage usage (GB/TB), annotated with risk levels
- **Discovery coverage:** Percent of known vs. unknown data stores
- **Sensitive data footprint:** Total volume of PII, PHI, IP, PCI data by region or classification type

Key Metrics Table:

Metric	Description
Discovery Coverage (%)	Percentage of scanned vs. known/registered data sources
Sensitive Data Stores	Count of stores with at least one classified sensitive object
Average Discovery Latency	Average time between store creation and detection
Dark Data Ratio	Proportion of data unused in the last 180+ days

Table B1: Data discovery and visibility metrics

Classification Dashboard

Objective: Evaluate classification engine accuracy and reduce alert fatigue from false positives.

Dashboard Elements:

- **Precision and recall over time**: Track changes in detection accuracy to identify model drift or improvements
- **False positive rate by category:** PII, PCI, PHI, source code
- **Regex vs. AI classifier comparison:** Effectiveness by data domain
- **Confidence score distribution:** High, medium, low buckets

Key Metrics Table:

Metric	Description
Classification Precision/Recall	Measures detection accuracy by evaluating true positives against false alerts. Critical for assessing overall model performance.

Metric	Description
False Positive Rate	Percent of benign data incorrectly flagged as sensitive. Directly impacts operational workload and trust.
Average Confidence Score	Mean confidence level assigned to classifications, by data type. Helps guide manual reviews and risk decisions.
Custom Taxonomy Accuracy	Accuracy in labeling user-defined or specialized data categories (e.g., genomic data, source code). Essential for domain-specific compliance.
Percentage of Known Data Classified	Proportion of total data estate that has been classified. Indicates overall coverage and helps surface untagged "shadow" data.
Classification Coverage by Data Source	Tracks completeness across environments and repositories (databases, SaaS, file shares). Supports prioritizing gaps in governance.
Sensitive vs. Non-Sensitive Data Ratio	Distribution of sensitive versus non-sensitive data. Useful for validating risk profiles and expected data sensitivity breakdowns.

Table B2: Classification performance and coverage metrics

Identity-to-Data Access Dashboard

Objective: Visualize and reduce excessive or unused access to sensitive data.

Dashboard Elements:

- Human vs. non-human identity access
- Dormant access paths: Permissions unused in the last 90+ days
- Toxic combinations: Identities with read, write, and download to critical data
- Access graph overlay: Identity-to-dataset relationships visualized

Key Metrics Table:

Metric	Description
Dormant Privilege Ratio (DPR)	Percentage of unused access grants
Sensitive Object Exposure Index	Number or percent of sensitive assets exposed to >10 identities
Overprivileged Identity Count	Identities with access beyond functional need
NHIs Without Ownership	Machine identities without assigned human ownership

Table B3: Metrics related to risks caused by access and privilege

Posture Management Dashboard

Objective: Track cloud misconfigurations and remediation efforts by severity.

Dashboard Elements:

- Misconfigurations by severity: Critical, High, Medium, Low
- Remediation SLA status: Percent of findings remediated on time
- Cloud provider posture breakdown: AWS, Azure, GCP, OCI compliance gaps
- Top misconfigured services: S3, RDS, IAM, Blob Storage

Key Metrics Table:

Metric	Description
Open Critical Issues	Total number of unremediated critical misconfigurations
SLA Breach Rate (%)	Percent of issues not resolved within defined SLA
Drift Count	Number of configuration items falling out of compliance
Average Time to Remediate	Time between misconfiguration detection and fix

Table B4: Posture and remediation metrics

AI Usage and Governance Dashboard

Objective: Monitor how AI models interact with enterprise data and detect policy violations.

Dashboard Elements:

- **Prompt activity summary:** Total queries sent to LLMs, by department
- **Training data approval status:** Approved vs. unapproved datasets used
- **Model output monitoring:** Alerts for hallucination, leakage, or inappropriate use
- **Violation tracker:** Unauthorized prompts, PII exposure, shadow model detection

Key Metrics Table:

Metric	Description
Prompt Volume	Total AI queries executed across all models
Unauthorized Prompt Rate	Percentage of prompts containing unapproved data
Model Hallucination Rate	Rate of inaccurate or policy-violating outputs

Metric	Description
Dataset Approval Coverage	Percentage of datasets formally approved for training
Prompt Logging Rate	Percent of AI prompts successfully logged and auditable

Table B5: AI usage and governance metrics

APPENDIX C

Sample AI Governance Committee Charter

Purpose

The AI Governance Committee is established to oversee the responsible development, deployment, and management of AI systems within the organization. The committee ensures that AI use aligns with corporate strategy, ethical values, data security, privacy, and regulatory obligations. It acts as the central authority for AI oversight, risk mitigation, and policy enforcement.

Scope

This charter applies to all AI systems developed, deployed, or procured by the organization, including but not limited to:

- Machine learning (ML) models
- Generative AI (e.g., LLMs, image generators)
- AI copilots or assistants
- Autonomous or agentic systems
- AI-powered analytics or decision-making platforms

It includes oversight of AI systems used in customer-facing services, internal processes, cybersecurity operations, and data analytics.

Committee Composition

The AI Governance Committee shall be cross-functional and composed of representatives from the following domains:

Voting Role	Responsibility
Chief Data Officer (CDO)	Data stewardship and quality oversight
Chief Information Security Officer (CISO)	Alignment with cybersecurity policies and controls
Chief Technology Officer (CTO)	Technical guidance and architectural governance
Chief Privacy Officer / DPO	Regulatory compliance and privacy enforcement
General Counsel or Legal Lead	Legal risk mitigation and contract oversight
Business Unit Representative(s)	Domain-specific use case validation
AI/ML Lead or Principal Data Scientist	Technical insight on model behavior and development
HR or Ethics Officer (optional)	Fairness, bias, and cultural alignment

Table C1: AI Governance Committee roles and responsibilities

Additional experts may be invited as needed (e.g., auditors, procurement, compliance, etc.).

Responsibilities

The committee is responsible for the following core functions:

Governance and Policy

- Approve and maintain the Enterprise AI Usage Policy.
- Review AI model documentation, including training data lineage and intended use.
- Define ethical principles and ensure alignment with company values.

Risk and Compliance

- Conduct impact assessments for high-risk AI use cases.
- Approve model use in regulated domains (e.g., HR, healthcare, finance).
- Monitor compliance with data residency, usage, and retention policies.
- Review third-party and open-source model risks.

Security and Safety

- Validate that AI systems follow internal data classification and security protocols.
- Enforce access controls and audit trails for training and inference pipelines.
- Approve exceptions to AI usage controls and document justifications.

Transparency and Documentation

- Ensure model versioning, source documentation, and usage logs are maintained.
- Oversee implementation of AI FactSheets (e.g., per IBM/NIST guidance).

Monitoring and Auditing

- Commission periodic audits of AI model behavior and drift.
- Investigate potential AI misuse or unintended outcomes.
- Recommend remediation for governance violations.

Meeting Cadence and Procedures

- **Frequency:** The committee shall meet quarterly, or more frequently as needed (e.g., during audits, breach events, or major deployments).
- **Quorum:** A quorum is achieved with 50%+1 of voting members present.

- **Voting:** Decisions will be made by majority vote. In the event of a tie, the CDO or designated Chair will cast the deciding vote.
- **Minutes:** A designated secretary will maintain meeting minutes, decisions, and action items.

AI Model Review Workflow

All new AI use cases, models, or tools must be submitted via a Model Intake Form, which must include:

- Business purpose and sponsor
- Training dataset sources and approval status
- Risk assessment (bias, explainability, impact)
- Technical architecture and model type
- Access controls and data classifications
- Deployment method (internal, cloud, vendor-hosted)

Each submission will be reviewed and either approved, conditionally approved, or denied by the committee at the next scheduled AI Governance Committee meeting, provided it was submitted at least two weeks in advance of that meeting. In exceptional cases where urgent review is required, the committee may convene an off-cadence meeting to evaluate the submission sooner.

Charter Review

This charter shall be reviewed annually or upon material change in AI regulations, corporate policy, or operational scope.

Approval

This charter is approved and adopted by executive leadership on:

Effective Date: [Insert Date]
Approved by: [Insert C-level Executive Name and Title]
Reviewed by: AI Governance Committee

APPENDIX D

Sample AI Acceptable Use Policy

Introduction

The advancement of Artificial Intelligence (AI) technologies presents unprecedented opportunities for innovation, automation, and productivity enhancement. However, the adoption and integration of AI into enterprise environments bring with it a range of security, privacy, ethical, legal, and operational risks. The purpose of this policy is to define acceptable and responsible use of AI systems across [Your Company Name] and its affiliated entities.

This policy governs the development, deployment, and use of AI technologies, including generative AI, machine learning (ML) models, and AI-driven services (internal or third-party). It is designed to:

- Prevent data leakage or misuse
- Ensure ethical, secure, and fair use of AI technologies
- Safeguard confidential and sensitive company or customer information
- Maintain trust in AI-powered decision-making systems
- Meet legal and compliance obligations

This policy applies to all employees, contractors, consultants, partners, and vendors who create, manage, or use AI technologies on behalf of [Your Company Name].

Definitions

- **AI (Artificial Intelligence):** Computational systems capable of performing tasks that typically require human intelligence, including natural language processing (NLP), image recognition, and predictive analytics

- **Generative AI:** AI systems that generate new content (text, image, code, etc.), such as ChatGPT, Google Gemini, and image generators like DALL·E
- **Public AI models:** Models hosted by external providers (e.g., OpenAI, Google, Anthropic) and available over the internet
- **Self-hosted models:** AI models deployed within [Your Company Name]'s controlled infrastructure (on-premise or private cloud) with strict access and security controls
- **Confidential data:** Information not publicly available, including but not limited to PII, PHI, financial records, source code, strategy documents, trade secrets, and customer data

Core Principles

All AI use within [Your Company Name] must comply with the following core principles:

- **Privacy and confidentiality:** No confidential or sensitive data shall be used in ways that could expose it to public, unvetted AI systems.
- **Security by design:** AI use must be proactively risk assessed and hardened against common AI threats.
- **Transparency and accountability:** AI use must be auditable, explainable, and documented.
- **Permission-based data use:** Any data used for training or fine-tuning must be legally acquired, authorized, and documented.
- **Governance and oversight:** AI usage must be monitored by approved teams and audited on a regular basis.
- **Documentation:** All AI systems, processes, and decision flows must be documented in IBM AI Factsheets format to ensure traceability, facilitate reviews, and support compliance obligations.

Authorized AI Usage

The following use cases are considered acceptable, provided they meet all security, privacy, and governance criteria:

- Internal process automation and summarization using internal data (external exposure not allowed)

- Code generation and productivity tools (if non-sensitive)
- Internal analytics, dashboards, and forecasting models
- AI-enhanced customer support (e.g., chatbot assistants using sanitized datasets)
- Responsible experimentation in sandboxed environments, governed by this policy

All use cases involving AI must be submitted to appropriate data governance or security review teams for evaluation and written approval before deployment.

Prohibited Activities

The following uses of AI technologies are strictly prohibited:

- Inputting any confidential, customer, PII, PHI, or regulated data into public AI models, such as ChatGPT, Google Gemini, or Claude, unless explicitly authorized and protected by contractual and technical safeguards
- Using AI models to generate or infer personally identifiable information or conduct profiling based on sensitive attributes (e.g., race, health, political views)
- Training or fine-tuning any AI system on datasets without explicit, documented permission or license rights
- Bypassing security or data governance review processes
- Using AI to support decisions with significant legal, financial, or employment implications without human review
- Allowing AI models to autonomously deploy actions in production environments without appropriate human-in-the-loop controls

Prohibited Use (Expanded)

In addition to general restrictions, the following categories are explicitly prohibited:

Unauthorized AI Tools

AI tools that lack contractual agreements or vetted data-handling controls are not approved for use with Controlled or Confidential company data. This includes free or consumer-grade versions of AI tools such as ChatGPT, GitHub Copilot, or other unmanaged SaaS-based AI offerings.

Sensitive Information

No data classified as Confidential or Controlled, including PII, PHI, customer records, source code, financials, or proprietary company materials, may be used in unauthorized or unvetted AI tools under any circumstances.

Non-Public Output

AI tools must not be used to generate or manipulate non-public information, including:

- Proprietary or unpublished research
- Legal analysis or legal advice
- Hiring decisions or performance evaluations
- Academic evaluations or intellectual property generation
- Creation of confidential training materials or business documentation not intended for public release

Fraudulent or Illegal Activities

AI tools must never be used to:

- Conduct or support fraudulent schemes
- Engage in plagiarism or impersonation
- Facilitate phishing, spam, or misinformation
- Violate federal, state, local, or international laws
- Breach internal company policies or contractual obligations

Data Protection and Confidentiality

Public AI Systems

- Confidential or regulated data (e.g., PII, PHI, PCI) must never be entered into publicly available AI models unless:
  - Explicit contractual protections are in place (e.g., private tenancy, model isolation, non-training clauses)
  - Use is approved by legal and security review

- Usage of tools like ChatGPT, Google Gemini, or other cloud-based models should be restricted to non-sensitive content unless behind enterprise-managed controls.

Self-Hosted AI for Sensitive Data

- AI systems that process or generate outputs using confidential data must be self-hosted or deployed in a secured, enterprise-controlled environment.
- Examples of acceptable platforms include: custom fine-tuned LLMs deployed in a private cloud (e.g., Amazon Bedrock with dedicated endpoints), open-source models hosted on internal infrastructure.

Responsible AI Training Practices

Training Data Permissions

- No dataset may be used to train, fine-tune, or reinforce an AI model unless the following conditions are met:
  - The data is either public domain, open source (under proper license), or internally owned and authorized for this use.
  - Legal, compliance, and data privacy teams have approved the use.
  - Consent has been obtained from data subjects where required (especially for customer or employee data).

Data Minimization and Anonymization

- Before training or fine-tuning:
  - Data must be de-identified or anonymized wherever feasible.
  - Avoid training on raw logs, chat messages, or unstructured user content unless scrubbed of sensitive identifiers.

AI Inventory and Documentation

- All AI systems and tools in use must be cataloged in an AI Inventory, managed by the team responsible for the model or use case.
- This inventory must contain:

    - Description of the AI system or tool
    - Model type and version
    - Data sources used for training/inference
    - Purpose and business function
    - Risks identified and mitigated
    - Approval history and owners
    - Dates of deployment and review schedule
- The inventory will be regularly audited by the Security and Data Governance teams.

Collaboration with Security Teams

Teams deploying or using AI systems must partner with Information Security to:

- Conduct AI-specific threat modeling
- Implement defenses against:
    - **Data poisoning** (malicious training data corrupting model behavior)
    - **Hallucinations** (fabricated or false outputs from generative AI)
    - **Evasion attacks** (inputs crafted to bypass AI detection)
    - **Model tampering** (unauthorized modifications or adversarial perturbations)
    - **Confused deputy attacks** (misuse of AI services via indirect invocation)
- Ensure:
    - Logging and monitoring of AI activity
    - Role-based access controls
    - Encryption of data at rest and in transit
    - Incident response playbooks specific to AI risks

Examples

Scenario	Allowed?	Notes
Using ChatGPT to generate boilerplate marketing copy	✅	No confidential data should be entered
Using a public LLM to summarize client contracts	❌	Violates data sensitivity clause
Training an internal chatbot on HR policies	✅	If hosted internally and data approved
Fine-tuning LLaMA 3 on product support logs	✅	Logs must be scrubbed of user data
Running AI analysis on financial transactions	✅	Must be done on approved, secure models
Using AI to screen resumes based on inferred gender	❌	Violates fairness and bias principles

Table D1: Example AI usage scenarios and allowance guidelines

Enforcement and Violations

- All employees are expected to review and understand this policy.
- Violations of this policy may result in:
  - Formal warnings
  - Revocation of AI access privileges
  - Disciplinary action up to termination
  - Legal or regulatory consequences depending on severity

Training and Awareness

- All personnel involved in developing or using AI tools must complete mandatory training annually.
- Training modules will cover:
    - Acceptable use
    - Security threats
    - Governance processes
    - Ethics and bias mitigation

Policy Review and Updates

This policy will be reviewed bi-annually by the Security, Legal, and Compliance teams and amended as required by:

- Emerging threats or incidents
- Changes to data protection laws (e.g., GDPR, HIPAA)
- New enterprise AI capabilities or technologies introduce
- Shifts in industry best practices or compliance frameworks
- Organizational changes impacting data or AI governance

INDEX

Made in the USA
Las Vegas, NV
19 April 2026